FOR
ALL
OUR
DAYS

FOR
ALL
OUR
DAYS

POLLY CURRY

MARINER
PUBLISHING
Buena Vista, VA

1 3 5 7 9 10 8 6 4 2

Library of Congress Control Number: 2009930764

For All Our Days
By
Polly Curry

p. cm.
1. Memoirs 2. United States Marine Corps, World War II 3. World Travel 4.
Military Life 5. Military Wives

I. Curry Mary, 1913— II. Title

ISBN 13: 978-0-9841128-0-7

(Hardcover : alk. paper)

ISBN 10: 0-9841128-0-4

Book Cover Design by Melanie Wills
Book Design & Cover Concept by Tracy Lee Staton

Mariner Publishing
A division of
Mariner Media, Inc.
131 West 21st ST.
Buena Vista, VA 24416
Tel: 540-264-0021
http://www.marinermedia.com

Printed in the United States of America

This book is printed on acid-free paper meeting the
requirements of the American Standard for
Permanence of Paper for Printed Library Materials.

The Compass Rose and Pen are trademarks of Mariner Media, Inc.

Dedication

This book is dedicated to my Grandchildren and Great-grandchildren who will carry the family memories to future generations:

Laura, Stephen, Jonathon, Serae, Noah, Kael, Michaela, Zeff, Brady and Sasha may you carry on the traditions of our family. May the Lord bless you and keep you.

Table of Contents

Acknowledgements

To the people who were such a help to me in writing, compiling, editing and revising this book, I offer grateful thanks.

Susan Cain, Katherine Glenn, Katie Letcher Lyle, and Sharon Sherrard.

Foreword

This is the story of my family. I should say my story of the family for it would most certainly read very differently if someone else had written it. I remember so vividly my sister, Betty, arguing with me about something that had occurred to both of us during our childhood. We recalled the event quite differently; each thought the other had a bad memory. Now I realize that we do remember things differently, sometimes uniquely.

This is mostly my story, because I lived it, but it is also an account of many other people who were part of my heritage or became part of my life. How I recall these people and experiences, is pure Mary Marston Curry because I am doing the remembering. I wish now that I had asked more questions of my parents, siblings and other relatives, saved more letters and been more aware of what was going on around me but I didn't and I wasn't, so this is all there is as almost everyone my age and older has died and I can no longer call on their memories. You might find it interesting for I was told by my husband that a story never suffered from my telling it, the implication being, I suppose, that I have a tendency to embroider the details. Is my account true? It may not be absolutely accurate but I would swear on a Bible that it is because that is the way I remember it.

I started writing this about 30 years ago when I was 65 years old. At that time, most of the people that I reminisce about were alive. Now they have all died. I have achieved my ninety-fifth birthday, so I think the time has come to put an end to this voyage of remembrance.

I entitled this memoir "For All Our Days," a quote from Psalm 90, verse nine. "For all our days are passed away in thy wrath: we spend our days as a tale that is told."

1

My Ancestry

Now for my roots, which are thoroughly British. I think this explains why I like English literature, English humor, English movies. Sometimes, when I am watching a British film, I'll start laughing at some situation on the screen that the general American audience does not seem to find amusing. Do we carry genes for centuries that are retained in the future generations of a family? I wonder; because I have never lived in England nor known many British people.

First, I want to introduce you to my father's forebears. I suffer dreadfully from pride of ancestry because my father was so enamored of his ancestors that he continually impressed upon us children that they were worthy of our respect and that we should be proud to have them.

According to my grandfather, John Marston, who compiled a family genealogy, my ancestors probably originated in Normandy. At all events, some of that name crossed over to England from that country with William the Conqueror in 1066, and to one of these gentlemen that monarch granted, for military services rendered, a large estate in Yorkshire, whereon is situated Marston Moor, the scene of a famous battle.

The first Marston that we have any record of came to this country in 1634 from England and settled in Salem, Massachusetts. He became a Master mariner, a ship owner. His parents' names are unknown as well as that of his wife. There is not much in the court records in Salem about him, as he apparently owned little real estate. Being a mariner, what wealth he had would have been in ships, I guess, and the old town records list only property transactions and court actions. There is a recorded instance of one of the latter against a Captain Thomas Clarke in 1658 for nonpayment of "frayeht" on three "tuns" of wine from Barbados to Boston. John Marston was awarded six pounds, five shillings.

This ancestor married and had six children. A member of my family, Douglas Chinn, who has been active in investigating our genealogy, says he has discovered that the mariner had children by an earlier marriage. That would explain why two of them, John and James, born in 1660 and 1662 respectively were born when he was in his middle forties. Both became mariners like their father. The family lived in Salem, Massachusetts and attended First Church, Anglican, where their children were baptized and entered in the church records.

In my papers I have an account of the family genealogy, copied from a paper read before The Society of Colonial Dames, at Bristol, Rhode Island, by a Louisa Gibson Pratt. She was certainly a Marston relative but I know nothing about her. She did a lot of research so I thank her for that.

Another John, (there are a lot of them) my great-great grandfather, the son of the mariner John, was baptized in 1715. When he grew up, he became an officer in the British Army and settled in Boston in June 1740. He was appointed Lieutenant in the British Army under a Captain Timothy Ruggles.

Five years later, he was commissioned a 1st Lieutenant in the Third Massachusetts Regiment under Colonel Jeremiah Moulton, for an Expedition to Louisburg, Cape Breton, Nova Scotia, October 27th, 1745, and at the battle of Louisburg he won the rank of Colonel. He was then but thirty years old. In 1755 he married Elizabeth Greenwood. His first two wives had died, leaving no living children. Elizabeth was a great-granddaughter of Miles Greenwood, who was a Lieutenant and Chaplain in Oliver Cromwell's army. By her John had nine children, six sons and three daughters.

In the Proceedings of the Massachusetts Historical Society, John Marston's name appears in a list of The Sons Of Liberty, who dined at Liberty Tree, Dorchester, August 14th, 1769. By that time he had become a rebel and wanted to separate from England.

There is also a description of a silver punch bowl, made by Paul Revere, one of their members. This bowl was owned by fifteen associates in Boston. Their names were engraved around the circumference, John Marston's for some reason being most prominent among them. Upon the front of the bowl was inscribed, "To the memory of the glorious ninety-two members of the Honorable House of Representatives of the Mass. Bay, who, undaunted by the insolent menace of 'vilians' in power, from strict regard to conscience and the liberties of their constituents, on the 20th of June, 1768, voted to rescind." Paul Revere's name as craftsman is modestly inscribed below.

My family had the opportunity to buy this bowl but my father couldn't afford to.

This John Marston assisted in throwing overboard the tea at the Boston Tea Party in Boston Harbor, and some of the tea was accidentally carried away in his shoe. He kept this as a memento of the famous occasion. (His portrait by Copley eventually was in the possession of my father until his death when it was inherited by my brother, John Marston, who sold all thirteen of the family portraits to a decorator in Atlanta, Georgia. Two of the portraits, one of the son of the Boston Tea party John Marston, and the other, of his wife, Ann Randall from England, now grace the walls of the Governor's mansion in Atlanta, GA.)

This son, the oldest of the six, was born in Boston, March 27th, 1756. At the age of nineteen he took an active part in the Battle of Bunker Hill.

After the Revolutionary War, this John went to London several times. Upon one occasion he saw the Prince of Wales, the future George IV, take his seat in the House of Lords for the first time. While in England he met Anna Randall and became betrothed to her. In 1784 she and her parents and brother came to America and she and John Marston were married in Newport, RI in the Old Church.

Following their marriage, John and Anna lived for years at Franklin Place in Boston. This was a rather elegant group of attached homes. They have long since been destroyed but I have a pen sketch of the original development. These homes were built in a great semicircle, facing a lawn that stretched from one end to the other. In this hospitable home, General Knox and Eldridge Geary often dropped in for a game of chess.

In April 1844, John Marston and his family moved to Quincy where an old friendship continued with the Adams family. Each Saturday John Adams and John Marston dined together and played chess, alternating the role of host.

Two years later John Marston removed to Taunton, MA, where he died in 1846.

Commodore John Marston, U.S. Navy, son of John Marston and Anna Randall, was born February 26, 1796. This John was a Midshipman on the Constitution before the Naval Academy was in existence. He sailed on sailing ships before there were steam powered vessels.

He was a young officer on the frigate "Brandywine" that took General Lafayette back to France after the American Revolution in 1825. The French general was quite taken with him and introduced him to his four daughters who greeted him when the ship docked in France. Since John was in love with Elizabeth Brackett Wilcox, a recent widow, whom he subsequently married, the Lafayette girls didn't make too much of an impression.

At the beginning of the Civil War, he was the senior officer of the Union Blockading Squadron at Hampton Roads, Virginia, commanding the Merrimack, the frigate Cumberland. The Union Monitor was on her maiden voyage to Norfolk from New York to join her Squadron. Captain Marston received orders to send the Monitor to Washington. He disobeyed and sent the ship to attack the Merrimack. By so doing, he was threatening his long career, but the outcome was so successful, he was promoted to Commodore.

When he retired from the Navy, he lived in Philadelphia, PA. He and Elizabeth had five children, two boys, John and Henry, and three girls, Katherine, Anne and Margaret.

One of the boys, John, my great grandfather, lived in Philadelphia and was an attorney. His son John was an engineer and you will hear more about him later as I remember him and his sisters very well.

Now, on to my mother's ancestry.

Elizabeth Barroll Worthington's forbears on her father's side (also English) came to America in the early 1700s. The patriarch was a Captain John Worthington, who settled in Annapolis, Maryland. He arrived there from England, less than fourteen years of age, without his parents. Did he run away? Was he an indentured servant? I find his story fascinating because he was so young. Whatever the circumstances that led this boy to leave England and come to America, and settle in Annapolis, Maryland, which was probably where the ship landed, in manhood he became prominent in political and military affairs. He married Sarah Howard, and he and his wife had six sons. Our direct family link is to Thomas, their second child.

My mother, on her mother's side, was descended from a James Taylor, an immigrant from Carlisle, England, who came to this country in 1660. His son, Colonel James Taylor, 2nd, was a member of the House of Burgesses from King and Queen County, VA.

In 1933, the homestead of an old grant of 1722, Meadow Farm, Orange, Virginia, was still occupied by a Taylor and he was the owner of about one thousand acres that had never been out of the Taylor family. Whether or not there are Taylors residing there today, I know not. I must admit I have been tempted to make a trip to Orange to contact the Historical Society. Who knows? Maybe I shall yet do so.

Colonel James Taylor's grandson, a Dr. Charles Taylor, had 10 children and only a daughter, Elizabeth, who married a Thomas Jenkins had any issue. Their son, George, who married an Elizabeth Hands Barroll, was my mother's grandfather. Their daughter was Evelyn Morton Jenkins and she was married to my Worthington grandfather, Eugene, about whom I shall tell you more later.

Now to the relatives that I knew and remember. My grandfather, John Marston, was born in 1856. He graduated from the University of Pennsylvania with an engineering degree, married a Mary Roberts from Somerset, PA. I think he met her when he was involved in building a railroad in that area.

We always called Grandmother Marston "Muvvie." I don't remember visiting them ever, but they came to stay with us on numerous occasions. Muvvie was sweet and quiet. My memories of her are sparse because I was about six years old the first time I remember seeing them but I recall she was great at finding four-leaf clovers. She frequently wore a pin that I admired which was a four-leaf clover in green enamel with leaves outlined in seed pearls. She told me it was going to be mine someday because I was her namesake, but I never saw it after she died.

Grandfather was just the opposite from his wife in personality. He was loud (maybe because he was so deaf, a family failing) very talkative and, as I remember, quite bossy. When they came to visit, we did everything exactly the way Grandfather liked. The household schedule had to suit his routine, every activity revolved around his preferences. I don't think Mother liked him very much. For one thing, their visits lasted so long, which must have been trying, to say the least. Fish and house guests spoil after three days?

My grandparents would, on occasion, stay a month! Travel was not easy in those days, the mid 1920s. Making such an effort, they had to make the trip worthwhile. I think their home was in Kentucky as grandfather retired there.

On their last visit that I remember, I had just graduated from elementary school in Annapolis. That would have been in 1925. As usual they were to stay for about a month. Thirty of us seventh-graders had tested high enough in the state examinations that the school authorities were going to allow us to skip the eighth grade and enter High School the following fall. This had no pluses and some minuses. One of the latter was that Betty, my sister, who was two years my senior, and I entered high school and graduated together, for I had skipped the fifth grade also. That mightily bruised Betty's self-esteem, although, to be honest, at the time I thought little about it.

Another minus was that freshmen in High School were supposed to have already had a year of algebra, an eighth grade subject. Since I knew no algebra, Grandfather offered to teach me. That was very kind of him, but at the first session I discovered that he had terrible halitosis. Sitting so close to him was painful. I was on the horns of a dilemma. How was I to get out of these lessons and not hurt his feelings? I decided I couldn't. He had the book, the paper, the time and the inclination, and I knew Mother would never let me off the hook. The only solution was to learn algebra in a hurry! And I did. I think I completed one year's study in those four weeks he and Muvvie were with us.

Grandfather decided I was a whiz at math. Actually, I forgot most things just as fast. My memory was excellent, but I decided early in life to remember only important things. What is the use of cluttering up your brain with math? Telephone numbers, birth dates, addresses, people's likes and dislikes, relatives' clothing sizes, remembering how to get places by the color of the house on the corner where you turn—now that's useful information. Remembering who was President 100 years ago, the population of New York City, how much grain we export or the dates of famous battles, or algebra. Who cares?

The third minus that accrued to me as a result of skipping eighth grade was I never learned United States geography which was also an eighth grade subject. To this day, my geographical ignorance of my country is appalling. Although I have crossed the continent three or four times, I couldn't find Nebraska on the map if my life depended on it. Or Iowa. Or Wyoming. I have no excuse except my own laziness.

What I remember most about Grandfather, (besides his dreadful bad breath) was his love of family history. He was so proud of his heritage, he continually, like my father, reminded us that we were very special, important people. He composed a Marston genealogy, making copies in his beautiful longhand for both of his children and all of his grandchildren. He must have worked on it throughout his entire adult life. When I was married, he gave me my copy, rendered in exquisite script. It proved, to anyone who cared, that I was a direct descendant of John Alden and Priscilla Mullins.

The first thing I discovered when I read through the little volume about the Marstons, was that women didn't count for much in genealogies, certainly Marston genealogies: they were mentioned as offspring, but when they married, that was the last you heard of them. When they lost the Marston name, they were dropped.

Like a lot of women in my and previous generations, there were times when I wished I had been born a man, but eventually I discovered how to get around men and rather liked being female. That must be the way women have solved this problem of male supremacy throughout the centuries; they learned how to outmaneuver members of the opposite sex. And believe me, some women in our family have learned to do this extremely well.

At my august age of 95, I think today's women are misguided. I do agree that men and women should get the same pay for the same work, but in striving for equality with men, women have lost a tremendous advantage; they have to compete with men in the marketplace. What a man does is who he is but this is not true of a woman; her relationships are who she is. I've read that men are so competitive because they can't have children, which is considered the supreme accomplishment for humanity. Today women with careers sometimes claw their way to the top of their profession. Do they find success satisfying as they grow old? I don't know, but I doubt it. I would love to discuss this with later generations of my family.

The second thing I discovered in reading this little family history compiled by Grandfather was that it had no action. There was not enough conflict or drama, at least recorded, for me. All my forbears were so hardworking, worthwhile, and patriotic; nobody left home to be a pioneer or live a life of crime. I was disappointed, to say the least. I couldn't find a pirate or a horse thief in the whole volume. We probably had some, but they are not mentioned by my grandfather.

John Marston, my father, was born in Somerset, Pennsylvania, on August 3rd, 1885. He grew into a tall, slender young man, with blue eyes and thick brown hair. Some snapshots taken when he was in college show him with his hair parted on the side, but later he had it cut in the style so favored by military men then and now, a sort of crewcut.

I never heard that he was a rebellious youth but he did love playing practical jokes, and anything to do with all animals. As a teenager, he often went to the Zoo in Philadelphia. He had noticed that the house cats at Merion, PA, where his grandparents lived, loved catnip. On one occasion, he took some to the Zoo and threw it into the lions' cage. The big cats seemed to go mad, tried to roll on it, and they roared so loudly that a crowd gathered and the guards were perplexed at the animals' behavior. It was quite a performance and amused my father and the other visitors to no end.

In the early 1900s, Philadelphia had street cars, and a favorite past-time of my father was to put firecrackers on the tracks at night and then hide until a trolley arrived and ran over them, causing them to explode. The conductor would stop the car and make the passengers get off while he investigated the noise. Of course, it was not easy to find any evidence at night and the passengers were momentarily frightened, to my watching father's delight.

He had an uncle who hated dogs and complained if one of the family pets came up to sniff him or made any gestures of friendliness or curiosity. Just to annoy him, my father once put an ad in the Philadelphia paper, which read, "Wanted: small yellow dog. Apply at, and he named his uncle's residence, between five and six o'clock Saturday morning." When the day dawned, there in the early morning were about thirty people, bringing small, yellow, yapping dogs, milling around outside this uncle's bedroom window, awakening him on the only day that he could sleep in. Sticking his head out the window, he yelled at everyone to leave, but no one was in any hurry to comply as they had hopes of selling their dogs. It was quite a while before the crowd dispersed and the irate uncle could go back to bed.

On another occasion, my father's then fiancée, Elizabeth, (not the Elizabeth Worthington he eventually married) held a masquerade ball at her home in Philadelphia. Her father was a surgeon. My father decided not to wear a full costume but only an eye mask. On the day of the party, he spent the afternoon experimenting with theatrical makeup, creating a nose of gigantic proportions, complete with hair-growing warts. That evening he attended the ball in black tie, wearing the eye mask. Since he was not recognized even by his fiancée, he was elated until he noticed the surgeon looking at him and talking about him to another man. Disappointed, Daddy approached his host to ask him when he had penetrated his disguise. Before he could open his mouth, the doctor said, "Young man, I am a surgeon, and I think I can help you. Your nose might be operable. If you are interested, here is my card. Make an appointment and come to see me."

Daddy was in seventh heaven! Even his future father-in-law had been fooled by his outrageous nose.

A bright boy, he entered the University of Pennsylvania, his father's alma mater, at sixteen to pursue an Engineering Degree, following in his father's footsteps. Being so young may have been a handicap. He was probably emotionally immature and socially gauche. No one ever told me that but I just have a feeling about it. When he was older, he could be the life of the party but he often made jokes at others' expense. This gauche trait, since it is always hurtful to someone else, but it is very British and greatly admired in English stories. And I suspect, English circles.

He studied civil engineering, fell in love with that doctor's daughter, Elizabeth, and on graduation went to work for the Pennsylvania Railroad. Their policy was to start their engineers at the bottom of the trade to learn all the dirty jobs so that they would have a thorough knowledge of the Railroad operations.

While he was still in this railroad apprenticeship, his life took a different direction. He ran into a classmate from college who invited him to come to his house for a visit. When he arrived, he discovered that his college mate had just become a Marine officer. Displayed on his bed were all his brand-new uniforms. My father looked at them. He was so tired of being dirty and greasy. There before his eyes was a complete full dress outfit: dark blue evening jacket with brass buttons, gold epaulets, braid and insignia, dark blue trousers with a gold stripe down the side, a red silk cummerbund, a beautiful sword in a polished scabbard, a dark blue cape with a velvet collar and frogs at the neck. And, wonder of wonders, it was lined in *red*. There were other uniforms there, of course, the everyday variety, but that particular finery captured his heart. After all, he was descended from a family with a long military tradition, dating back to the American Revolution. Entranced by what he saw spread out before his eyes, he asked his friend, "How did you get to be a Lieutenant in the Marine Corps?"

"It's easy," he said, "I wrote to Marine Headquarters and told them I was interested in taking the exams to be an officer and requested they send me the study materials. When they arrived, I studied. When I thought I knew enough to pass, I went to Washington and took the exams and, Voila! I passed the tests, a physical exam, and a personal interview and I became a 2nd Lieutenant."

When Daddy returned home he followed through on his friend's directions. Everything happened just as he said it would. In due course Marine Corps Headquarters informed him that they were ready to confer on him a Second Lieutenancy. He went to Washington, was interviewed, took the tests, and was sworn in. He deserted the Pennsylvania Railroad and embarked on his new career. I don't think he ever regretted his decision. He did well in the Corps and eventually attained the rank of Major-General. However, he never lost his love for trains, and when we lived in Quantico, Virginia, he would walk down to the station, which was two blocks away from our quarters, and watch the trains arrive, talk to the engineers, ask them about their runs, and wistfully watch them leave.

Daddy's first tour of duty was to the U.S. Naval Academy in Annapolis, Maryland. He attended a training course, probably a Basic School, indoctrinating the fresh-caught Second Lieutenants in the fundamentals of Marine Corps discipline and tradition.

Mother was 19 when she met Daddy, and he was 24. He became a 2nd Lt. in 1908 but they were not married until June 8, 1910. After Basic School, he was ordered to sea duty. When he left Annapolis, they were engaged.

Mother was a "crab," an affectionate term for people born in Annapolis. Her full name was Elizabeth Barroll Worthington. She was born February 18th, 1889. Libby, as she was called, was vivacious and quick mentally. Her sense of humor was delightful, and all her life that I remember, she preferred being around young people. I think they made her feel young. At nineteen she was pretty, with hazel eyes, dark reddish-brown hair, worn in a high pompadour, and she had what was called in those Victorian days "high color." Her waist was ridiculously small. In the photographs I have of her; she looks like a Gibson Girl, the archetype of a beauty of the period, made famous by the illustrator named Charles Dana Gibson. (Incidentally, he used to visit at my father's home in Philadelphia when he was a child. Daddy said the boy artist would sit and cut out animals from a piece of paper and they were remarkably well-executed.)

Mother graduated from Annapolis High School and had no particular goal in life that I know about except to have a good time with midshipmen at the Naval Academy and the students at St. John's College, all male. Even though this sounds shallow, she wasn't. College was not an option for most females in the early 1900s. Besides, her father didn't have much money. No girls from "nice" families worked in Annapolis in those days. Nothing was expected of her except that she find a good husband, and she was well situated to do that! At the Naval Academy and St. John's College, there were dances, picnics, tea dances, parties and more parties. She and her sister, Evelyn, were both pretty and lived in a big house close to the Academy. Midshipmen had so little free time to amuse themselves, and they never seemed to have much money. Since out-of-towners came to visit so infrequently in 1908, local girls were much in demand. The midshipmen had "leave," a navy term for vacation, so seldom that they were literally starved for female companionship. Mother had been socially active for at least four years when she met Daddy and I guess that she was tired of the dating routine and ready to get married.

Mother and Daddy's first date was a blind one—and a disaster. I don't know how they met but on their first date, they attended the theater with another couple. In those days, and really much later also, military men hardly ever wore civilian clothes. Since they always wore their uniforms, I can imagine Daddy arriving at Mother's door. He was probably wearing his "blues": dark blue jacket, high collar with shining insignia, and brass buttons. The trousers were bright blue with a red stripe down the side. Was he the first Marine she had dated? Maybe, maybe not. Mother was certainly accustomed to uniforms but I surmise she was properly impressed.

The trouble started at the theater. He embarrassed her by making no effort to buy tickets, so that his friend had to buy enough for the four of them. She told me he was quite raucous in the theater during the play and that she didn't like him very much.

After the performance, it was the local custom to go to an ice cream parlor next to the theater for refreshments. When the other couple mentioned it, my father refused, making some excuse about having to work late. This put him lower than ever in Mother's graces. Bidding the other couple "good night," they started walking to her home.

On the way, they passed a little store. Daddy asked Mother if she would like some candy. Surprised, she said she would. They entered the store where boxes of assorted bonbons were displayed. Mother knew the storekeeper so they chatted while my father investigated the merchandise. Finally he gestured to some loose candies in jars at the bottom of the case and asked Mother which she preferred. She was mortified, and that "high color" must have flooded her cheeks. She had expected him to buy one of the boxes of chocolates. She gulped and said, "Oh, anything." Then my father pointed to a jar and asked, "How about these?" She nodded, and my father said, "Five cents worth, please."

Even back in 1908 a nickel wasn't worth much. He handed her the little grey paper bag of lemon drops and they left the store. Mother was embarrassed to death. The proprietor must have been mortified for her! They were not far from her home, and when they arrived at her door, Mother did not invite her date in. She vowed to herself never to see him again.

The next morning, a dozen roses arrived from the florist with a note. "Dear Elizabeth," it read, "please accept my apologies. Last night when we arrived at the theater, I discovered I had left my wallet at home. I had one nickel in my pocket, and so I was forced to ask my friend to buy our tickets. I didn't want to embarrass him further by making him pay for our ices too, so I refused to accompany them to Wiegard's Parlor. I couldn't resist spending my last nickel on you though and you were a good sport. Can we try again? John."

That was the beginning of their courtship. I have no idea what happened to his first fiancee. Did she or he break up the relationship? Mother also had been engaged to another man, Lightfoot Harrell, a very attractive half-Spanish, half American from Mexico. Why they broke up will remain a mystery.

I met Mr. Harrell when I was a teenager. I was about thirteen and visiting some cousins on King George Street in Annapolis. My Aunt Sophie told me to go across the street to a certain house, to walk in and call out, "Is anyone home?"

I did what she asked and suddenly, standing in that dark hall, someone grabbed me and kissed me. It was Lightfoot and he thought I was Mother. Our voices were identical. When he found out I was her daughter, he kissed me again! I remember he had dark eyes and blond hair and that he was a large, good-looking man. I wonder if Mother saw him that time when he was in Annapolis visiting? I doubt it.

Daddy's courtship must have been a whirlwind one for when he was ordered to sea duty at the completion of the Basic School, they were engaged and making wedding plans.

When Daddy was on board ship he must have been very bored. He was on his way to the Philippines. In order to amuse himself, he wrote his bride-to-be a long letter, confessing that he could not marry her. "It is so awful," he wrote her, "I can barely bring myself to tell you the details." The more she read, the more upset she became. What could he have done? On the last page, he finally came to the point; he had a mole between his shoulder blades. She reread that sentence and decided not to marry him; she couldn't spend her life with a man like that!

She did forgive him, we know, for they were married in Annapolis at St. Anne's Church on June 8th, 1910, and like thousands of others at that time, they went to Niagara Falls on their honeymoon.

The Philadelphia Navy Yard was their first duty station. All I know about their life there was they lived in a section of Philadelphia called the Girard Estates and they had a maid who once cooked a roast chicken without removing its innards. Did they eat it? I doubt it! They also were amused because she couldn't pronounce "crisp;" she spoke of bacon as "crips." They laughed themselves silly when she left the dining room.

A year and one month later, my sister, Betty (Elizabeth Worthington Marston, the second) was born on July 27th, 1911, at 110 Duke of Gloucester Street, the home of her Worthington grandparents. Mother always went back to Annapolis for the delivery of her babies. All of us were born "at home," but a doctor was in attendance, not a midwife. Although boys are preferred in the Marston family, I know Betty was welcomed with plenty of love. There are lots and lots of snapshots of her and formal pictures too.

Mother returned to Philadelphia after the usual birthing convalescence, and stayed there until Daddy was ordered to sea duty again in early December 1912. She was pregnant again, so she rented a house in Annapolis on the corner of King George Street and College Avenue. She would be near her parents while Daddy was gone.

In due time the writer of this story made her appearance on June 26, 1913. Alas! No John Marston, the umpteenth (15th in succession, I believe.) Poor Mother! She had disappointed the Marstons a second time around.

Grandmother, (Gag-Gar as we called her) and her sister, a maiden lady named Ellen Jenkins, (we called her Aunt Ellie,) lived with her sister and brother-in-law and must have been a help to Mother. In those days, elderly female relatives always helped with small children. I was either spoiled or difficult. I had to be rocked to sleep every night, and I screamed bloody murder if the rocker slowed for an instant. I never understood that Mother did the rocking. Wasn't she blessed to have those older women around?

I have seen just one photo of me as a baby, taken at ten months. I'm in a romper, quite plump, my nose crinkled up in a grin, and my hair standing up all over my head. Since this was a studio portrait, I'm sure Mother tried to make me as attractive as possible. My hair is a disaster in the photo so I gather it was impossible to do anything with it. (It still is.) I am told I combed oatmeal into my locks if anyone spoke to me while I was eating, so maybe someone had been conversational that morning at breakfast. There are loads of snapshots and many portraits of Betty as an infant but only that one of me, so I am led to the conclusion that I didn't inspire photographers.

When I was about nine months old I fell out of my high chair, knocking out one of my baby teeth, which resulted in my nickname, Toothless Tillie. The Tillie stuck and my family called me that all their lives. That gap in the front of my mouth could have done little to enhance my looks in that photograph, which Mother was most likely having made to send Daddy who was still on duty in Mexico when I was born and had never seen me.

When I was about 2 years old, Daddy finally came back from Vera Cruz, Mexico, with a beautiful fire opal ring, some black pottery and two matching Indian serapes for Mother. She didn't wear the ring often. She said it was bad luck unless the opal was your birthstone. When she died, I inherited it. I didn't wear it either. I gave it to my daughter, Posy, and someone stole it from her in her sorority house at the University of Indiana in Bloomington, Indiana. It was bad luck for her too. She hadn't owned it more than a few months. It wasn't her birthstone either.

Were Mother and Daddy in love? How does one ever know? I'm almost sure they were. How they felt about one another later is a mystery. Do children ever know? They had loud arguments sometimes and that scared us children to death. When they entertained, Mother was the frequent butt of his humor. This infuriated her, but in polite company she smiled. What she said later in the privacy of their boudoir is anyone's guess; Mother was never a wimp. I remember one argument they had was about whether or not we children could live with them after we had married. Mother said we could and Daddy vehemently disagreed. Betty who was 15 at the time was alarmed enough to think they might get a divorce. I remember that I thought that was ridiculous.

There were some fun things too. Once, Mother sent Daddy, who was on duty in Nicaragua, a pussy willow bud in a letter. He sent it back with some quip. Then it returned to Nicaragua with a pink ribbon around it. Back it came with something else added. That pussy willow traveled a lot.

They both were very loving parents to us children. We kissed each other good morning and never went to bed at night without embracing. I loved both of them very much and I always felt perfectly secure. Now that I am old, I know they did without many material things, trying to give us half the things we wanted. Those were the Depression years and we were poor. The Marine Corps had cut everyone's pay 10%. I didn't appreciate their unselfishness until I had children of my own and had to forgo a lot for their sakes.

I was a terrible teenager and fought some *battles royale* with them over issues they were right about and I was wrong. I was feisty and fought for whatever I wanted. I guess I gave them sleepless nights and I'm sorry. I could be sneaky and I wasn't above lying if I thought I could get away with it. They were always fair, but I guess they worried about me. I am blessed that I didn't do anything illegal.

Betty, a first child, was much more passive than I and had an overgrown conscience. They knew she would never get into trouble. If they worried about her, it was because she took life so seriously. It interfered with her good times during her teen years. Mother depended on her company mightily when Daddy was out of the country on foreign duty.

As I told you earlier, Daddy was as proud as his father was about his Marston forebears. Nothing much was said about our Worthington and Barroll ancestors, although I eventually discovered they were very commendable indeed.

The Marston coat-of-arms had crowned lion heads and the War of Roses rosebushes on it. Mother's Barroll coat-of-arms had a wild boar, which Daddy called a pig, which, to him, indicated that Mother's people were pig-farmers. He was teasing her, of course, but this enraged her. Arguing with Daddy was hopeless. He yelled louder than she did and he had dates and figures to back up all his claims about his forebears. She was defeated before she started because she didn't have many genealogical records. As she grew older, she did acquire some to back up her claims and fight back.

Now I shall tell you a little about Mother's father, Eugene Worthington, who must have been a delightful person. I don't remember him at all as he died when I was one year old. He was raised on a plantation called Belvoir, somewhere in Maryland, near Baltimore, I think. His father was the Honorable Nicholas Brice Worthington, a State legislator. His mother, Sophie, played the piano and practiced six hours a day. (I am told!) Mother told me her grandmother would attend the opera in Baltimore, then return home after the performance and play the music by ear that she had heard. She was the mother of 13 children and my mother had 43 first cousins. The Worthingtons must have had plenty of house slaves as servants. If Sophie was playing the piano, someone else had to watch those thirteen children and do the housework.

Eugene, the eldest of the children, was tall and slender, very gentle and soft-spoken. He demonstrated a talent for painting at an early age and won a scholarship to Paris or Rome, I don't know which, but he never had a chance to use it. The Civil War erupted, and Grandfather enlisted in the Confederate Army at the age of 19. His outfit was the First Maryland Artillery, also known as Dement's Battery. That battery fought throughout the war but never lost a gun. (From the family archives.) Eugene was in twenty-one battles before his twenty-first birthday. Eventually, he was captured by Union troops and spent time in a Yankee prison until the War ended.

Sometime after the end of hostilities, Eugene married Evelyn Jenkins from Baltimore, Maryland. She was twelve years his junior. The family estates were gone, and there was no money, so Grandfather learned to be a pharmacist and opened a shop on Main Street in Annapolis. Mother told me he educated all of his brothers and sisters from his earnings as a pharmacist. His obituary refers to him as Dr. Worthington, although I doubt that he had a degree.

He invented an anti-acid powder, which was very popular with the winos and others who imbibed too much or ate too heartily. It was known in Annapolis as "Dr. Worthington's headache powder." At one time he had a young apprentice working for him, who eventually left and went into business for himself in Baltimore. Years later he patented an anti-acid product and called it Bromo-Seltzer. It was Grandfather's headache powder with a tiny change in the amount of one of the ingredients. If Grandfather Worthington had been an entrepreneur, we might have inherited a lot of money!

I'm sure he was a lovable person. When his children were little, he would take them for walks in the woods, "looking for the gingersnap tree." Eventually he would point out a cookie on the ground. "Look," he'd say, "that gingersnap tree must be near."

Then the children would run around shaking all the trees. Eventually, gingersnaps would start tumbling and they would have a feast. Mother thought for years those cookies grew on the trees and couldn't understand why they couldn't find them when her father was not with them. I think I would have loved him if I had known him. I know Mother did.

Grandmother, Evelyn, was everything Eugene was not. He was very tall; she was just four feet, ten inches. While he was blond and blue-eyed, she had snapping black eyes and masses of dark hair. Where he was mild mannered, what we would call today "laid back," she was quick and energetic. I imagine he spoiled her and let her have her way since she was so much younger than he.

Mother told us that he never spoke a cross word to any of his three children. If one of them did something horrendous, he would write the offender a letter, liberally sprinkled with charming illustrations, to soften the admonition.

Grandmother, on the other hand, must have been the disciplinarian. She was not equally eulogized by Mother; who never spoke of her with much affection. She was what some today would call a "do-gooder" but others, a great Christian lady. She never turned away a tramp from her door without feeding him, or a person begging without giving him or her money or clothes. The Worthington house was marked with a special symbol by the tramps, designating it as a "soft touch." Mother told us that Gag-Gar, as her grandchildren called her, gave Grandfather's heavy overcoat to a beggar and that Grandfather went out in the cold without enough clothes and caught pneumonia, which resulted in his death.

She also had a prison ministry. What role she played at the jail, I don't know but both she and Grandfather were very active in St. Anne's Episcopal Church. When she died, every pew there was filled. Besides her relatives and friends, the bums, winos and beggars were out in full force to mourn her passing.

I would like to have known her. I feel a kinship with her because I also worked in the local jail where I was surprised to find the inmates were just like other people; I had expected them to be a different breed. For the first time, I realized jail mates happened to get caught doing things many others have escaped being punished for. I accept virtuous folk. We know there are people who live exemplary lives and would never do anything to warrant their going to prison. Most prisoners I came in contact with were losers and not too smart.

Back to my father! Daddy had a younger sister, Anne Randall Marston (named for that other Anne Randall from England) and she was known to us children as Aunt Anna. She married a Theodore Green of East Aurora, New York. She and her three children came to my wedding. I don't remember much about her or my cousins. That was the only time that I remember seeing any of the Greens, my Aunt and first cousins.

Mother told a funny story about Aunt Anna and her first-born, little Teddy.

She and Daddy were visiting the Greens and the two women walked to a nearby shopping area with Teddy, who was three years old. They bought a cake and started home to fix lunch. Teddy discovered the contents of the box and demanded a piece of cake. Anna said he had to wait until they returned home because she had nothing with which to cut it. This brought on a kicking and screaming tantrum. Anna said very quietly that he would have to wait. The screams got louder and Teddy lay down on the pavement and refused to get up. Then Aunt Anna left him lying there, walked up the steps of the nearest house and asked the perfectly strange lady who came to the door to lend her a knife. The woman's mouth dropped open but she went away and came back with one. Anna returned to where Teddy was yelling. She opened the box, cut a huge piece of cake and stuffed it into the child's mouth. He stopped screaming and began to chew. Anna returned the knife to the staring housewife. When she came back to where Mother and Teddy were standing, crumbs smeared on his tearstained face, she said in a quiet voice, "Don't be cross, dear." And they continued on their way home. Mother never got over that.

Mother's sister, Evelyn, (we called her Mamie) married a Naval officer named George Keester. They were very lucky or else they knew the right people at the Navy Department, for with the exception of one time only, they always managed to have duty in Annapolis or Washington, D.C. When it was Washington, Uncle George commuted to work by train and they continued to live in Annapolis. In between times, he was on sea duty and she just stayed in her home. Most Naval personnel are ordered from coast to coast and never stay anywhere for more than two years so that was quite a feat.

They had three children, two girls and one boy. My two female cousins, Evelyn and Mary Ellen lived at 110 Duke of Gloucester St. Their parents inherited the old house when Grandmother Worthington died. Mother and Uncle Eugene, her brother, received their shares of the estate in cash. My cousins, Mary Ellen and Tootie, (Evelyn the third) now had a historic landmark as it was built in 1786 or thereabouts. I thought they might leave it to the Historical Society when they died. (Mary Ellen never married and Tootie has one son by her Naval aviator husband, who was killed in World War II.) It is built of bricks, brought from England as ballast on sailing ships, returning to the Colonies for tobacco and cotton. The floors are wide planks, the window panes are of old glass and the mantels and woodwork are quite lovely. The house is one of four row establishments built by a Mr. Rideout for his children. I am almost certain Rideouts still live in the main one the original owner built for himself. It is a large colonial and attached to the row houses. David, Tootie's son, has built himself a modern home. 110 Duke of Gloucester will probably pass out of the family in this century.

I don't remember ever seeing Mother's one brother, Eugene. He was the youngest of the three children. He inherited his father's artistic talent and was a painter. He never married and lived at 110 with his parents. When WW I broke out, he was 28 years old. When America became involved, he enlisted in the Army. I am told he never went overseas; he had duty at various bases in the U.S. When the war ended, he came home and went back to painting. His father had died and he continued to live with his mother. When she died in 1923 and Mamie and her family moved into 110, they invited Uncle Eugene to stay on and live with them.

After a few years, the Keesters were ordered to California, their first and only duty station away from the Annapolis area. Uncle Eugene went out to visit them. While he was there, the Keesters received orders back to Annapolis. They had bought a house when they arrived in California but had put it on the market when they were ordered east. When they left the West Coast, Eugene stayed behind to facilitate the sale of the property and to take care of it. The house didn't sell right away and the poor man stayed there with practically no furniture, just camping. The neighbors noticed that he kept the blinds down and hardly ever came out. When Mamie told him to come back east, he arrived in a taxi. (Mary Ellen says this is not true but Mother swears it is.) He was mentally ill and not rational. He was suffering from paranoia and had to be hospitalized. At that time he was thirty-three years old. As he had been in the Army, a Veterans Hospital accepted him as a patient, where Mother and Mamie would make trips to visit him from time to time. I am told he was a mild-mannered person, rather small and not prone to any violence, although he was diagnosed as having dementia praecox. His jobs in the hospital were in the gardening line and in the library. He never painted again. His new love and hobby became his stamp collection. Poor Uncle Eugene was never released because no one wanted the responsibility of taking care of him.

In 1981 he died. He was ninety years old. He had been institutionalized for fifty-seven years. We, Lamar and I, had come to Virginia to live and the Veterans Hospital was at Hampton, VA. I was asked to be the executrix of his estate because I lived in the same state, which facilitated the legal end of things. Buzz, Betty's husband, and I went to Hampton to retrieve Uncle Eugene's effects. There was nothing in his room except a few pieces of worn clothing, some toilet articles, a battered old wallet, which held nothing except his hospital I.D. and a sparse amount of hospital store script (coupons with which to buy merchandise) a folder with some clippings from the Annapolis newspaper. On a table in his room were six heavy volumes of stamps. The last was his "life work." We signed the release for his things and left, marveling how little there was to show for a life of ninety years although he did leave some paintings.

We finally located a stamp appraiser in Washington who was reliable, and we went to see him. After looking over the albums carefully, he told us he appraised the value of the collection at $471.00. We must have looked incredulous. He saw our expressions. "After fifty-seven years of collecting, this is all it is worth?" I asked.

He replied, "It's strange. Your Uncle has some wonderful stamps but none of the series is complete. If he had just completed some of the sets, the collection would be worth a lot of money. As things stand, I can't do any better."

Later I found out that Uncle Eugene had left an estate of $65,000. I still wonder if he ever knew he had that money and if he would have spent some of it to complete his collection if he had known he could afford it. Was his mind clear enough? I am told the policy in mental institutions often is to keep the patients sedated. I once asked Mother if her brother was dangerous. She said he was as sane as you or I but he couldn't cope alone with life in the world outside the hospital. Neither she nor Mamie felt they could have him live with them. I still feel remorse when I think about him. Would he have liked to have seen me if I had gone to see him? Betty never did and she lived pretty close by in Lexington for forty years. I think she used to send him a fruitcake every Christmas after Mother died, but no one ever suggested that I do anything. How cold we sound. There was a stigma attached to mental illness in those days and perhaps that is why Mother was shy about discussing him with her children.

He was buried in Annapolis and his 57 years of illness and his funeral never cost anyone except the government one penny. Uncle Sam had footed the bill and even bought him a tombstone. My cousins in Annapolis bought him a nice suit and outfitted him for his burial. His estate paid for that wardrobe. I am glad that at the end of his life he was not buried in rags. My cousins told me he had always been a sporty dresser when he was a young man. I wonder what Mary Ellen and Tootie would have said if they had seen those rags I threw away down in Hampton?

After her aviator husband was killed during World War II, Tootie had come back to Annapolis with her son and she had lived with her parents and sister, Mary Ellen, who never married.

Her brother George inherited the artistic ability of his grandfather and great-grandfather and became an artist. He did beautiful etchings and taught at the University of Illinois. He died several years ago. Alice, his widow, lives in Ohio.

How I do get carried away, remembering things that no one else living today knows.

In 1916, Daddy was ordered to Haiti. He had been promoted to First-Lieutenant, and was assigned to the Haitian Constabulary with the temporary rank of Captain. We went by Naval transport to Port au Prince with him. I read in some Marine Corps publication that during his tour of duty in Haiti, he took part in operations against the bandit Cacos, whoever he was. Bandits (members of another political party?) were always trying to overthrow the governments of Central American countries. This duty could not have been considered dangerous by our government because my father was allowed to take his family with him.

I have no memory of that trip; I was three years old.

2

Family History
(early childhood)

My earliest recollections are of Port-au Prince, Haiti. We lived there from 1916 to the middle of 1918. Daddy was in command of the American occupying forces in Haiti, sent by Uncle Sam to quell the frequent revolutions that threatened American business interests in that country. The Marines worked with the Constabulary of Haitian troops that was trying to keep peace on the Island. (Landing Marines is *not* an act of war but sending Army troops into a country is considered such.) The Marines were reinforcing the Constabulary, not fighting them.

We lived in a big pink stucco house with a red tile roof. There were covered verandas on two, maybe three, sides with polished, blood-red tile floors and grass blinds. The house was a three or four-storied building. I remember the kitchen was in the basement and we ate almost all our meals on the veranda of the main floor. There was a staff of Haitian servants that consisted of a cook, several maids and gardeners, and our nurse, Celie, who had a slim, wiry figure and graying hair. She was perhaps 45 years old.

There was a handsome dining room, painted with murals of black cherubs, scantily clad, floating around on clouds. I have no memory of ever having a meal in that room. Breakfast was the only meal we ate together as a family. That was always served on the back veranda. Betty and I ate lunch and dinner alone at an earlier hour than our parents.

Our bedrooms were upstairs on the second floor but there was no bathroom. We took our daily bath in an outdoor covered pool, called a piscine, which was close to the house but not attached to it. Betty told me in later years that she remembered it was full of slime and who knows what else. For some reason, tadpoles come to mind. Where we went to answer the calls of nature, I don't recall. Maybe we had those old-fashioned chamber pots, but there was most likely an inside toilet.

For All Our Days

The house sat in a walled garden, which was spacious enough to allow Betty to have a pony. There was a large vegetable patch there too. In the pictures I have of that era, there are towering palm trees and the driveway is laid out in neat squares of grass between flagstones. Daddy always loved flowers and there were some beautiful beds of tropical ones, most likely his idea, but he didn't work them. We had gardeners for that. His favorite flowers were his roses. They were in front of the house and the gardener had arranged little paths between the beds, outlined in rocks. Daddy tried to inculcate in Betty and me a love of gardening but my plot was always dried up with an occasional dead or sick flower to reproach me. I dreaded looking at it. It was a proof that I had failed to please Daddy. Betty's wasn't much better but, remember, she was only five years old.

Natives lived across the street (which was dirt in dry weather and mud when it rained.) We were fascinated by what we could hear coming from across the road, and by what we were told by Celie about our neighbors performing voodoo ceremonies; killing chickens, spraying the blood around as they shouted and chanted in Creole, the Haitian dialect. Celie talked a lot about "gree-grees," which I believe is a voodoo term. They were marks made by sucking your skin. They were supposed to do you harm, as was also the custom of sticking pins in little handmade dolls, that represented people they were trying to hurt.

Betty rode her pony around the garden on the roadway. I was terrified of it, perhaps as a result of having been strapped to it once when Daddy decided I should ride it. He gave it a smack on its haunches and it took off with me yelling bloody murder. In later years I learned to ride but I blame that early experience for instilling in me a fear of horses that was hard to eradicate. I never was as enthusiastic an equestrienne as I should have been although I had excellent instruction in equitation when I was older.

Because my name was Mary, Daddy bought me a little black lamb. We didn't keep it very long as it had been taken from its mother too early and it baaed all night and disturbed everyone's sleep. It soon disappeared.

Family History

We had beautiful peacocks that were decorative and very noisy but they evidently didn't bother anyone's slumber. They were loud and raucous, but apparently only in the daytime.

The servants being Haitian, of course, spoke no English. Celie soon had us speaking Creole, a mixture of Indian and French, and we had little difficulty understanding the natives as children learn languages so quickly.

Mother made a stab at learning the language because she had to run the house and speak to the servants. There is a story afloat that she went to a dinner one night and sat next to the President of Haiti. The host worried that these two would not be able to converse but protocol demanded that they be seated together; he knew neither one spoke the other's language. As the dinner progressed, the host glanced over to see how el Presidente and the wife of the senior military Officer were getting along. To his amazement, they were laughing and talking. Later, he inquired of the President if Madame Marston could speak French? The President said, "Before dinner, Madame Marston spoke no French; after a glass of wine, she spoke a little; after two glasses she spoke better; and after three glasses she spoke no English."

I'm surprised that she could say anything in either language; one glass of anything alcoholic made her so dizzy she couldn't do anything but giggle. The alcohol must have released her inhibitions and she was rattling off her kitchen French.

Every afternoon after our naps, Celie would dress Betty and me and take us out in a carriage. We had a coachman and the buggy was an open horse-drawn one. Sometimes we would go around a plaza which had a statue of a man in the center of it. Celie would point to it and say, "If you are not good, that man will come and kill you." Betty and I were very afraid of him. His name was Dessalines. I searched him out in the encyclopedia and found out he was a black dictator who at one time had slaughtered every white person living on the Island of Haiti – probably one of the historical reasons my father was ordered there for duty.

For All Our Days

One night when I was about three and a half years old, I had a terrible nightmare. I dreamt I had been down in the kitchen and a giant was chasing me up the steps to the main floor. He was huge and my feet wouldn't move very fast, the way they act in dreams, as though one is running through molasses. The giant was on the verge of grabbing me when I screamed and woke up. Mother came to see what had frightened me but I was so hysterical I couldn't tell her. She took me back to her room and I slept between her and Daddy the rest of the night. I remember how safe I felt. I don't believe I ever had that comforting experience again. But then, I don't remember any other nightmares either.

Nineteen years later, Lamar, my husband, and I were in Scotland and we stopped for the night at a hotel with the name, "Mortal Man Inn." At dinner that evening, I asked the waiter where the inn's name originated. He said that a giant had been murdered there once and he had been hurriedly buried in the basement. Remembering my unique nightmare, which had been so vivid that I never forgot it, I was a little nervous. A giant in a basement? On the way back to our room, those long empty corridors looked foreboding. When we opened the door to our room, there in the bed was a FORM! I was really spooked out. The hump turned out to be a bed-warmer, filled with warm coals, which made those icy sheets quite cozy. We slept fine but I was glad to drive away from the Inn the next morning. I kept wondering if my dream could have been a forewarning about something that would happen in the future, and that's why I had never forgotten it. Lamar was not very sympathetic.

Back to Haiti. One morning before breakfast, I arrived at the table before anyone else. It was set with the usual oranges, peeled and stuck on forks (those oranges were so sweet and juicy, and big!) and butter plates with squares of canned butter. (We never had any fresh dairy products in the Tropics.) No maids in sight so I scooped up the butter from all four plates and ate it all. It was rancid and shortly afterwards I began vomiting. I must have been pretty sick. It turned me against butter and I have never knowingly eaten it since. My parents repeatedly tried to bribe me to eat some in later years. They once offered me five dollars, which was a lot of money then, when I was six to eat a buttered roll. I tried but ate the roll around the edges and then couldn't put the middle portion in my mouth. They gave up. All my growing up days, my portion of vegetables was always served on a separate dish or bowl, butterless. If anything on my plate looked shiny, I wouldn't touch it. When I grew up and was married, I still didn't butter anything. I am told I am psychotic on this subject and I guess I am. It's too bad but I'm 94 years old and I don't believe I will ever change now. I managed to cook for Lamar all those years and he never complained. My psychosis will go with me to the grave.

The food in Haiti was different from the food we were accustomed to eating back in the States. The staple for the natives was arroz y frijoles, rice and red beans. They were delicious and we had them every day for lunch. The beans were cooked in lard and had tomatoes and onions for seasoning.

Breakfast was usually cream of wheat with butter melted on it or eggs prepared in some fashion. I can't recall if corn flakes had been invented. That was the only cold cereal on the market for years, until puffed wheat and puffed rice appeared. After the rancid butter experience, I ate my hot cereal plain but I can still remember how it tasted buttered, sort of salty.

We ate fruit all day long; oranges, grapefruit, mangoes, bananas, papayas, other tropical varieties which grew in the garden. When we were hungry we picked anything we could reach. The mangoes fell off the tree when ripe, so we just picked those up off the ground. We did get a rash from them. Our mouths and chins broke out if we didn't wash our faces after eating them, and what kids would do that? Bananas were picked in a great bunch called a "hand," which usually hung from a nail on the porch.

A special treat for dessert was evaporated milk; the can boiled for hours in water. It tasted like sweet caramel. I'm not sure but I would bet a bundle we never ate lettuce, tomatoes, anything raw, out of the fear of getting dysentery. Perhaps in our garden my father had control, and didn't let the natives use human manure which was their custom. We also had plantains, a cross between a banana and a sweet potato, and various native greens from the garden. I suppose we depended on canned vegetables and fruits a lot. We learned to love papaya which was new to us.

Once, when an American Naval Ship came into port, Mother was having the officers to dinner. When they were invited, one of the guests sent word to Daddy to tell Mrs. Marston that he would be bringing her a special present for dinner. When he arrived, guess what it was? A block of ice. Mother had not seen any ice since our arrival in Haiti. She was so excited. Her guests had iced drinks as a special treat.

I don't ever remember drinking or liking milk. Betty told me we drank canned milk straight, with no water added. No wonder cow's milk tasted watery when we returned to the States. I do remember the smell of warm boiled milk, probably Carnation canned, after Jack was born. That must have been his formula.

We had all the usual meats, plenty of pork and chickens, probably tough beef. Fish was delicious because it was fresh caught, Port-au-Prince being right on the ocean. My father was fond of the doves and pigeons that were so plentiful. He would try to teach Betty and me how to carve our very own birds. He was a terrific carver and was put off by men who weren't as talented as he was in that line. He considered it one of the signs of a gentleman to carve properly.

When Betty was six and I was four, Mother took us back to the States. She was very pregnant but we didn't know it. In those days, no one ever mentioned pregnancy. Back to Annapolis we went, leaving Daddy for two months by himself. Mother rented a different house this time, less than a block from her Mother's house, on Duke of Gloucester Street. Eventually, she was delivered of a fine bouncing boy, John Marston, the seventeenth. He was born on July 24th, 1917. The family rejoiced and Great-Grandmother Marston in Philadelphia at the age of ninety, fell to her knees and gave thanks to God for His great mercy and goodness, when she heard the news. After this satisfactory feat, Mother gave up childbearing.

The day Jack was born, a nurse hired to keep Betty and me out of the house dragged us, yelling our heads off, down the street for a walk which we didn't want to take, and which lasted quite a spell. I guess Mother had hired her to help with the expected new baby. Maybe labor had started unexpectedly but that nurse was in a hurry to get us out of there. I don't remember being told why we were going out. Babies were never mentioned in those days until they were born. We hadn't the slightest idea where they came from or that Mother had much to do with it. When we made the acquaintance of our new brother, he could have dropped from the sky for all we knew or cared.

When Jack was six weeks old, we returned to Haiti on a naval transport called the Orange Nassau. It left from New York so we must have gone there by train from Annapolis. Mother had bought a beautiful new wardrobe to impress Daddy and her friends in Haiti. She was so relieved not to be pregnant anymore. All the baggage she had with her for the four of us was packed into one wardrobe trunk, which would be put in our stateroom for the duration of the voyage. Because she was traveling with three small children, she went aboard the ship in an old maternity dress, planning to throw it out a port hole when we were at sea. Then she intended to break out her gorgeous new wardrobe. Unfortunately that trunk fell when it was being loaded onto the ship and landed at the bottom of New York harbor. The ship sailed without it. Poor Mother! None of us had anything to wear. She lived in that old dress for the entire ten day voyage. Passengers loaned her clothes for us and diapers for Jack but no one offered her a thing to wear. Some bachelor officer on his way to Panama remarked to a mutual friend, "Mrs. Marston is such an attractive lady. What a shame that she is so dowdy. If she dressed herself up a little, she would be a beauty."

On our trip to Haiti we had a submarine alert. A German sub was located in our vicinity and we had to leave our staterooms and go up on deck in the middle of the night. All ship's lights were out and the engines were cut off. The passengers were in life jackets, children included. It was quite exciting but I don't remember being frightened. After a couple of hours we all went back to bed. The sub had not spotted us.

In due course we arrived back in Port-au Prince. I'm sure Mother looked pretty good to Daddy in spite of the old, worn maternity dress. The male child, who was always as cute as any infant I have ever seen, must have filled his heart with joy.

Since mail took forever to arrive, our parents ordered toys for us months before Christmas. When they were delivered, they were immediately hidden in some remote room in a wardrobe, since there were no closets. On one occasion, all the toys arrived in September. Our parents hid them as usual but one day Betty and I were discovered playing with them. We had uncovered the loot. It was too late to order more so Mother took them away from us and hid them someplace else. Christmas Day we didn't recognize a thing. We squealed with delight over every gift. Our parents were relieved but thought we were awfully dumb!

Betty and I would play house in the garden. We liked to fry eggs on a flat rock, (it was hot enough to do this rather quickly.) Then we would eat them and pretend we were having a dinner party. I was carrying my rock with a nicely cooked egg for Betty to eat when I fell and tripped. I had torn off a fingernail and blood was streaming from the end of my finger. I ran in screaming to Celie and she poured a bottle of iodine on it. If I had been screaming before, this brought forth bellows and I remember being held in her arms, and being rocked until the pain subsided, which must have been quite a while.

We loved all the servants but we contracted some skin disease from one of them. Betty and I underwent some medicinal douches which were not unpleasant as they relieved the itchy rash. We were finally pronounced cured and I suppose more precautions were taken with sanitary measures.

After two years in Haiti, in 1918, we returned to Annapolis, where Daddy was ordered to the Naval Academy, where he attended or taught at the Post Graduate School. This time Mother brought Celie back as a nurse for Jack. She used to tell me she often wondered what New York looked like to a forty-five-year-old Haitian woman, who had never been out of

Port-au-Prince in her whole life. Celie never was able to describe it. She would just shake her head when asked. Mother said it must have been like Lazarus trying to describe heaven.

I don't believe Celie ever learned a word of English. Life must have been lonely for her. She had a trunk in her room, (all living quarters had a servant's room and bath) into which she put everything that was ever given her, saved perhaps as gifts for her family when she went back to Haiti. Every piece of candy, every cookie was stashed away with all the clothes and things Mother had given her. Mother saw them years later when she helped Celie pack to go back to Haiti.

When I was five years old, Betty, who was seven, started going to real school. I was entered in a preschool, run by two elderly sisters, old maids that Mother had known all her life. The first day I guess I was homesick for I was found trying to turn the knob of the door to get out and go home. Someone asked me where I was going. I knew I had to have a good reason to leave or they wouldn't let me go. I said, "I have to go home. My mother's dead!" It was the worst thing I could imagine happening to anyone. It didn't work. I had to stay until someone came to get me. That's my one memory of preschool. Maybe I never went back.

Daddy thought he could save money by cutting his daughters' hair himself since we had Dutch bobs. He bought some barber's shears and went to work on us. First he put a bowl on our heads and cut around it. Since shingles were "in" he attempted to cut the hair up the back in layers. We must have looked terrible. Everyone laughed at us. My reaction was to pack my doll and my nightgown into my doll carriage and leave home. I went quite a distance to my best friend's quarters where I hauled my doll carriage up the steps and announced that I had come to live with them. The whole family received me with open arms. It wasn't long before Daddy arrived to take me home. They had naturally called my family! I learned at five that you can't always trust people, no matter how nice they act towards you. I can't pass that set of quarters today without feeling betrayed.

For All Our Days

The Naval Academy cemetery was very close to our house. As the gates to the Academy always had guards, anywhere in the Academy was considered safe for us to play. We wandered all over the place. The flowers on the graves were so beautiful, I would pick bouquets for Mother. She never asked me where I had found them. Looking back, I think she must have suspected but I didn't realize it was wrong and I was not scolded. Eventually someone caught me and told me not to pick flowers off graves. I was mortified.

Daddy lost his watch walking to the office through the cemetery one day. He found it gone when he arrived at work. Maybe the strap broke. Anyway, he returned and retraced his steps but couldn't find it. This was in the fall. The following spring, one night he dreamt he saw his watch lying in the snow, the gold gleaming where the sun's rays hit it. The next morning, he walked through the cemetery again, taking the same path he had in the fall when he had lost the watch, and there he saw it lying just as he had seen it in his dream. He always said this was his one and only psychic experience.

The year was 1918 and the war was still on. Such ridiculous things impress children. Someone asked me once if I was having a nice day. I said, "Oh, it has been a wonderful day. My cousin was killed in France and we found a dead rat behind the piano." I hope we didn't have many days like that.

About this time it was decided that my tonsils and adenoids should come out. I was not informed of the upcoming event. Mother made me a rose colored, smocked dress and when I asked her why she was doing it, she would only say, "You'll see. It is for a very special occasion."

One morning I was dressed in the beautiful new garment and Mother and I were taken by car to the Naval Hospital by Daddy. It was just over the hill from our quarters. As he waved goodbye, I noticed Mother was carrying a small suitcase. "What is that for?" I asked.

"I should have told you," she said. "We are going to spend the night." Still I was not alarmed.

When we went to the doctor's office, he acted as if this was going to be great fun. He laughed and teased me as we went up in the elevator. When we arrived at my room, I noticed there was just one bed.

"Where am I going to sleep?" I asked Mother.

"In this bed. I'll be right here with you." She was taking off my beautiful rose-colored dress and I was beginning to panic. A corpsman wheeled in a stretcher trolley and I began shrieking bloody murder. The doctor came in then, his face covered with a mask. Somebody slapped an ether cone over my face. It smelled sweet and sickening. Then I died. When I woke up Mother was sitting at a desk, eating from a tray and I remember the lamp was on so I figured it was nighttime. I spoke to her and noticed my throat was sore. "When do I get my dinner?" I asked. (Like all Marstons, nothing kills the appetite.) I was starved.

Mother gave me a dab of mashed potato in a spoon and I had difficulty swallowing it. "How about some crushed ice?" She was holding a glass and I nodded. When the cold ice hit my throat, it felt wonderful. I was more thirsty than hungry. After quite a few spoonfuls, I promptly threw up. Then I went to sleep again.

When I woke up the next morning, Mother was still there. She must have slept in a chair. She had breakfast of some sort and then we went home. I used to wonder why no one ever prepared me for this terrible event but the truth is I think I know. The least little thing threw me into a tizzy and they would have needed to knock me out to get me into the hospital that morning. I would have kicked and bitten anyone I could reach with my feet and teeth.

I remember Christmas in those quarters in the Academy. There were sliding doors between the hall and the living room. We believed in Santa Claus, of course, and never were aware of a tree being set up or any decorations or visible presents until Christmas morning. Santa Claus was supposed to do it all. This year we were awakened and escorted downstairs. The sliding doors were closed and Daddy opened them. There we beheld this beautiful huge tree, decorated with tinsel, popcorn strings, baubles and lights. Our eyes popped as we saw all the presents, some wrapped, some not. Our stockings were old hose and they held a lot. They were bulging. That was an unforgettable sight. Santa Claus had come. It was so grand, I tried to reproduce that moment for my own children when they came along. I wanted so for them to feel the awe I had as a child. Some of my grandchildren have been taught that there is no Santa Claus and have never believed in the old Saint, and to me, that's a tragedy. Mother said her mother told her if she even suspected that there was no Santa Claus, he would bring her nothing. When her friends told her he was a myth, she would put her hands over her ears and scream, "Don't say it. I don't hear you!"

In reality, the moment you discover that Santa is not real, you do go into a decline but the magic you sense before that is worth the pain of perception. Fantasy is a lovely part of childhood. (Your father, who is more emotionally mature than I, said he would handle Christmas differently today. He would tell you the truth. But I wouldn't!!)

The next year we went back to Quantico. I considered Quantico home more than any other place we were stationed, we had duty there so often. Our first house was the second one going up the hill to the officers' quarters and Club, as you entered the Base. The first house was clapboard, ours was stucco. I think they are still there.

The town of Quantico is to the left. It was so dinky when we first went there, it consisted of one main street and a couple of cross streets. I remember only the main drag. After you crossed the railroad tracks and passed the station, there were a few shops. There was a barber shop where Daddy had his hair cut for a quarter. Then you arrived at Mama and Papa Gratz' variety store. If they didn't have what you wanted or needed, you had to go to Fredericksburg, which was the nearest town, about twenty miles away. If I were blindfolded I would recognize the smell of that store. It was one of many in that period; a small variety emporium, usually owned by Jews, operated like a family store. I don't believe anything was ever dusted. An item stayed in one spot until sold. One could buy material, thread, shoes, socks, underwear, toys, kitchen utensils, towels, ribbons, scissors, hats, bathing suits, you name it. It was heaven to us children. The Gratzes were friendly, loving people who would give you the coats off their backs if you needed them. I remember Papa Gratz loaned his own dress shirt to some officer once who needed one in a hurry. We spent many hours and all our allowances there.

The town had one bank, which took care of lots of Marine families all over the world. If an officer or enlisted man went on foreign service, he would leave his account in that bank and draw on it from the foreign country. I would bet money that the Quantico Bank still operates like that today. Lamar and I had our account there when we went overseas. Once in a tiny town in Scotland, a store took our check on the Quantico bank without demanding any other identification. Europe was farther away in those days and that Scot was very trusting.

There must have been car dealers, beauty shops and even a food store downtown but I don't recall ever going into them the first time we lived there. Of course, there were houses where people lived but nobody I ever knew. The town children went to school somewhere in the County, not to the Base school. Only service brats attended that center of learning, which was tiny. It was a long, narrow temporary structure, about fifty feet from the Administration Building. I guess we had six grades.

I do remember a frowzy little restaurant on Main Street. A friend took me there one day to get a box of candy, she said. She had been before with her Daddy and had punched holes in a card. A small piece of paper came out and the man behind the counter gave her a box of chocolates. Now I could do the same thing, she told me. We entered the restaurant and asked for the board to punch. He gave it to us and I excitedly punched one of the spaces and a tiny little roll of paper was pushed out the other end. The man said it was no good, I had to punch another one. I did, but that wasn't any good either. I punched until I won a box of candy. Then he said, "Little lady, you owe me one dollar and thirty cents." Of course we didn't have any money and we told him so. He threatened to get the police and wanted our names. We told him and soon Daddy appeared at the door. He was mad and scolded me, saying the police were coming for me. I was terrified and started crying. He took me home where I promptly crawled under my bed and wouldn't come out even for dinner. After a time, I was reassured that I wasn't going to jail so I left my hiding place. That experience made me afraid of the police, which I have never really conquered. When a cop stops me for any reason, I panic. My first thought is, "What have I done now?" Incidentally, Daddy put that place off limits for quite a while to punish the proprietor for taking advantage of six-year-olds.

At that time, in 1919, there were just 10,000 marine enlisted men, (no women, no blacks) and 1000 officers in the entire Marine Corps. It was so small that you knew your father would have duty again and again with the same people and so partings were never really sad. We learned to make friends quickly and to say good-bye to them with few tears.

When I was a little girl, life on a Marine Base was a country club existence. There were tennis courts, horses to ride, a golf course, (the first tee was a marvelous sledding place in the winter) woods in which to build forts, a different movie every night, (I think they were free) and a bus that came and picked you up and brought you home from school, movies and swimming in the summer. There was no pool in those days (1920) so a launch would take us across the Potomac River to swim. We even had a lifeguard, a marine who operated the motor on the boat.

I was six years old and I was in first grade. I thought my teacher, Miss Moncure, was beautiful. I loved her. I had my first sweetheart, Johnnie Clapp, who lived next door to us, show his ardor by cracking me over the head with an eraser at school. When I was told he had a crush on me, I was not impressed.

We would walk to school on a wooden boardwalk which ran along the side of our quarters, down the hill to that little temporary war building, next to the Base Headquarters. The school is long gone. So is the boardwalk. Now there must be a sidewalk. The Base bakery was across the street from the school and every morning about 10 o'clock, we would smell that wonderful aroma of fresh baked bread. At recess, we would all run across the street and beg for samples. We would usually get them and that bread, still hot, would taste heavenly. So much of memory is taste and smell. When I smell fresh bread, I mentally go back to Quantico, remember begging for some from the Marine baker.

Soon after we moved into our house, we discovered that the school bus would pick us up at our front walk. It was a marine troop bus and had bench seats along both sides. Like all Marine Corps trucks, it was a dull dun color, had canvas sides and heavy duty tires. A marine stood on the steps of the bus, to keep order and see we didn't kill ourselves or each other.

There was just one road which wound along a ridge, climbed the hill up to a series of apartment buildings, then slowly descended into what we called Guinea Pig Alley (Double decker apartments or smaller four-in-a-boxes, where junior officers lived with their families.) Then it continued downhill to the main thoroughfare which was on flat ground. The road ran along the top of a ridge and the officers' quarters were scattered along both sides of the road and behind them were deep woods, dropping downhill into gullies.

The bus started its round by stopping at our house. Being the first children aboard, we got the end seats, which allowed us to see out and talk to the guard. How the other kids envied us our seats. The bus would go up the hill, grinding down from high gear to second and then into first, stopping at all the quarters where there were children. Finally, with the last moppet aboard, we started downhill, the driver coasting and braking with jerks and squeaks until we arrived at the main street and school, which was the equivalent of two blocks away from our house. This routine took about twenty minutes. Sometimes Daddy would get his back up and make us walk to school. Then the two Clapp children next door got the prize end seats.

We followed the same routine with the movie bus. Our parents drove their cars or walked but we never seemed to go with them. The theater, a big barn-like building, had folding seats, with a section assigned to the officers; another for the warrant officers; and in front of those two sections, places for the children of both, segregated by rank, of course. The warrant officers' children were well-behaved; the officers' offspring were brats. The guards were eternally threatening to throw us out, which quieted us down temporarily. Looking back, why didn't the authorities make us sit with our parents? I'm ashamed to say we kids were very conscious of our rank, which we appropriated from our parents. We wouldn't be caught dead, sitting in the warrant officers' section even if we had a friend from school sitting there.

The movie was always preceded by a songfest. The words and music of the popular songs would be flashed on the screen and a bouncing ball would guide us from note to note. Those marines made a wonderful noise; they sang their hearts out. I remember a huge redheaded sergeant always led the singing.

When the movie was over, there would be a mad scramble among us children as the lights came on. Smoking was permitted and we kids were saving foil for the war effort. As the marines and officers and their wives emptied the building, we would dash to retrieve empty cigarette packages. There were candy bar wrappers too. We all had our individual balls of foil and would compare their weights. I wish I could tell you that those balls of foil helped our country but that would be a lie. No one ever collected them. We kept them for years.

Sometime during this year I had my second experience with crime, the first being that pegboard. Mother found a dollar bill in my room lying on my bureau. That was a lot of money then. She asked me where it had come from. I lied and said I had found it. Actually, I had stolen it from a little boy who was showing me how much money he had.

Mother had taken me to visit her friend, Ethel Butler, the wife of the Commanding General, and the little boy was her son. He entertained me by showing me how much money he had accumulated. He had a lot of money; a heap of dollar bills and a box full of quarters, dimes and nickels, more money than I had ever seen before. His mother called him away for some reason and I was left to gaze alone in awe at such wealth. I couldn't resist. I took one bill and stuck it in my pocket. I was sure that he would never miss it. And he probably didn't. When Mother discovered it and asked me where I had found it, she didn't believe my story and eventually got me to confess the whole crime. She made me go back to that boy's house, ring the doorbell and ask to see Tom Dick, the boy I had robbed. When he arrived at the door, I had to confess my thievery and ask his pardon and hand him the dollar. It was a wonderful lesson. My mortification cured me of stealing, at least for a long time.

Very shortly after this my father was ordered to Managua, Nicaragua. There was continual unrest in that country and U.S. Marines were assigned there to guard the native troops against the bandits that periodically made attacks on the government forces.

Mother and Daddy knew Celie would never be happy in a Spanish-speaking country so the idea of taking her to Managua was out of the question. They must have taken her to New York and put her on a ship to send her back to Haiti. Besides, Jackie was four and didn't need a nursemaid anymore. The trunks were brought up from the basement, goodbyes were said, toys discarded and we were on our way again.

3

Later Childhood

We went to Nicaragua in 1919 when Betty was eight years old, I was six and Jack was four. The whole family traveled to Central America on a transport. I remember the ship going through the locks of the Panama Canal. Mother told us that this was an important experience and we should pay attention. We soon lost interest as we thought it was boring; it took so long and the ship moved so slowly through the locks. Finally, we arrived at Corinto, a Nicaraguan seaport on the west coast. We stayed there overnight with a Doctor and his family. They had a daughter named Marion, who was Betty's age. She was one of the few white children we ever encountered in Nicaragua. The family would visit us later in Managua.

We knew just two other white children in Managua, where Daddy was stationed; one was just a baby and to Betty and me, she was like a live doll. Her parents lived in the same part of the castle that we did, but down on the first floor. She was a beautiful, dainty, blue-eyed, blonde ten-month-old named Nancy. Her father was a Lieutenant on Daddy's staff.

I remember an incident one day when Betty and I were sitting on the floor of the living room of her parents' quarters, playing with her. Suddenly she spotted something on the grass rug that intrigued her and she went crawling in its direction. We saw no toy but there was a dark something. We looked more closely and there was a scorpion, poised for action with his tail curled to strike. Even we children knew what a scorpion was. Betty grabbed Nancy away and yelled for help. Someone came and killed it. I dread to think how sick she would have been if it had stung her.

The only other white child was a little boy about Jackie's age, named Buster. He was red headed and freckled. His father was attached to the American Legation. The two boys played together incessantly.

The castle we lived in was located in a walled compound in the city of Managua. It was called Campo del Marte. To gain access to our Quarters, we had to go through a gate which was guarded at all times by a Marine sentry.

Our living quarters were on the second floor of this small fortress. I have pictures of it and, from the outside, it really resembled a castle; there were two battlements, connected by a long recessed veranda, with a series of rooms opening off the back. Daddy's offices were in those rooms, where he, a couple of officers and enlisted men worked at typewriters all day, dispensed discipline and interviewed workmen. Our living quarters were in one battlement and the kitchen and servants' rooms in the other. All of our meals had to be carried from the kitchen, along the porch to the dining room, which was quite spacious. Daddy had a heavy table made for the quarters. He always hated wobbly tables. This one was solid mahogany. It took six marines to bring it up the steps to our quarters and once centered in the dining room, to my knowledge, was never moved. Daddy regretted leaving that piece of furniture when later we returned to the States but, of course, this was government property. He didn't have one made for himself for it weighed as much as all the rest of our household effects put together. When we exceeded our household traveling allowance in weight, we had to pay for shipping and that cost a lot of money, which we never seemed to have much of. That's why all our childhood treasures were discarded every time we moved. Our wonderful children's books always went to the Salvation Army and secondhand bookstores. I remember when we made one move, Mother sold our original Oz books for a dollar apiece. They would be worth a mint today.

Betty and I slept on a long screened-in porch. We had cots with mosquito nets, which we would tuck in under the mattresses on all four sides, once we were bedded down for the night. Those cots would often slide the length of the porch during our frequent small earthquakes; we would wake up and find our beds in different spots, usually up against the porch railing. The quakes were never severe during the time we lived there but eventually there was a terrible one in 1931 that practically destroyed the city of Managua. I have pictures of our castle home and the terrible damage done to it at that time.

There was a bathroom with all the comforts of home, a distinct improvement over Haiti. Betty and I had a huge bedroom together where we dressed and kept our toys and clothes.

One incident that occurred in that room resulted in one of my two remembered spankings. One afternoon Betty, who considered herself a budding artist, decided to draw me in the "buff." We saw enough 1920s adult movies to know certain parts of the body must be hidden from the viewer. The only garment she could find to drape me in strategic spots was a heavy wool scarf, about five feet long. She wound this across my breast area and trailed it around my waist and across my crotch. In the Tropics, the temperature is normally in the nineties. Having posed me the way she liked, she started to draw. While she drew, I was in a state of dripping perspiration.

Once in a while I would ask her to let me see the drawing. She would say, "Not yet. In a minute."

When I was on the point of passing out, my whole body wet, she suddenly said, "Oh, that's no good." And promptly tore her drawing into shreds. She NEVER let me see it! I was so mad I grabbed a hair brush, lying on the floor beside me and heaved it at her and struck her on the side of her head. She yelled bloody murder and I could see blood running down the side of her face, which really scared me. Mother came to see what Betty was wailing about. That brush was soon swatting my wet rear and I was yelling as hard as Betty.

Since we had no other children to play with and were so heavily influenced by the movies, which we attended almost every night, sitting out on the grass in our folding chairs, our ideas about life were pretty distorted. Betty could sew a little and made us both boudoir caps (ridiculous little bands ladies wore around their heads at night) which we wore to bed, aping the sirens in the films. They were made out of silk and lace and were tied around the forehead.

We often pretended we were much older than we were and, probably because of the films we watched, both of us had crushes on Marines. Mine was named Williamson and was probably a nice, clean-cut person. He had blonde hair and smiled a lot. Betty's was greasy-looking and spent a lot of time in the Brig, the military jail.

Marion Sanstrom, the girl we stayed with when we arrived in Corinto, sent me a valentine, signed, thank goodness, in pencil. I spent one afternoon erasing all evidence of her name, then replacing it with mine, and finally delivering it to the barracks for Williamson. He never acknowledged receiving it. It must have made him nervous that his commanding officer's seven-year-old daughter had a crush on him.

Once, Betty and I put on a show for the marines. Our theater was our front steps. We sang, we danced, we told jokes and stories and ended the performance by serving lemonade and cookies to the assembled house. We charged admission, I think about a nickel, and were gratified when eight or ten marines attended. The hit of the show was "The Sheik of Araby" complete with gestures. That brought down the house. We wore scarves over our noses and wiggled our skinny hips.

The Marines' Mess Hall was across the street from our quarters. Chicken and turkey were often on the menu. The cooks brought the birds out in the yard to chop off their heads. When we heard squawking, we would dash out to watch the operation. It was fascinating to see those poor birds run around with no heads.

Our diet again as in Haiti was mostly rice and beans but something new and wonderful had entered our lives. Kremel! It was the forerunner of Jello puddings. It came in two flavors, chocolate and vanilla. We had it almost every night for dessert. Since there was no cream available, the cook would whip an egg-white, sweeten it and add a dash of vanilla, similar to a meringue. Some days the cook would whip it very early in the afternoon so that by the time we had supper, about 5:00 p.m., it would be liquid. We didn't care; it tasted good anyway.

In Nicaragua Betty and I learned to drink coffee. Daddy gave us our choice of a full sized cup on Sunday or a demitasse every day of the week. Betty, who was very smart, figured we got a lot more coffee with the little cups every day than we did with the bigger ones once a week, and as usual, I was impressed. I thought she was the smartest person I knew. She made all decisions for both of us about what we'd play, where we'd go. Once in Nicaragua, someone asked me what my name was and I said, "I don't know. Ask my sister. She knows everything."

Back to that coffee. It did not stunt our growth. Later, at thirteen, Betty was five feet, nine inches tall and, at eleven, I was five feet, five inches. We did develop a love for caffeine that lasted all her life and through 90 years of mine. And I am convinced that Nicaraguan coffee is the best in the world.

The first year we were in Managua, Betty and I attended a Roman Catholic Convent school. All our lessons were in Spanish and we attended Mass every morning, learned to read, in Spanish, of course.

The convent had an open patio onto which classrooms and the chapel opened. At recess the most important Sister, whom we called Mother Superior, would walk around the patio with us and proselytize us. Also my teacher would ask me from time to time, if I wanted to see my little friends again when I died. I said I did and she told me I wouldn't unless I became a Catholic. She was very nice to me and let me have some of the scraps of wafers from the communion bread, which the nuns made and cut out into little circles. This was considered quite an honor; a sort of prize for doing something well. She made a mistake by trying to make Catholics of us but she truly thought we would never go to heaven unless we were converted. She was European (I don't remember any of the nuns being Hispanic.)

One day, I learned to whistle. I couldn't stop doing it. My teacher kept telling me not to do it but I couldn't stop; I was afraid I would forget how to do it. Then she hauled off and smacked me across the face. I was so surprised, I did the same thing to her. She made me go outside the classroom and kneel on the tile floor. There Mother Superior found me. I was supposed to be praying for forgiveness. She asked me what I was doing, kneeling there. I gave her some cock-and-bull story which did little to get me back in my teacher's graces. My classmates were convinced I was going to hell.

One of my classes was sewing. I learned to embroider and finally worked the American flag as a Christmas gift for Mother. It was so filthy from my sweaty hands, the Sister had to wash it before she could frame it. I learned to write in English and Spanish. My speller was in the latter language and I can see it now. It was a very small black book with a picture of one thing on each page in black and white. On one page the word looked so long to me; it was "mariposa." I was so proud when I learned it.

I was being taught to write with my right hand. Since I was left-handed, this promptly resulted in my stammering. I learned that I could write backwards with my left hand as well as I could write forwards with my right and do both simultaneously. That has been useful as a parlor trick over the years but I never figured out anything useful to do with it.

Betty learned a dance routine carrying a garland of paper flowers. As the children danced, they sang, "Uno, dos, y tres y quatro," counting, "one, two and three and four," all the way up to sixteen. Each number told them where they were supposed to be on the stage so they could memorize the routine. The dance was performed at a school assembly. We younger children marched in and took our seats. The curtain was about six inches too short and I could see Betty's big gringo feet. The Spanish girls were all so much smaller than we were, it wasn't hard to identify my sister. The dance went off well and later Betty taught me the routine at home. In my old age, I remember that tune and can count to sixteen in Spanish.

One day, I happened to tell Daddy about my walks with my teacher. When I related how I was going to hell unless I was confirmed a Catholic, my father nearly had apoplexy. Of course, I would have loved being confirmed as the girls involved wore beautiful white dresses and lacy veils and their families had wonderful parties to celebrate the occasion. But no, we were removed from the convent and some sergeant's wife tutored us for the rest of the time we were in Nicaragua. With just two children to teach, she covered a lot of ground. Later, when I was confirmed at twelve in St. Anne's church in Annapolis, we never had the plush treatment those Roman Catholic Nicaraguan children received; my dress was a simple white cotton one and the veil was suspiciously similar to a discarded curtain. I was given a Bible by an uncle and aunt, which I put on the bookshelf and never opened. I was not spiritually inquisitive. I think I had expected a real dove to descend and sit on my head but I felt nothing.

I must tell you about all the animals we had in Managua. Daddy wrote to the director of the San Diego Zoo in California and offered to procure for them any animals they might want that were available in Central America. Native hunters were always bringing animals in to camp to sell. The zoo authorities gave him a list and my father put out the word. Soon we were inundated with animals that were being brought to the Camp. Betty acquired a pet anteater and a toucan, the bird with an enormous beak. She walked the former so it could find ant hills to snack on, and she tied a string on the latter and tied him up in a tree when her arm got tired of carrying his weight. That toucan had a sad end; he fell off the tree branch, hanging himself as he couldn't free himself from the rope around his neck.

My pet was a macaw, one of those gorgeous red and blue and green parrots. His name was Don Diego but I called him Challie-pot, which was, I think, macaw in Nicaraguan. He slept on the iron headboard of my cot and became very possessive about me. He talked up a storm, but it was all Spanish obscenities as he had originally belonged to some sailors. He was five feet long from his head to the tip of his tail. His only perch was my headboard. I taught him to whisper and we did that a lot in bed when I should have been sleeping. He ate up all our straw blinds, the grass rugs and an occasional straw hat. Finally, the Marine carpenter made him a perch and he was chained to that but he gnawed that off too. I was desolate but Daddy finally sent him to San Diego. We were told he was later shipped to Australia and was traded for some of their animals.

For a while we had a kinkajou. Mother kept it in the bathroom. Like the Haitian lamb, it cried all the time; I guess it was too young to leave its mother. So back to the jungle he went. We had a leopard cub for a few months. When it started drawing blood when we played with it, then it too had to go.

One day, some natives brought into camp a huge boa constrictor. It was tied on a pole about fifteen feet long. Since this was one of the requested items from the San Diego Zoo, Daddy had a pen built for it and planned to send it back to the States on the next transport, which was due in a couple of weeks. When the ship arrived and the Captain received Daddy's request, he refused to take it aboard. He told my father, "I'm not such a damn fool as to go to sea with a fifteen-foot boa constrictor." So the snake stayed in its pen, waiting for a braver Ship Captain.

One night almost everyone in camp was watching a movie, which was being shown as usual, after dark out on a grassy sward in front of our quarters where the Marines set up folding chairs every movie night. A guard came up and whispered to Daddy, "The boa is not in its cage!"

Daddy jumped up and yelled for the lights to be turned on. I think everybody's feet came up off the ground when they heard the news. The cage was about fifty feet from where we were sitting. A search party was organized, but no one could find it. That snake's whereabouts were a source of worry to everyone until it was discovered a week later curled up in tall grass not far from its cage. It had burrowed out under the wire fence and gone looking for food. It must have found dinner and gone back to sleep for it seemed pretty content.

The natives brought in some giant lizards. The zoo wanted them too, so a cage was built for them. A captain on another ship offered to transport them to San Diego. (I don't remember if Daddy ever talked anyone into transporting the boa.) Because the curiosity of sailors is well known, precautions were taken. The cage was not padlocked for the lizards had to be fed but a sign attached to the top said, "Danger. Do not open under any circumstances."

One evening, some sailors assigned to feed the creatures came up on deck to do so. Curious to see what they were feeding, they couldn't resist opening the door of the cage so they could peer in. The huge lizards dashed out and ran around, looking for some escape route. They found it in a gangway down to the cabins. As they started down the steps, a sleepy ship officer, going up on deck to stand his watch, collided with them. They looked like dragons to him, and in his sleepy state, he had a slight case of hysterics. The story, as told to me, was that he had to be relieved from duty when they docked in San Diego. What happened to the lizards? They eventually threw themselves overboard. Too bad. Daddy said they were such fine specimens.

We had a series of monkeys. One, a capuchin, black with a white face, Mother tried to tame. Unfortunately, she decided to give it a bath. She drew water in the bowl in the bathroom and gently lowered him into it. He was sitting on her wrist and when he felt the water, he bit her finger hard. It hurt like everything and we found her standing in the middle of the bathroom, swinging that monkey around in the air, trying to get him to release her finger. When he finally dropped off, he was relegated to the orchard, where the marines kept pigs. There he made friends with a pig and rode him all over the orchard, swatting him on the fanny when he didn't run fast enough.

Another monkey I remember also lived in the Orchard. We gave it some chewed chewing gum. That was a mistake. He kept moving it from one hand to the other, each time leaving long strings of gum in his hair. When he tried to wipe his hands on his chest, he left gum there. Finally, he was a mess; gum on his face and all over his body. I don't think anybody cleaned him up; the gum just wore off in time.

Another monkey had twin babies. She was found with them in the forest. They finally made the trip to San Diego to the zoo as well.

Once we were involved in a revolution. Some bandit with his outlaw soldiers threatened to attack the Campo in order to unseat the Government of Nicaragua. The Legation Staff came to our quarters for protection, and the Marine troops were all in battle dress, milling around out in front of our quarters. Maybe the opposition looked too formidable to the attackers (they could see everything from the top of a hill, overlooking the city) for after sending numerous messages to the Legation and firing a few nervous shots, they backed down and went away. Daddy said later the Marines had plenty of weapons which were on display but he had no ammunition. He was lucky. Happily the enemy retreated. As for us kids, anything to relieve the monotony was fun. Some of the Americans sitting around our living room were close to hysterics, which was interesting to watch.

Little Jackie was a very cute and handsome little boy. He had coal black hair, olive skin and brown eyes, and after being exposed to that tropical sun daily, he was as dark as any native in Nicaragua. His friend, Buster, had exceptionally fair-skin which was always beet-red and peeling. The two boys had the run of the Campo and made it their playground. The enlisted men loved them. They made them toys, found them puppy dogs, allowed them in their barracks, gave them food from the Mess. They were the mascots of the company and definitely free spirits. Their faces were habitually broken out with mango rash, brought on by consuming too much of the free-fall fruit from the numerous trees in the camp. Jack was the original personality kid. He was loved by and loved everybody all his life. Maybe those early years of being friends with so many men formed his personality. Throughout his life he remained popular with people of all ages. He was a true social animal.

On one occasion, Mother took us three children to Corinto to the beach. We stayed again with the Sanstroms. We went to the beach and spent the whole day there, playing in the surf. In those days, there was no such article as sunscreen except baby or olive oil. I suppose we put some of that on our faces and shoulders before we went swimming. After two or three hours, we went back to the house for lunch. Dr. Sanstrom had very bad table manners, so bad even we children noticed them. When we mentioned this to Mother, she told us not to look at him at the table. We tried not to do so but he fascinated us and Betty and I would steal glances at him and giggle.

After lunch we returned to the beach and played in the waves all afternoon. That night I discovered that I was sunburned. I hurt so much I couldn't sleep. I cried and Mother tried to put something on my back, which was the worst area. When she touched my skin, I yelled and wouldn't let her do anything to help me. My back was so red and hot, I was miserable. The next morning everyone else went back to the beach but I lay in that bed and whimpered. We returned to Managua without my ever going back in the ocean. Eventually, I peeled like a banana. I remember the skin coming off in sheets.

Whimpering was my thing. Mother told me I started when I was about three years old and didn't stop until I was seven. Then I decided to become good-natured. I'm sure everyone was relieved. I have been told that I had a pleasant disposition from then on. That Corinto beach episode taught me a healthy respect for the sun and its toll too.

Betty and I each had one doll. They were made out of pressed sawdust and painted. They had china heads with movable eyes and stiff hair which took a lot of mistreatment. We played with them all day long. Our dolls were on tight schedules: feedings several times a day, a daily bath, a daily promenade around the camp in their carriages. Betty's doll had brown hair and mine, named Mary, was blonde. Since we fed them flour and water so frequently, the moving works in their eyes shut down and they were eternally awake. For Christmas, Mother sent them to a doll hospital in the States and they were returned with new hair and eyes that closed. Mother made them extensive wardrobes for the season and Betty and I were happy as two bird dogs. They were alive to us. Now when I see the large doll collections children have today, I feel they are missing something that we had, a true bonding with our one that we would never have had with an assortment of dolls.

When we returned to the States, the dolls were packed in one of the trunks. I worried to death that Mary would suffocate in there and asked repeatedly if she was all right. Mother reassured me she was fine. Dolls had special gifts.

We learned to ride horses in Nicaragua. One of the Marine grooms would take us out on the trail. One time we stopped by the lake to let the horses drink, and the groom we had that day tried to take off Betty's riding pants. She refused very firmly. When we arrived home, Betty told Daddy she didn't like that particular Marine. When he asked why, she told him. I think that was our last equitation lesson in Nicaragua.

We had another sexual experience in Managua. One of the native workmen would lie in wait for us when we took our dolls for their walk. The first time he saw us, he beckoned to us where he was sitting under a tree, and when we approached, he exposed himself. We thought that was a little strange, but we weren't particularly shocked. When he repeated his exposure several more times, we told Daddy. Then he disappeared from the camp. Looking back on the freedom we had, we were fortunate not to have had a really bad experience.

When I was eight years old, we returned to Quantico, VA. We occupied a different set of quarters. These were larger, quite close to where the Ridge Road split, one road descending into Guinea Pig Alley. Now when we boarded the school bus, it was pretty full and we never got the end seats. Betty was in fifth grade and I was in third. We had lots of new friends, but by now we each had different ones. From this point on in our lives, Betty and I never had close friends in common. We never liked the same girls, we never competed for dates. Betty's friends were older, of course, but the differences in our personalities drew us to entirely opposite types of people. Betty was worthwhile, conscientious and bent on improving herself. I seemed to have nothing on my mind except to have a good time. Now that she had other friends, she stopped bossing me around. I was more of a nuisance than an associate.

Betty was so tall, the school cast her as Marley's ghost in the Christmas play at school. I have memories of her coming on stage with tin cans tied to her arms and legs to rattle and make a ghost sound. I bet she was reaching her full five feet, nine inches by then. She was always self-conscious about her height because all the boys her age were much shorter than she.

I had my first "best friend." Her name was Francita Butler and she lived across the street in quarters that we occupied on a later tour of duty. We were inseparable. We made a blood pact to meet in 1950, which to us was an eon away, and tell each other everything that had happened to us in our entire lives. I don't even recall what she looked like except she was dark and probably had Latin blood. Mother complained that her neck was always dirty but I would never have known that if it had not been brought to my attention.

Our favorite game was poker. We would play, as many as ten or twelve of us, sitting on our concrete-floored screen porches and play with three or four packs of cards. Who taught us the rules? Mother and Daddy never played cards. We used dried beans as money. How we fought and argued over those beans. We also played "pick up sticks" and "tiddley-winks." These were bad weather games. Most of the time, we were outdoors, involved in more strenuous stuff.

There were three or four groups of kids that hung out in packs. Each gang had a fort down in the woods behind our houses. No one seemed to mind if we chopped down underbrush or cut off tree limbs. We had flags, (handmade, usually with pictures of skulls and cross bones.) In these lairs we laid plans to attack each other's forts and steal supplies. That must have been food. I'm sure we had no weapons.

We did not have bicycles. The terrain was too hilly and the many-geared bike was in the future, at least for us. We did have roller skates, two-wheel models that were harder to learn to use but went much faster when we got the hang of it. Maybe today's roller blades are comparable.

I guess I was eleven when a boy asked me to go to the movies with him. Bill Sullivan was older and fascinating because he went to a private boys' school and just came home for holidays. Mother and Daddy thought it was funny that I was going on a date but they didn't object particularly. Movies were "silent" then and I spent the entire afternoon before my date making a list of things that I was going to talk about. That evening when he came to pick me up so we could get on the movie bus together, I started referring to the list as soon as he arrived and I never stopped talking until he dropped me off at home that evening. I would whisper throughout the film such inanities as, "Where did you spend your vacation last summer?" or, "What is your favorite color?" The poor kid never had the chance to follow the plot of the movie or read all the subtitles. That was my first and only date in Quantico on that tour there. I think I looked older than I was for I was developing breasts and I was bigger than a lot of my classmates. I guess my date thought, "If they are big enough, they are old enough."

At Easter that year Mother bought Betty and me navy blue taffeta dresses. Betty's was trimmed in pale blue velvet ribbon and mine had red cherries and a bit of red velvet ribbon. They sound so awful, even for that period. We thought they were gorgeous.

That summer, Daddy received orders to Washington, D.C. We would not have quarters so Mother went house hunting and came back with the news she had rented a house in Alexandria. In due time we were packed up and on our way. The day we left for our new home, it poured cats and dogs. When we arrived at our destination, the house, brand-new, was afloat in a sea of mud. The grass seed had not sprouted, there were no plantings and a narrow plank was the walk by which we entered the house. All our effects came in the same way. Soon the floors were muddy and Mother was close to tears. We should have guessed we wouldn't be there long. We made a few hurry-up friends, enough to be invited to someone's thirteenth birthday party. The day stands out in my memory for two reasons. We had FRESH grape ice cream (a first for us) and Betty started menstruating and had a spot on the back of her white dress. (I had started the year before and was not allowed to tell Betty. Now I was relieved for we could talk about it together.)

By September 15th, we had moved to Annapolis. If Uncle George, (Aunt Mamie's husband) could commute by train to DC, then, by golly, my father could too. Mother found a house on Southgate Avenue, number 35, telephone number 91-J. (The things we remember!) It was a nice house, two-story stucco, where we all had our own bedrooms and it was only a mile from the schools. The back yard was grass and fenced in. We loved it. Poor Daddy, for four years he rode that bumpy Washington, Baltimore and Annapolis electric railway. He deserved a medal. I think it was an hour trip to Washington.

We soon found ourselves caught up in a whirl of social activities. Mother knew everyone in Annapolis and we were Navy Juniors (Marine Corps, but what's the difference?) Subteenagers had as many parties as the High Schoolers. The first dance we were invited to was on an old ship that was tied up to the dock at the Naval Academy. It was called the Reina Mercedes and was used as a jail for the Midshipmen who misbehaved. The officer in charge had two teen-aged daughters and held the party up on its tiny deck. Betty and I wore our Easter dresses. All the other girls were in light colored dance frocks, white shoes (with heels), silk stockings and some even wore earrings. No one knew us. I was told later that everyone wondered who those two big girls in black were. I don't believe anyone danced with us. We didn't know how anyway. We ate our weight in sandwiches and cookies and drowned ourselves in watery punch. Then we went home to think about this new life and decide what we should do about it. It was sure different from life on a Post.

4

Girlhood

Our residency in Annapolis lasted six years. Daddy's four years of boring and tiring duty at the Dept. of the Budget at Marine Headquarters, Washington, DC came to an end. He was ordered back to Central America, to Bluefields, Nicaragua, where there were no adequate schools for us children. As a consequence, Mother stayed in Annapolis where all three of us children continued to attend the local schools. This resulted in being the longest period we had ever lived in any one place and, we thereafter thought of it as home.

The first year, Betty entered the seventh grade and the school authorities decided to let me skip the fifth so I became a sixth-grader. I stammered very badly for a while, the result, I think, of learning to write with my right hand. When the teacher would ask a question, I would raise my hand, stand up to answer and not be able to get out a word. That was the weirdest feeling; I could say all the words in my head! The other students would snicker and the teacher would say, "Sit down, Polly. I'm sure you know the answer."

For some reason, I was not too embarrassed; always able to laugh at myself, I would giggle along with the rest of the class. One day, I don't remember exactly when or why, I just stopped stuttering. It was as simple as that. I never had any speech therapy; I just got over my handicap.

Jackie, my brother, was not so fortunate. He stammered all his life and he wasn't left-handed. There were certain letters and sounds he never could say but he became adept at finding substitutes. When he would tell a story, "There was this man standing there with a re--re--,uh a pistol, when a cu-cu-cu, pretty girl came up and grabbed it." Everyone in the family tried to help him by talking for him. He never improved. Later, when he attended St. James Academy in Baltimore, an Episcopal School for boys, he sang the lead in "The Pinafore." Gilbert and Sullivan lyrics are difficult to sing and we were amazed that he could do it. He could sing lyrics and very fast, too, but not say them.

Jack was inconsequential in Betty's and my lives. He was so much younger than we were, four years my junior and six for Betty. He always smelled like a rabbit and wore corduroy knickers that would stand by themselves as they probably were washed so seldom. They were thick and heavy and we didn't have dryers in those days. Mother said he still smelled like a rabbit after a bath and a shampoo. He was a poor student but unconcerned about it; to him, life was a bowl of cherries.

Betty and I considered him a great pest. He was always a natural actor; he would hide behind the draperies and jump out at us when we came home with our dates. Or, he would hide outside and pretend to be a cat yowling or a dog barking. I guess you would say he was a normal active eight-year-old.

We all walked to school, walked home for lunch, walked back for the afternoon session and then walked home. At one time I had a bike but not for long. There were trolley tracks in the main streets, although Annapolis had not had street cars for years, and one day, coming home from school in the rain, my bike skidded on the wet tracks. I was thrown off and landed against a curb. Of course, I was scraped, dirtied and bruised. I walked the bicycle home and never got on again. Looking back on my early life, it seems to me, if I failed at something, I quit. No one ever insisted that I get up and try again. I did only the things which I could do easily.

Speaking of walking to school, I think I was a strange girl. Younger children seemed to like me and would wait in the mornings until I came down the street to accompany me to school. Sometimes, there would be as many as four little girls, vying with one another to go arm and arm with me. There was one poor child who had a missing hand. When she stuck that stump against my bare arm, I nearly jumped out of my skin. I just hope she never sensed my reaction.

One reason, I suppose, for my popularity with those younger girls could have been my membership in the Girl Reserves. They were comparable to Girl Scouts but were sponsored by the Y.M.C.A. We met once a week and bragged to one another about our good deeds. Pride was always a sin with me. My favorite deed that I religiously related was how I went to the Old Ladies' Home, The Chase Home, and read to some of the occupants. They probably were bored to death and put up with me because their lives were so barren. Anything was better than just sitting there, looking at the walls. I was the oldest in my group at the "Y" and the biggest, so the littler girls made me their leader.

When I was twelve, one of these little girls was killed in an automobile accident. I didn't know her very well, but I became involved in her funeral since she was a member of my Group. The grown-up in charge of us thought it would be a nice idea to include us children in the service and asked us to attend the funeral in uniform. Then she asked me to be ready to recite the Girl Reserves creed. I didn't know how to get out of going to the funeral, and I was scared to death. I had never been to a funeral, never known anyone who had died except two of my grandparents, both of whom had expired when I was very young. I didn't attend their funerals as I never saw or knew them.

The day of this child's funeral, that lady drove us out in the country to a little wooden church. There were about five of us. The season was close to Thanksgiving and it was a cold, blustery and overcast day. When we entered the church, the smell of flowers was overpowering and almost sickening. I have hated the scent of freesias ever since then.

We were escorted to the front pew, where we sat solemnly in a row, not knowing what was coming next. What came was a small, white child's coffin (I had never seen a coffin before.) Some men wheeled it in and stationed it right next to me. I began to think about that little girl being in there and I just wanted to go home.

There was a service, but I didn't seem aware of anything except the coffin and the overpowering smell of those flowers. When the last mournful hymn was sung, we all went out in the churchyard where the coffin was put down in a deep hole in the ground. Then someone handed me an American flag, took me over to the edge of the pit and told me to recite the Girl Reserves' Creed. I was terrified, but I got through the recital. All these strangers, relatives and friends, I suppose, came over and thanked us and then that lady took us back to Annapolis.

When I arrived home it was dark and I was still scared. I had discovered that death was real and it actually happened to people. I realized for the first time that anyone could die, Mother, Daddy, Betty, Jack, little children, ME. The idea was terrifying. I couldn't sleep that night. I kept seeing that little white coffin floating around in my room. For days I worried about Mother or Daddy dying. When I saw a hearse, I ran. When I noticed a funeral in progress at some church, I ran. This experience gave me an early horror of death that I have never completely overcome.

Thank goodness, in our church we have closed coffins. I have never been to a viewing of a deceased person and I don't intend to do so if I can possibly avoid it. I take that back. I went to a funeral once where the coffin was open but I didn't realize it until I noticed some clasped hands among the flowers. I never went any closer, when the rest of the congregation was invited to view the body, but stayed frozen in the pew.

When I was thirteen I joined the Girl Scouts. We met in the State Capitol, where we sat in the entrance hall on the floor in a circle. That seems strange to me now. I don't remember having any leader. We had books to go by, and learned to make knots, identified trees and practiced Morse Code. We tapped it out on the floor. Once we hid under the balustrade and smoked a cigarette!

My chief reason for joining the group was to get out of the house at night. For some reason, going out after dark was not very usual and therefore exciting. Eventually Morse Code was my downfall; I got behind and quit. Tom Stone, one of my admirers, walked me home from Scout meetings. I wonder what excuse he gave to get out at night? Maybe he went to a Boy Scout meeting.

Mrs. Stone, Tom's mother, invited me to dinner on his thirteenth birthday. She was a large, loud woman and a little intimidating. When I arrived and rang the doorbell, she gave me a horsey smile as she let me in. Then she frowned and yelled up the steps to the second floor, "Tom, Polly is here. Get down here but be sure to wash off the ring around the bathtub first." I was mortified for him. How could I ever feel romantic about anyone who left a ring of dirt in the bathtub?

When I had a birthday, Tom gave me one of those little shiny wooden oak chests, filled with home made fudge. He probably made it himself. We were all poor, but we didn't know it. I kept that box for jewelry for years. It even had a little key so I could lock it. I bet he never bought it. Those boxes were common then and usually held maple candy or something.

Tom carried the cross at church and I sang in the junior choir. He was going to be a missionary so I steeled myself for a life in the Mission field. In my mind, The Field was always Africa for that was the worst place I could imagine being. It still is, although everyone who has been there says it is lovely.

I was very pious, just having been confirmed. I congratulated myself for attending the entire three-hour Good Friday Service at Saint Anne's. We newly confirmed looked down our noses at anyone who left before it was over or arrived late although there were periods during the service every half hour for people to come and go as they wished.

Tom was not a Navy Junior so he didn't belong to the "in" crowd. He attended Annapolis High School. All the other boys I was interested in went to preparatory schools for the Naval Academy; Severn School, or a private preparatory school which was located in town.

Once our high school beat Severn and we yelled all the way back to Annapolis with our schoolmates on the Washington, Baltimore and Annapolis, the electric train which we called the Wobble, Bump and Amble. We wouldn't have been caught dead going to a high school game of any sort unless Severn had been playing. We were horrible snobs, but we surely loved beating that boys' school.

When I was in the seventh grade, I had my first kiss. Betty and I had gone to a party at one of our friends' house which was located in the Naval Academy grounds. We always danced to a phonograph in a parlor where all the rugs had been rolled up and stashed at one end of the room. The wooden floors were great for dancing with some wax or cornmeal sprinkled on them. By this time Betty and I had made the grade: we could dance and we wore the proper pastel taffeta evening dresses (not navy blue!) Some of the boys were ogling us and we felt perfectly at home with the "in" crowd.

Refreshments were always served at intermission and a very cute boy, Tom Morton, asked me to sit it out with him. We went halfway up the stairs to the second floor to sit and eat. As my male friend joined me, carrying two plates heaped with melting homemade fresh peach ice cream, he maneuvered his face so it brushed mine. He managed a quick smack on the lips. (That was quite a feat, now that I think about it.) I was so surprised, I just gasped. Guess what I said to him? "I'm saving my kisses for the man I marry."

I was truly upset. Never again could I say when I was sweet sixteen that I had never been kissed. For some reason this bugged me a lot. Incidentally, I dated this boy for six years, off and on, even wore his Naval Academy miniature when he was a midshipman until I became engaged to Lamar, who would become my husband. He was a Navy Junior and looked a lot like Gary Cooper. Every girl should have a first love like Tom Morton. Our romance was as clean as a hound's tooth. A few fumbling kisses took care of our needs as we grew up together. I might easily have married him if our paths had not separated us. After I did marry Lamar, Tom married an English girl and he eventually became an Admiral in the Navy during World War II. I remember a friend told me he had described his wife as someone he could get caught in the rain with. I deduced from that remark that she had naturally curly hair as no one with a permanent wants to get caught in the rain! I'm sorry I never met her as she was probably a lovely person.

That year, 1928, I had a new best friend, Claire King, a Navy junior whose house was just three blocks from ours. Her father was Admiral Ernest King later of WWII fame. She was one of six girls and they had one little brother, the youngest in the family. After this male birth, Mattie King, the mama, quit childbearing. Claire was right in the middle, having two younger sisters and three older ones. Captain King, seemed always to be on Sea Duty, which meant he was always on a ship and I never saw him. Mattie, his wife, was an easy going mother. After all, she had seven children and a husband who was never at home; you couldn't expect her to keep much discipline. We could do anything we liked in their house, such as make fudge, cocoa, sandwiches, iced tea, or play cards, or mess up the house.

At my house we couldn't cook ever, play cards or dance on Sunday, or do much of anything else for my father was usually home. My friends were terrified of him. He was a large man and had a booming voice, which he was not averse to using. The King girls had a distinct advantage with no man in their house.

I know Claire's home was not as well maintained as ours, although that never occurred to me at the time. Good housekeeping was not my "bag" so I wouldn't really know. One Easter Sunday I had a new hat, a lovely electric blue felt cloche. After church, I stopped by Claire's and took off my hat. When I was leaving, I couldn't find it. Everyone helped me look for it but it never surfaced. I never found it. Mother asked me repeatedly where it was, which was embarrassing. I never told her. How do you say, "I lost my new hat at Claire's house?" No one could lose a hat in MY house. They probably found it behind the piano years later when they were transferred to another duty station.

I loved going to the Kings. One of Claire's sisters was married and two others, Martha and Eleanor, were dating midshipmen. They were both popular, pretty, and they wore snazzy clothes and jewelry, very high heels, lots of make-up, smelled of perfume and had slews of middies hanging around. We younger ones learned a lot by watching and imitating those older girls. I'm sure they were the reason I learned to smoke a few years later.

I guess I was "in love" with Claire. I was jealous if she paid attention to other girls; I did everything she did; if she went out for basketball, so did I; if she took Latin, I did too; if she didn't like someone, I couldn't stand her either. I thought she was so sophisticated and she even smelled good. I would love to ask her how she remembers those years. I know I was her "best friend" too. We were absolutely boy-crazy, of course. We were always trying to "get" boys. After we did, we never let them go or released them emotionally so some other girl could enjoy their attentions. We collected them the way you collect baseball cards or match boxes. It's so different today with teenagers or was even in my daughter's generation. Today, girls want to go steady. What a bore! It's funny but the boys didn't seem to mind how we girls controlled them. They carried the torch for us for months until they caught on that they were not getting anywhere. Our affairs were so pure. No heavy necking, just an occasional virginal kiss. Most of the youths today would have a hard time believing how young and naive we were.

Remember, I said we were poor. My school shoes were worn down to the pavement. I used to put cardboard in them to save my socks and hose but, come Friday or Saturday, I would need another party dress, Betty too. Our closets were full of clothes for dances but not so many changes for school. We danced so hard, we wore out our silver or gold dancing pumps very fast. They did get hard wear. Dancing was quite strenuous in those days and we would work up a dripping perspiration, hopping, kicking, flying around the room. None of this slow cheek-to cheek stuff. What we did was real exercise.

I skipped the 8th grade and sailed into high school at age 12. I recall some of my teachers. I had a Miss Marking for Latin for four years. She had the widest hips I ever saw on a woman. One year, she took a correspondence course in Spanish in order to teach it and I was one of her first pupils. She was so unsure of her pronunciation of the words that she would turn to me for help because of my two years in Nicaragua. I had the poor woman in the palm of my hand; she had to give me an A. I liked languages and took four years of Latin with her. I became quite fond of Miss Marking.

Mr. Leach was one of my Math teachers. On his desk was one of those spikes to hold papers. He would take the homework we turned in and stab the sheets on that spike. When it was empty, he would do some home dentistry, using it in place of a toothpick. I guess we would say today that he was "laid back."

He lolled at his desk with his feet up on it so some of us couldn't always see his face as his feet were quite large. I don't believe he ever went to the blackboard to demonstrate or write assignments; he wasn't big on energy. He was my first male teacher and, believe it or not, I did not have a crush on him.

I don't remember the name of my chemistry teacher. He had mounds of red hair and was literally frightened of his students. He demonstrated many experiments and told us to write down the formulae, which we did. Half the time they were failures. He would put some substance in a beaker, heat it and add another element, saying, "Watch it turn blue!" It didn't and he would mournfully tell us to write in our notebooks that it had. He would never turn his back to the class. What was he afraid of? Writing on the blackboard was a real hassle for him for he couldn't see what he was writing, always standing sideways and nervously watching the class.

One year I took Zoology. Amoebae and such were OK, but eventually, I had to dissect a frog. We were told to dissect the eye, which didn't appeal to me at all; I tried and landed on the floor in a dead faint. When I was revived, I found myself in the principal's office, lying on a couch. I hadn't the slightest idea why I had passed out. When I was sent home, I told Mother what had happened. (Mothers were always home in those days.) She told me other members of the family now dead had the same trouble with eyes; I must have inherited a family weakness. Suffice it to say, when I went back to school the next day, I was excused from dissecting my frog's eyes.

My ancient history teacher, Miss Bennett, was ancient. We suspected she wore a wig. (In those days wigs looked awful and were something you didn't talk about.) But she knew her subject thoroughly and managed to create enough interest in her class that passing was no problem.

When we studied modern history, we had a teacher, Mrs. Leech (no relation to the Math teacher) whom we suspected of smoking. That was against the school rules for faculty and pupils. We would make excuses to go to her desk and see if we could detect the smell of cigarette smoke when we were close to her. We decided she definitely did, but since we were rebels, we admired her for it; she had dared to defy the Establishment.

Betty started going with midshipmen when she was fourteen. I was twelve and barred from a party Betty gave one Saturday afternoon. When I thought it was safe to go home from Claire's, I arrived to find the "tea dance" still in progress. A very attractive midshipman started talking to me and asked me to dance. We were enjoying ourselves when Betty spotted me and in horror, went and told Mother. In the interim I gave this attractive young man a long bull story which he swallowed hook, line and sinker. Since I was big for my age and didn't want him to know how young I was, I told him I went to Wellesley College. When he asked what I was doing home that time of year, I said that I had been sent home for disciplinary reasons; I had climbed up on the chapel steeple and rung the bell at midnight. I had been apprehended, so for punishment I lost half a semester at college. He was entranced and asked me for a date. Then I got scared and told him I was going back to school the next day. The poor guy wrote me at Wellesley. The letter was returned with the information that there was no student enrolled there under my name. After doing some detective work, he found out who I was and sent me a letter which I cherished for years. It was on beautiful Naval Academy crested paper and it contained one sentence, "Thanks for the buggy-ride." He didn't even sign it. Mother had soon let me know that I was too young for midshipmen and that I was not to crash Betty's parties.

When Daddy left for Nicaragua we had moved to another house, probably because it was cheaper. We liked it just as well; it was closer to school and the Naval Academy. It was one block from Spa Creek and the canoe rental place was at the end of our dead-end street. Betty's best friend, Page Robertson, lived just around the corner, on Shipwright Street. Page's mother took a great liking to Betty and so my sister practically lived at their house. When Mrs. Robertson made a trip, she always included Betty with her girls, Page had a much younger sister, paying all her expenses.

My sister and I had one terrible cross to bear; neither of us liked dogs. Was that because we had never had one? Daddy told us people in the Service shouldn't have them unless they had a place where they could run. Mrs. Robertson, had two smelly cocker spaniels, which had the run of the house and were fed from the same plates the family used at the table. Page and her mother were lousy housekeepers and, in the days before dishwashers, Betty did not want to eat from the same plates the dogs did. How she schemed and lied to keep from having to eat a meal in that house. She would come home to eat lunch and then return for the rest of the day, coming home just in time for dinner.

When Jack was ten, he became quite entrepreneurial. Once he sent away for a case of soap which he had undertaken to sell, door to door. Mother had a fit and threatened to sue the company for sending merchandise to a minor. She finally spent quite a sum of money, mailing the case back to the sender, minus three or four cakes which Jack had managed to sell. Another time he sent away for some firearms. He received a letter, demanding proof that he was over twenty-one. In his childish writing, he wrote back, swearing he was old enough to sell firearms. They believed him and sent a representative to talk business terms. Imagine that man's surprise when Mother met him at the front door and told him how old Jack really was.

My brother had a beautiful boy soprano voice. He sang all the solos in St. Anne's Boys choir for several years. One night he came home from choir practice in disgrace but he was reluctant to tell Mother the reason. Finally he blurted out, "Well, if you must know, we were playing hide and seek in the bleachers!"

Mother was upset that he called the pews bleachers and that the boys would be what she called "skylarking" in Church.

He did sing like an angel for a few years until his voice began to change. Then when he sang a solo, we in the family would all have sweaty palms, expecting his voice to crack. When it did finally change, he still sang well. He had a beautiful baritone and he sang in choirs throughout his life.

During those high school years, when we woke up and heard the patter of rain, we rejoiced. We could stay at school and buy our lunch. Mother gave each of us a quarter and with that we could buy a hot dog and either a cold drink or a mug of cocoa.

In addition to dogs, Betty hated worms. In wet weather Betty would leave for school an hour early so she wouldn't step on a worm on the way. She made the trip, walking ever so gingerly, her eyes glued to the pavement. A few hours after the rain stopped, the wiggly things would be dried up but if there was any sign of life in them, she would walk around them; she had a horror of feeling one squash under her shoe.

The most memorable thing for me about Annapolis High School was that half of it burned when I was a senior. There was no other place to hold classes so while the building was being repaired, half the school attended classes in the remains of the building in the morning and the other half in the afternoon. School work that year consisted of six class sessions: Math, English, Latin, Spanish and two study periods, all forty-five minutes each. Because of the fire, some subjects were dropped, such as Home Economics, Music and Physical Education. As a senior I attended in the afternoons. My first and last periods were study hall, so for almost a full school year, my class hours were from 12:45-3:45. The rest of the day was mine to do what I wanted. Most of the time I was hanging around the Naval Academy as I had discovered Midshipmen. I had sort of oozed into going with middies as some of the Navy Juniors I had known earlier were now in the Academy. I had no interest in studies as no one expected me to go to college. I just wanted to graduate, so it was necessary that I pass everything.

One small item was on my conscience, *sewing!* That was my Home Economics class. I chose it because I yearned for an extensive wardrobe. The things we made in class were a great disappointment to me; first, a pair of cotton under panties, which I wouldn't have been caught dead in; I wore rayon. Second, a cotton slip; ditto, I wouldn't be caught dead in. Finally a dress! We could choose our own pattern. Mother said she would teach me how to smock, so I had chosen a darling pattern, smocked at the waist, at the shoulder and neck, and at the cuffs.

When I cut out the dress I was distressed at the size of it. I was skinny as a rail and this voluminous garment, unsmocked, was very discouraging to contemplate; it was enormous. It looked more like a crib sheet! I took it to Mother and she told me it had to have all these dots pressed on to it to guide the smocking stitches. When I tried to iron the pattern onto the material, it didn't show up very well. Completely overwhelmed, I put pattern and material plus embroidery floss, needles, thread and scissors in my bottom drawer and went down to watch the plebe football practice.

Whenever I remembered the dress, I put it right out of my mind. Then the school burned! We had no more sewing classes! I was free, free! But I had underestimated my teacher. One day I ran into her in the hall at school. She called me over and asked me how far I had progressed in my dressmaking. I told her I was doing fine. She said it would have to be completed before I graduated. That was a long way off so I didn't think about it again.

One day in the spring she accosted me again and said, "Polly, there's something I wanted to ask you but I can't remember what it was. Never mind, it will come to me one of these days." The brown paper bag filled with materials was still in my bureau drawer. I smiled weakly and said, "I'm sure you will remember it someday, Miss Swetzer."

Time went on and occasionally I would see her and she would smile and shake her head. I would smile back and pray her memory was gone forever. It never did return. I graduated with a "C" in Home Economics, which suited me just fine; true sinners have no conscience. I told this story once to a friend and she shocked me by saying she thought Miss Swetzer knew all along I hadn't made that dress. She kept trying to get me to redeem myself but I never did.

Graduation Day finally arrived. Since our auditorium had burned, the Naval Academy allowed the school to use Dahlgren Hall, the same place exactly where the midshipmen received their degrees and tossed their hats into the air. I later loved telling people I had graduated from the Naval Academy. The seniors practiced for months singing "Kentucky Babe." That was a weird choice. There were no blacks in our school and this song was all about a Negro baby putting its wooly head on its mammy's breast. I guess it was a Negro spiritual. I failed to go to the rehearsal for the Graduation and didn't know where I was supposed to sit. On the big day I finally chose a random spot which happened to be vacant but was not, of course, my assigned space so we got our diplomas fouled up. Everyone after George Larsen, starting with me, received someone else's diploma and there was a scramble to exchange them all later.

I have no memory of going to a Graduation Ball. I do recall that a Michael Finkelstein, invited me, which I found so ridiculous I had to tell all of my friends, who were convulsed with laughter at the thought that I would be caught dead with him. What unfeeling snobs we were and what courage that poor boy had to ask me and expose himself to being rejected.

Betty, at least, had the glory of getting better grades than I. That was small consolation for having a kid sister, two years younger, getting a diploma the same day. She never said anything mean to me but that circumstance must have hurt her. Of course, she didn't like me much. I can't say I blame her. She had enough conscience for both of us so I let her carry the burden of good character alone. Whereas she would worry to death about how Mother could afford to buy a new dress for her, I would wheedle one out of her without a twinge of conscience.

Betty taught herself to sew and became quite proficient as a dressmaker. Once she made herself a black velvet evening wrap, lined it in white satin and put a white fur collar on it. I was really impressed. She was neat too. All the hangers in her closet faced the same way. She had given me explicit orders NEVER to wear anything that belonged to her. Since she weighed 145 pounds and my weight was 115 pounds, that makes sense, doesn't it? Not to me. I had plenty of safety pins.

On one occasion, Betty went out of town for a few days. I was going to a dance so I rummaged in her closet and found an evening dress I thought I could wear. It was a little big so I pinned it up in several crucial places and went out on a date. That night I had a ball. Such popularity. What I didn't know was that the dress was cut so low, anyone dancing with me could see down me all the way to my navel. This was pointed out to me by

Mother when I returned home. The dress was a mess after all my wild dancing so she advised me to take it to the cleaners. When it came back, it looked gorgeous. I put it back in Betty's closet, congratulating myself on getting away with something. When Betty returned, she pranced into my room with fire in her eye, "What do you mean by wearing my aqua lace dress?" she asked.

I was so surprised I just gasped and said, "How did you know?" "I always put my hangers back facing forward. I found that one facing back. You do both so I can tell if you have been fooling around my clothes." It probably didn't cure me but it did make me more careful.

Betty and I shared a bathroom. One time I had run a bath full of hot water with the intention of bathing as soon as I got my clothes off. I heard Betty sloshing around in the tub and went in to complain. There she was, lolling in my hot water, soaping herself. In retaliation for taking my hot water, I went to the washbasin, drew some cold water and started sprinkling it on her with my fingers. She told me to stop but I continued. Then she rose up like Venus on the half-shell, stepped out of the tub with fire in her eye and started after me. Instead of running (I was in my slip), I just stood there and pleaded, "Don't hit me! Please don't hit me!" Of course she did, all 145 pounds of her. It never occurred to me to walk out of the bathroom. You have heard of rabbits being paralyzed with fright?

Betty was so neat, she lined up bobby pins on her dresser. Once I took one and she missed it! A whole package cost a nickel. What a big deal. I guess, to her, it was the principle of the thing! She had such high principles.

My room was always a shambles. Finding a bobby pin in a hurry would have taken me fifteen minutes. I had twin beds, one I slept in and the other was a repository for the clothes I had worn. At the end of the week there would be seven orderly piles of garments, each representing one day's wear. Every Monday our black laundress would come in, scoop up the seven piles and wash and iron them. When we had a maid, which was most of the time, she would clean my room but not straighten up. This resulted in my room being a constant disaster area.

For All Our Days

Now that I had graduated from High School, what did I do all day? I slept late every morning, played tennis and swam in the summer, went canoeing from early spring to late fall, planned weekends which always included midshipmen. By this time I was deeply involved with Earle, a Third Classman, who considered us engaged. I was wearing his miniature and I dated him exclusively, at least when he was around. When he left town, I dated others with alacrity. Earle, the midshipman in question, was eight years older than I was and I should never have been allowed to go with him at all, much less as a steady. He had been a sailor before he was a midshipman and was pretty sophisticated.

Mother disapproved of our dating exclusively and put limits on the number of dates we could have monthly. She might have worried that our relationship was too intimate but she never mentioned sex to me in my whole life! This limiting our dates enraged Earle and confused me since he brought a calendar of the year's activities and circled every event of any importance as dates with him. Other midshipmen soon stopped asking me out for I was always with him. Eventually Earle won; we were going steady.

We had met at St. Anne's Church. Midshipmen were compelled to attend Church, either at the Chapel in the Yard or one in town of their choice. They marched to and from in formation. Earle was not an Episcopalian but he was church-hopping, looking for one that he might like. The Sunday he came to St. Anne's, he saw me singing in the choir and told his buddies that I was the girl he was going to marry. He joined St. Anne's and lost no time beginning his courtship. He was Irish, every inch of him, not tall, about 5'8" but very aggressive, as many small men are, volatile and so jealous of me he even resented my girl friends. I never knew how he would react to anything. He looked like Bing Crosby with respectable ears. He must have driven Mother crazy. Once he arrived at the house and asked her where he stood around there. She answered, "About as low as a snake's belly."

I'm sure if my father had been around, I would never have become so involved with a man like Earle. Daddy would have broken up our relationship. Earle was not what he would consider husband material, and I think he would have intimidated this young man. They never met until after Earle had graduated.

The first summer after I had met Earle, Mother took Jack and went to Bluefields, Nicaragua to visit Daddy. She enticed an elderly distant relative named Cousin Lizzie Trescott to come and chaperon Betty and me. She was an old dear and seemed to enjoy being with two young girls. I remember she loved her toast in the morning, lavishly spread with anchovy paste. That's pure salt! I bet that caused her demise when her end finally came.

Earle was on a Midshipman cruise so I had a ball, dating everybody I knew. There was a whole new class of plebes and lots of them were cute! Then a few civilians entered my picture. One was wealthy and had his own Buick roadster. He ended up in later years as a spy and was caught while he was in England during WWII. I don't think he was shot but he was imprisoned.

Another was the son of a well-known Baltimore artist. He was sort of fey. He would send me letters full of foreign money which he designated as alimony. He also was known for skulking behind the bushes when I had a date with someone in Annapolis. I would catch glimpses of him peering at me from the greenery bordering the sidewalks. Then my longtime admirer, Tom Stone, reentered the picture when he came home from college for vacations. He was always his usual attentive self. You don't have any trouble recognizing that I was a boy-crazy teenager.

That was a lovely summer. I had males running out of my ears. Like all good things it came to an end when the upperclassmen returned from their cruise and I found myself in bondage to Earle again. To make matters worse, Earle decided I was too thin and tried to force me to drink milk. I hated it and fought him at every turn. He would take me into an ice cream parlor for a sundae and not let me eat it until I had downed a glass of milk. I would be embarrassed with so many people around, so I wouldn't make a scene. I would drink the horrid stuff, hating every mouthful and Earle most of all. I didn't gain an ounce, which irritated him and suited me just fine; no one can be too thin or too rich. I managed the first but not the second.

The next summer when Mother and Jack went to Nicaragua to visit Daddy again, she insisted I go with them. My parents must have been worried with good reason about this enduring affair I was having with Earle. Betty probably stayed with her friends, the Robertsons. I sort of doubt it because of the eating problem. It's possible Cousin Lizzie came for a second summer and stayed with her. I just don't remember. Mother never was concerned about Betty's beaux. She always yearned for someone who wouldn't give her the time of day such as the captain of the football team, the five-striper (the regimental commander), or the star of the basketball team. She hated to be seen with men who were shorter than she was but she dated some anyway. One midshipman she dated was so short, she got a charley-horse from keeping her knees bent when she walked beside him. I don't remember my sister ever being in love with anyone who dated her at the Academy except two; one turned out to be homosexual, which was tragic because they were very well suited to one another in every other way. The other was a big man on campus and eventually dropped her for some other girl.

In 1930, Mother, Jack and I traveled to Bluefields out of New Orleans on a United Fruit Company boat. But first we traveled by train, the Crescent Limited, out of Washington, DC. It was nonstop to New Orleans except for a ten minute pause in Atlanta, Georgia. This was the most luxurious train I ever traveled. It was quiet and moved very fast and smoothly. We had a compartment which was comfortable, roomy and had three beds. For dinner that night in the candlelit fancy diner we were served, believe it or not, thirty-one items of food; I counted them. The entree was roast leg of lamb, which was served with mint sherbet. At home we always had mint jelly with lamb, but sherbet! The table had snowy white linens, fresh flowers and we had our own black waiter. I have no yen to travel today's Amtrak; I have known what it was like to be "high-regarded."

Breakfast was equally impressive: fresh orange juice, wonderfully strong coffee and anything you might want such as waffles, hot cakes, eggs cooked to order, bacon, sausages, served with grits to please all the southerners on the train.

Poor Jack, he never traveled well; all that great food was wasted on him. He had motion sickness and spent most of his time lying around our compartment reading comics. No matter what means of locomotion, car, train, boat and later planes, he was always nauseated. He inherited that from Mother, who although perfectly fine on planes, cars or trains, went to bed with a bag of oranges as soon as she stepped on a ship. Even the smell of the paint made her sick.

The next day in New Orleans, some friends took us to Antoine's famous French restaurant for lunch. I ordered broiled chicken, mashed potatoes and peas, my favorite meal at fifteen. When it came it looked and smelled delicious. I had just put a fork into the chicken, getting ready to cut it, when the waiter poured half a cup of melted butter over the whole plate. I just looked at it. Remember me and butter? My meal that day consisted of two dry rolls and iced tea. Mother kept looking over at my plate, frowning, signaling me to eat something. She was so embarrassed for the meal was very expensive. I didn't dare ask for another plate of food, so I went hungry.

The ship we boarded was Norwegian and the crew did not speak English. We ate our meals with the captain and his officers. All I ever remember having for dinner was fish stew, which was served for lunch and dinner every day. I liked it, thank goodness. We must have had other things but the stew was the center of the meal. Dessert was canned fruit. One day I offered to make a pie, so I was allowed into the galley and there I put together a lemon meringue pie from memory.

We ran into foul weather and the captain told us our ship radio was dead; there were no lifeboats either. For some reason the crew was not alarmed so we weren't either. We didn't like to complain. We were traveling free, being what they called deadheads. Daddy was in command in Bluefields and an office of the United Fruit Company, was situated there. To be nice politically, the Fruit Company gave us free passage. They must have been making face with the U.S. Government.

One night I went back to my cabin and found a small bottle of perfume under my pillow. I knew one of the crew made up our bunks and I asked the captain to point out our steward. He was a nice looking young boy, so I approached him to thank him for his present. He turned and grinned and he had only about four teeth. Then I noticed all the crew had the same need of dentistry; I hope Norwegian sailors have better teeth now.

Meanwhile Jack just stayed in his bunk and complained that the mosquitoes were biting him. Mother told me later that they must have been lice or fleas for there are no mosquitoes at sea. Mother herself was so sick she couldn't do much about it. She just lay in her bunk and ate oranges.

When we arrived in Nicaragua we found ourselves in a small coastal town. I don't remember how we traveled to Bluefields. It was up in the mountains and very tiny. We were told this area was the second rainiest spot in the world. The only water supply available was collected in large metal cache basins on the roofs of the houses. It rained everyday, sometimes several times, so there was never a shortage of water. It was lovely and soft, of course, so it was wonderful for bathing and laundry.

Daddy had a small apartment in the same building as his office. There was no kitchen so we ate our meals at a little native hotel down the street. We stayed there with him the whole summer. My Spanish vocabulary returned with usage so I could read the newspaper and talk to the Nicaraguans.

I was fifteen years old and the officers made a fuss over me as there were so few white females around. I remember once going up the river in the jungle on a picnic on a boat about the size of "The African Queen." Mostly though, I played tennis every afternoon with the officers. We would watch a thunderstorm approaching but would continue to play until the first huge drop of water hit the court. Then we would dash for the clubhouse and drink large, wonderful fresh limeades. Very soon the rain would stop, the sun would come out and minutes later, the court would be dry. Back we'd go, reminding each other of the score, and continue playing until time to dress for dinner. My tennis improved immensely that summer as I played with men only and they were not overly kind; I had balls slammed at me almost as often as the men did.

One of my tennis partners received his commission as First Lieutenant and asked me to pin on his bars for him. It is customary to be kissed at that time and I remember his mustache felt so funny. We would walk to the hotel for our meals. On the side of the road there was a papaya tree which Daddy had coaxed into bearing fruit, sending someone out to water and feed it. He would watch the greenish-yellow melons ripen and when one was perfect for eating, he would take out his little pocket knife, cut it off and carry it triumphantly to the hotel and have it for breakfast. How he loved growing things. And eating them!

The food we were served was the usual rice and beans, plantains, chicken, pork, native greens, and fish, I suppose. Once we had a dish that was different and delicious. Daddy asked what it was. Our little waiter asked the cook who came out beaming and gave him a word Daddy had never heard before. When we returned to our apartment, he looked it up in a native dictionary. "Guess what," he said, "that was a mountain rat we ate tonight."

Several times we had iguana which tastes much like chicken. We lived in terror of being served unknowingly, dog, which the Nicaraguans considered a delicacy. As I remember, we had canned prunes every night for dessert; our waiter called them plumes.

One day we were having lunch when Daddy said he had received a postcard from Earle, who was on another Midshipman cruise. He told me Earle had asked him for my hand in marriage. This didn't surprise me as he had talked to me about doing this before he left. Then Daddy said, "What kind of nincompoop would ask a man he has never met for his daughter's hand in marriage *on a postcard?*" Nowadays I would agree with him but then I rose from the table and said icily, "I refuse to eat with anyone who is insulting the man I am going to marry!"

He did not mention Earle again and neither did I. Years later my father wrote me a letter and told me how proud he was of me for my loyalty to this man and how thankful he was I had not married him.

Daddy became so bored in Bluefields when his family was not there with him, he would play games at others' expense.

I told you he had a quirky sense of humor. One of his junior officers was so terrified of him that when Daddy asked him to look out and see what the weather was doing, he would read the thermometer and make a written report. All his C.O. wanted him to say was that it was a little cloudy or sunny or whatever. Since his desk was right across the room from this Lieutenant's and they faced one another all day long, Daddy started squinching up one eye every time the young man looked up from his work. After a week or two of this the Lieutenant asked some of the other officers how they stood the Major's awful tic. "What tic?" they asked.

"Do you mean you haven't noticed how he squinches up his right eye?" "No," they said, "you are imagining things."

Soon the Lieutenant was so busy watching Daddy that he couldn't do his work. He could not convince the others that he was seeing anything and he thought he was losing his mind. He finally went back to the States on "sick leave" and didn't return. I think Daddy felt remorse for a little while.

I have a picture of Mother and Daddy in Bluefields. The press (where did they come from? This was a small jungle town!) wanted a picture of him and since he was talking to the Chief of Police at the time, Daddy insisted that both the Chief and Mother be in the picture. No one knew how to tell him "nay" so they complied with his wishes. In the picture, Daddy is sitting in a large wicker chair with his puttee'd legs spread and he is holding his safari hard hat on his knee. Behind him and standing is the very fat Jeje de Policia on one side and on the other, Mother standing, holding a bouquet of flowers. The expressions of all three are definitely reminiscent of Grant Woods' Early American Gothic, absolutely dead pan. I just love it! I don't believe the Press knew Daddy was trying to be funny.

I think Daddy loved having us and we had fun too. In August we started home on another banana boat. This time Jack had no mosquito bites and there were no storms. Mother took to her bunk anyway with her bag of oranges. When we docked in New Orleans, there were no more invitations to dine at Antoine's, which was a great disappointment to me. I had planned to order the same meal I had before and to guard it with my life against a shower of butter. We boarded our train, again the Crescent Limited, and settled ourselves for the return trip.

Jack was so black from three months in the tropics, Mother had a hard time convincing the conductor that Jack was not Negro. In the late 20's, Blacks could not travel in a "white" car. She hauled out passports and he finally believed her and let us on the train. Everything was fine until we arrived in Atlanta. The year before, Mother had let Jack go up into the terminal to buy a comic book. The train stopped there just ten minutes, so she had watched impatiently for his return. He didn't come back and the train started to move. She became a wild woman; she called the conductor and tried to get him to stop the train. Finally he said he would make a search through the cars and if he couldn't find Jack, he would arrange to have the train stop so she could return to Atlanta to find him. Jack was found, sitting on the rear platform, quietly reading his new comic. By that time Mother's hair was half down her back and she was nearly out of her mind.

This year she refused to let Jack leave the train. He said I could go with him and *please*! Mother said she guessed that would be all right so we hurried off the train and dashed up the steps to make our purchases. I did make sure exactly which track our train was on. We quickly spent our money and ran down the steps so Mother would not have another fit. To my dismay the train was not there. I couldn't find anyone to ask where it had gone. Over on another track I saw a train ready to leave and when it started to move, I grabbed Jack and we hopped on. Entering the first car, I asked someone what train we were on. He answered, "Crescent Limited."

I asked, "Where is it bound?" He said, "Washington." I often wonder what would have happened if we had failed to board the moving train.

I beamed. We found Mother, unperturbed, reading peacefully. I wouldn't have said anything about our panic but Jack could hardly contain himself. He had to tell her how we had just jumped on any old train we could catch. We never returned to Bluefields again so our Crescent Limited days were over, but if we had gone back, I would never have left the train for anything. I'll never understand why they moved it or why it was facing the wrong direction.

The next year Daddy came home and had orders back to Quantico. When he arrived home, I burst into tears. His hair was grey at the temples; he was growing old. He might die! He laughed and said I was a silly because I cried when I was sad and I cried when I was happy. That's true. I have very weak tear ducts and I weep at movies, listening to music, at sunsets, reading books, you name it. I don't think he thought it was a weak trait; it's a Marston trait. That made it a good one in his estimation.

Daddy rounded up all of Mother's unpaid bills, some of which were being used for bookmarks, ranted about unreliable females, paid the bills with the money he had saved to buy a new car, and carted off the family in the old Buick to their new duty station, which was Quantico again. Mother carried on her lap a plant given her by our Chinese laundryman.

I was in no hurry to leave Annapolis at this time. I was seventeen and there was a whole batch of new plebes to conquer. I stayed with a friend named Charlotte Dugan, who lived in that beautiful Rideout House, which is an historical landmark, built by the original Rideout who had also built the house Mother had grown up in.

Charlotte and I slept in a huge four-poster bed and warded off bats at night by covering our heads with the sheets as the windows had no screens and the critters were attracted by the light of our kerosene lamp.

Breakfast was always wonderful: waffles, cooked on an iron on top of the wood stove down in the basement kitchen, then sent up on the dumbwaiter to the enormous dining room. If you think what you get now in the frozen department is a real waffle, I feel sorry for you. Those delectable ones that Charlotte's colored mammy sent up to us were crisp, hot, rich and browned to perfection.

I learned to eat crab that summer. Annapolis is noted for its seafood and it was fresh and plentiful. Lunch was crab salad and iced tea and homemade rolls everyday in that house that summer. I didn't eat crab when I arrived but I became so hungry, I broke down and tried it. After two days I was hooked for life. To this day I spend an inordinate amount of time looking for crab in markets, going to seafood restaurants, getting to the oceanfront every chance I get, collecting crab recipes, even crabbing if the opportunity arises. Nothing in the world compares with backfin lump fresh crabmeat.

Everything at that house was served on antique Willow ware and the food was so delicious, I can't see Willow dishes without getting an appetite. At Sunday dinner there was always a crowd of relatives and midshipmen, and the memories of huge platters of fried chicken and mammoth strawberry shortcakes will never fade from my memory. It is no coincidence that I use Willow ware myself. It is the only pattern I never tired of in sixty-six years of housekeeping.

One night that summer I had a date with good old Tom Stone. We were sitting out in the gorgeous colonial garden of the Rideout House, smelling the hedges of honeysuckle, watching a new moon rise over Chesapeake Bay with its myriad sailboats and fishing vessels, when he asked me to marry him. Everything was so romantic, I said yes! At the time, it seemed like a wonderful idea. We had been reminiscing about all our times together over the last six years and it seemed so natural. Who else could I marry? Why did I ever go with Earle in the first place? Tom and I embraced and swore undying affection.

The next morning when I woke up, I remembered the night before. Ye Gods! What had I done? In the light of day, Tom had retired to his usual hound dog spot in my list of eligible bachelors. I must have been crazy. I couldn't marry him, ever! I had to tell him but I couldn't, not to his face. I didn't have the courage. I would write him from the safety of Quantico. I left, like the coward I was, and joined my family in Quarters 345. One of my best friends in Annapolis, Ann Hall, who was supposed to look like me and eventually became one of my bridesmaids two years later, married Tom so he finally got himself a good wife. Am I happy about that? Not too happy. Annie turned out to be an alcoholic and died quite young.

For All Our Days

I was seventeen, soon to turn eighteen. Earle had graduated from the Academy and was in Florida, qualifying to be an aviator. Mother and Daddy had refused to let us get married for a year. He had always planned we would be wed on Graduation Day, in the Naval Academy Chapel with all his friends crossing swords over our heads as we exited from the Chapel. He was wild because he had orders to the West Coast after flying school. How could he keep track of me from there?

The first week I was in Quantico, someone came to the front door and rang the bell. When I went to answer it, I saw a Lieutenant carrying a large cake on a platter. The cake was tilted and the frosting was lying in pools on the plate. He beamed and asked if Miss Betty was at home. I told him she was and invited him to come in, I would fetch her. She was in the kitchen and when I saw her I said, "There is a weird Lieutenant out in the living room and he's carrying a large cake. I think he made it himself."

Betty laughed and said, "Oh, that must be Lamar Curry. He said he was going to make me a cake but I thought he was fooling."

I approved of this man for Betty. He was the first one she went with that I thought had promise. He was a southern gentleman, soft-spoken with a Georgia drawl. I thought he was quite good-looking, blond, blue-eyed with a trim physique. He could have been a little taller for her. Actually, he and Betty were the same height, five feet, nine inches, and weighed exactly the same, one hundred and forty-five pounds. Unless she wore high heels, she would not have to bend her knees when they were dancing or walking together on a date. As the weeks went by and Betty and Lamar would date, I would encourage romance by leaving only dim subdued lights on when I came home earlier than she did in the evening. Unfortunately, the relationship did not jell; Betty did not feel romantic about Lamar. After a while he started dating a girl across the road, that I considered a real "dog." I felt he was definitely wasted on her.

Meanwhile, I had "other fish to fry." I had met some aviators, one of whom I found very attractive, definitely worth pursuing. George was short for a man, not good-looking and very shy, but wow, how he could dance. We danced ourselves into a Fred Astaire and Ginger Rogers romance. We eventually went "steady." I wore his original "wings," his most prized possession, the ones he was given when he qualified as a flyer. I also wore his flying scarf, made from part of a parachute. He even gave me a flight one evening, which was absolutely against regulations. I went out to the flying field, put on a flying suit after everyone had gone home for the night, got into a two-seater plane and away we went. I was scared to death, more of being discovered than of the loops George was executing to impress me. We were not discovered but we never repeated our prank.

He lived in a set of quarters with two other Marine pilots and two other girls and I ate many dinners there. All aviators drank (we females did not, of course) and we worried about their dissolute lives. On dates, we three couples would go riding in three cars. Being aviators, our dates would drive in formation, the lead vehicle in the middle of the road, the other two behind, one on the left, the other on the right. The lead driver gave flight signals to the other two when he changed direction. Why we were not killed on that two-lane road, I'll never know. There was not a great deal of traffic but it was twisty and curvy and we could not see very far ahead. But we felt invincible! Nothing would ever happen to us. At least, that was what we thought. One day, Katie, one of the other dates, who was a nurse, told me she worked in the emergency room at the hospital and she had seen some terribly injured people, who would be disfigured forever; they were all victims of auto accidents. After that, I didn't feel so devil-may care about the formation driving.

Dancing was important to me. After all those years in Annapolis, I was a darn good dancer. George was one of the best partners I ever had. On dates we would go to the old Officers' Club, turn on the big bands on the radio and dance for three or four hours. He would always attempt to trip me up, trying new steps, turning and dipping unexpectedly. I was a limp rag mop, anticipating every move; I followed like a shadow. Gosh! It was fun! I have met only one other person in my life who could equal

George as a dancer. He was a scroungy little South American that I met on board the ship, "The President Coolidge," going to Hawaii. He too was short and quite Latin in appearance. I spotted him the first night aboard when he was dancing at the after dinner passenger get-together. He wore filthy white shoes and I couldn't take my eyes off him. He danced with oodles of people but he didn't ask me.

The next night, there he was again, flying all over the room with different partners. *Finally*, he appeared at my side and invited me onto the floor. As we were dancing, he complained that his shoes were holding him back. He excused himself and left. When he came back, he was wearing different shoes, white but even dirtier than the ones he had been wearing before. He grinned and said, "Now I can do you justice. You are a wonderful dancer."

He never danced with anyone else that trip; I had him all to myself for three nights. When we docked in Honolulu, he flew on to the Philippines and I never saw him again. I can't even remember his name. This occurred pre-Pearl Harbor. Later I used to wonder if he was a spy or involved in some unsavory business. He never told me what he did for a living.

Back to Quantico and my romances. As I said, Betty and Lamar dated but they also dated other people. My love life was confused. I dated George exclusively in Quantico but I went back to Annapolis frequently to date midshipmen, and then Earle was writing me daily from the West Coast. I was really unofficially engaged to three people and none of them knew about the other two.

Lamar's two sisters, Shirley and Louise, came to visit him that spring. They were ten and twelve years his senior and both of them had teenage children. He decided to have a dinner party at the Officers' Club. There was always dancing on Saturday nights. Mother and Daddy were invited as they were contemporaries of his sisters. He felt comfortable with them for he had dated Betty so much. Lamar asked Betty to be his date but she had another engagement. George was away on some flying expedition so Lamar asked me to go with him. I accepted and he arranged to pick me up a little early. He arrived promptly, his two sisters and a couple of teenage nieces in tow. When we entered the Club, Lamar escorted Shirley and Louise straight to the table reserved for us all but I went to the powder room to fix my hair.

When I came out, the orchestra was playing and a young Lieutenant I knew saw me and asked me to dance. I said I thought I should dance with the man who had escorted me. He asked me who that was. I said, "Lamar Curry."

"He's dancing with someone else." He said. "See, there he goes." I looked and there was Lamar dancing with Shirley. "OK," I said, "I'll be glad to dance with you." From time to time, I'd go back to our reserved table and someone else would ask me to dance. Lamar was very busy being a host and never looked my direction. Finally, it was intermission time when people paired off and had refreshments. Someone asked me to eat with him but I was so sure Lamar would expect me to be his partner, I refused.

When I saw him carrying plates of cake and cups of punch to where his sisters were sitting and then joining them, I accepted the next offer. As the evening wore on to a close, the band struck up "Auld Lang Syne" and I had yet to dance with the man who had brought me. He never appeared at my side or asked me and I danced the last dance with someone else, which was unheard of.

Now you are not going to believe this! Or maybe you will! As people were saying goodnight, Lamar appeared at my side and said, "Tillie, can you go home with your parents? It would be quite a help. They haven't left yet and I'll just go on back with Shirley and Louise and the girls. Thanks a heap."

I went out to Triangle Cafe with some of my friends to eat hamburgers and I regaled them with my date's inattentiveness. I'm sure I never intended to date Lamar Curry again; he was nothing to me and I was surely nothing to him. Little do we know what the future holds.

The following fall, George had been transferred to a different base somewhere in New York. Lamar was still playing the field. So was I. There were always new Lieutenants coming on the Base to get to know and entertain. Lamar had a "mess" in his Quarters, a dining pool with three or four other officers. It sure beat eating at the Club three times a day for them; they had a cook and home-cooked food. It was cheaper and better. And they would often invite girls to dinner. Lamar had a set menu for parties. This was when Pamelia, the cook, was not there. He could cook the whole meal by himself. It was good too: roast beef, browned potatoes, peas, cauliflower au gratin, store-bought rolls and ice cream for dessert. Those were the days of ice boxes and ice cream had to be bought at the last minute, otherwise it would melt before you could eat it. Someone would run down to the store after the first course to buy it. The rest of us would clear the table and wait for our host to return with the dessert.

We young women were living a hedonistic life; swimming, playing tennis, having bridge parties, sometimes even at night when the men joined us, putting on amateur plays, taking riding lessons, having dinner parties, going to dances, dating until the wee hours of the morning, sleeping late the next day. I don't know anyone who lives like that today except the "jet set." The year was 1932. We were in a deep Depression, our fathers had taken a pay cut, Franklin D. Roosevelt was president and launching a New Society. Everyone seemed to be poor except those in the military. If we were, we were all poor together; no one had any more money than anyone else. And we were living a country club existence.

About this time Daddy became Boppie. One of my friends, Betsy Ann Steele, started calling him "Pop" and he teased her and said he didn't pop. She said, "All right, I'll call you 'Bop' and you can bop me," or some such foolishness. For some reason, the name stuck and forever after he was "Boppie" to all of his children, his wife and his grandchildren. We never called him "Daddy" again.

Jack had been sent to St. James Episcopal School in Baltimore for boys. He was a terrible student but so attractive everyone loved him. He became president of the student body, captain of the football team, sang the lead in all of the school musicals, sang in the school choir, was voted the most popular boy in school and flunked almost every subject. When Boppie heard this last he nearly had a stroke. His schooling was not cheap and the family was living on short rations to pay his tuition. You could hear my father yelling all the way across the street, "I'm not going into debt so that boy can sing and play football! What do those crazy people think they are doing? I sent him there to get an education!"

He was so afraid Jack would never get into college when the time came. He did but he flunked his first year. Not that he minded. He had to repeat his Freshman year but he was a "social sophomore" and had many privileges denied to freshmen. Nothing ever bothered Jack that we knew. We didn't see him very much. Every summer some wealthy parent would invite him to spend time with their family, sailing, yachting, visiting at their summer homes. The boys loved him and so did their parents. He looked like Tyrone Power (a movie star of the period) tall, lanky with an up tilted nose, beautiful dark eyes and black hair. The girls his age were wild about him.

Jack had musical talent which surfaced when he went away to boarding school. He was allowed to play the organ in the chapel and he taught himself to play by ear. He couldn't read notes so he had to make a recording when he composed a melody he liked. He could play anything he could sing so he played all the popular songs of the day. Once he composed a religious piece which he called his Opus I. His musical know-how made him even more sought after than ever. Sit him down at a piano and he would happily entertain you for hours. It's a shame we never owned one. Mother played by ear also.

That fall Lamar, for some reason, asked me to go to a football game in Baltimore. I'm sure Navy was playing and that's the reason he wanted to go. (I just asked him and he says it was a Navy-Maryland game.)

Once or twice I had gone to the Army-Navy game in my Annapolis days, up at four a.m. traveling on the special train with all the middies, once to Philadelphia and once to New York. That was fun. Weather reports were iffy though and we never knew what the weather would be like by the time we arrived at the stadium. Once I sat through a game in Philadelphia in a light drizzle, the temperature hovering around 50 degrees, dressed in a tweed suit, sweater, winter underwear, coat, scarf, plush-lined boots and gloves. I was in a dripping perspiration and shed as much as I could. To me, football games were to be lived through because you had so much fun later, like dinner at a restaurant or a party somewhere.

When Lamar asked me to go to Baltimore with him, I offered to bring a picnic lunch. We had to leave pretty early in the morning for the highways were all two-lane or in some spots, three-lane in those days. It was a four hour trip. When we arrived in Baltimore, Lamar pulled into a gas station. While he was pumping gas, I pulled out my compact and started powdering my nose. Then he leaned in the car window and asked, "Do you want to powder your nose?"

Young women in my day were not supposed to have urinary tracts. Now that I had powdered my nose visibly, I had no excuse to go to the ladies' room. I sat there, waiting for him to use the facilities, slightly uncomfortable in the region of my bladder. What a dumb thing to ask me. He could have said something about freshening up. Anyway, I bled within my Victorian armor and we continued on to the stadium. I can't imagine any young person today being able to understand how repressed we were back then!

We ate our sandwiches in the parking lot and washed them down with hot coffee I had brought in a thermos. Halfway through the first quarter, I couldn't think of anything except going to the bathroom. I don't remember even suspecting the stadium had restrooms. I sure wasn't going to ask. I just had to wait until the game was over and we went to dinner, when I would have the ladylike excuse to "wash my hands."

At last, the game ended and we got back to the car and Lamar said we were going to a restaurant called the Colinswood. It was halfway back to Quantico! There was lots of traffic and we didn't arrive at the Inn until eight o'clock. When I finally reached the restroom, I was nearly ill. I felt clammy and faint. We had left Quantico about nine that morning. Eleven hours in chilly weather! I would like to tell you this was a unique experience but it wasn't. Once I spent a weekend at a beach cottage and never once went to the bathroom for it was an outhouse and everyone could see you approaching it. There's only one reason anyone goes to an outhouse. We were raised like that!

Sometime after the football game in Baltimore, Lamar started courting me. I thought he was too good to waste on that unattractive girl across the street. He was really kind of cute. He couldn't dance worth a hoot but for some amazing reason, I didn't care. George began to fade in my memory and as for poor Earle, I couldn't remember what he looked like. Lamar looked better and better to me. Another plus was that Boppie and Mother liked him so much. And his sister, Shirley, who had raised him since he became an orphan at seven, really liked *me!*

I wrote George that I didn't want to be engaged anymore. He flew down to Quantico to "talk it over." I told him I was sorry but I didn't love him. Poor George, he hated himself for falling in love with me and had fought valiantly against it for months. I had finally caught him and here I was telling him to forget the whole thing. He left to return to New York. He zoomed so low over our house, I was afraid he was committing suicide. We all ducked our heads as the plane roared overhead, clipping the treetops in our yard. Of course he didn't kill himself. He later married a nice girl, had two boys, brought them all to call on me in California, went to war and was killed.

One night Lamar and I were parked down on the dock and he made some remark about what if we were married, would such and such be, or words to that effect. I swear I thought he proposed. I remember I was wearing pink and I had read somewhere that a large number of proposals were made to girls when they were wearing that color. I was a statistic. Lamar does not remember proposing, but he didn't tell me that for many years. Although he doesn't think he asked me to marry him, he decided he ought to get married someday and being married to me wouldn't be so bad. Anyway, we found ourselves engaged. Mother and Boppie and Shirley were happy as bird-dogs and we were sort of pleased too. Alice Cushing, one of my friends, shook her head in amazement and disbelief. She had admonished me the month before by saying, "If you hurt Lamar by mistreating him, I'll never forgive you!"

So we were going to be married. I told Lamar I had promised to go to June Week with Tom Morton in early June and he didn't seem to mind at all. He told me not to change my plans; we could be married on July 1st. He didn't have any leave until then, anyway. I had to tell Earle, of course, and he threatened to commit mayhem, murder or something equally dramatic. He was still a continent away on the West Coast, so we were not alarmed. Distances were much greater in those days. California was halfway to the moon!

Quantico Base went wild. There had not been a real wedding there in years and everyone was invited and wanted to have parties for us. They lionized us to the teeth. Mother planned a big wedding with the Marine Band, three ministers, one from Annapolis' St. Anne's Church, another the local chaplain, and the third, a Rev. Heaton from Aquia Church, the closest Episcopalian Parish to Quantico. The last was invited as a courtesy to the Church in Virginia. (In those days, it was against the law to cross a state border to marry someone. You might be marrying a white to a black!) Mother had been baptized, confirmed and married at St. Anne's, I had been baptized and confirmed there but it was too complicated to get the whole wedding to Annapolis. We compromised by having their priest, my Cousin Edward Johnson, come to us. By inviting Rev. Heaton to participate, we did not have to post the $1000 bond required by law, insuring our intentions were honorable.

One amusing note. When Tom Morton read of my engagement in the Annapolis paper, he wrote and excused me from coming to June Week. Like the gentleman he always was, he congratulated me and wished me well. Isn't it strange? All three of those men I had seriously contemplated marrying, had military careers and I never saw any of them ever again. Earle was a war hero and Tom got to be an Admiral. They are all three dead now so I shall never see them in this life.

Everyone was lovely to us, giving us showers. There were teas, luncheons, dinners, bridge parties, and sandwiched in-between, trips to Washington for a trousseau. Quantico is the hottest place in the world in the summer. Nothing was air-conditioned so my wedding dress was the coolest one we could find, white organdy. When I was buying it at Garfinckel's department store in Washington, the sales girls thought I was graduating from high school. They said, "Doesn't the little girl look lovely."

When I put on the jacket with a train and long sleeves, I looked more like a bride; that made me feel better. The veil was a last minute affair. I was supposed to wear one that belonged to Mother's best friend, Ethel Butler. It arrived the week before the wedding and it didn't do at all. It was tulle and about twenty-five years old, so it looked yellow. We had to make three trips to Washington for fittings on an organdy veil. In that heat with all the social engagements that were scheduled, I was worn to a frazzle.

Presents were pouring in and Mother made me write ten notes a day before I could leave the house in the morning. She instinctively knew I would never write them after I was married. Lamar had received orders to Fort Sill, Oklahoma, six weeks after the wedding. She was determined that I would be socially correct and not embarrass her so I had to have every note written by the time we left.

The big day, July 1st, 1933, arrived, so hot you could fry an egg on the sidewalk. Out-of-town guests were billeted all over the Base, cousins, aunts and uncles, bridesmaids, friends. There was no hotel or consecrated church in Quantico so the wedding was held at the Officers' Club. The ballroom was decorated with a makeshift altar, complete with flowers and candles. There was a long white cloth for the wedding party to walk on and the Marine band played for the service as well as the dancing which followed the ceremony. I had six bridesmaids, Alice and Edith Cushing, Ann Hall, from Annapolis, Mary Louise Nutting, Sport Barber and Betsy Ann Steele, and my sister, Betty, was Maid of Honor. We dressed upstairs at the Club and the wedding party descended the staircase to the main floor. Horror of horrors! At the rehearsal, as we descended the staircase, someone discovered the light from the big window on the stairs showed our bodies as though we were not wearing slips. People were sent scurrying around the base for eight long evening slips, which would help block out the sunlight pouring through the window. They were collected but where they came from, I'll never know.

Lamar had a Best Man, Duncan Waller, and fourteen groomsmen. At the conclusion of the ceremony, the latter crossed swords to make an arch, the usual custom at a military wedding. The wedding party really filled up most of the room, and when the men drew swords, those people standing close to the wedding party drew back so they wouldn't be wounded. Every Marine General within a radius of three hundred miles was invited and they all came. Two of them were not speaking to one another so one climbed a lamppost outside on the lawn to watch the ceremony as he refused to enter the Club while his enemy was inside. Another General saw Lamar pacing nervously in the hall and said to him, "Settle down, son. No one pays any attention to the groom at a wedding."

The minute the ceremony concluded, a group of photographers appeared out of nowhere, uninvited, demanding to photograph the wedding party. I remember perspiring so much my flowers were sticking to my long organdy sleeve and I was miserable. All I wanted was a tall glass of punch. The photographers won out and took pictures but they were so poor that when we saw the proofs, we never ordered any. The original plan had been for us to go to Washington after the honeymoon and have studio portraits made but we never went. So, that's why there are no formal pictures of us in our finery. By that time, I know my parents were poverty-stricken and didn't want to spend any more money than they already had.

We cut the cake with Lamar's sword, which made my new husband very nervous. He was so afraid someone would put it back in the scabbard with crumbs on it, he hovered nervously until he saw it properly cleaned. It was dear to his heart as his Company at the Naval Academy had given it to him. We danced the first dance to "She'll be Coming 'Round the Mountain," which was Lamar's choice. I asked him why *that*? And he said it was the only song he could think of. I had definitely married a non-dancer.

We didn't stick around very long at the reception as we had a considerable distance to drive before dark. We were going to a Hotel Panorama up in the Blue Ridge Mountains, our first stop on the way to Mountain City, Georgia, where Lamar's sister lived and where we would spend our honeymoon.

Now that Lamar and I are really married, I think it is time to talk about his forebears and *his* family.

5

Lamar's Forebears
& His Early Years

L amar is, and has ever been since I first met him, the epitome of a Southern gentleman. Since his family members called him the "gold child" when he was young, I'm sure his nature has ever been thus. He is a gentle but strong man and I consider him one of the bravest people I have ever met. I don't believe he is afraid of anything or anyone. He has more integrity in his little finger than many people have in their whole bodies. The Lord was good to give me this man as a husband. Looking back on our life together, I think Lamar had a tough job turning me from a frivolous teenager into a more worthwhile creature with a conscience, but living with him all those years eventually paid off. Alice Shell, one of my bridesmaids, was right back in 1932 when she anticipated my mistreatment of him; I had been pretty flighty about the other men who had been in love with me. I would have been ashamed of myself if I had treated Lamar that way. He was so decent and expected nothing but the best from me, as he did of everyone. I thank God for bringing us together.

Who was he and where did he come from? He was from Macon, Georgia and had graduated from the Naval Academy in 1929, going into the Marine Corps.

All of his forebears in this country that I have heard or read about were from the South. Strange to relate, both his father and his mother trace their ancestry back to the same person, Thomas Lamar, a French Huguenot who came to this country in 1675 and settled in Maryland. I have a chart, showing how two sons of Thomas started branches of Lamars and after seven generations, Manly Lamar Curry from one branch married Augusta Lamar Bacon from another.

I shall start with his two grandfathers because I know something about them. They were both distinguished in their own fields. Both served in the Civil War as officers. Both served in their State Legislatures. Both had more than an ordinary share of intelligence. And both continued to serve their country in peacetime. They were very different in personality although they were both essentially politicians

I'll start with Grandpapa Curry. His full name was Jabez Lafayette Monroe Curry. At some point in his life, he changed the Lafayette to Lamar. He was born in Double Branches, Lincoln County, GA on June 5, 1825. Not long after his birth, he lost his mother and in 1838 his father moved to Talladega County, AL. He graduated from the University of Georgia in 1843, then he studied Law at Harvard. After practicing Law for a year, he served as a private in the Texas Rangers in the war with Mexico but had to resign because of ill health. He married Ann Alexander Bowie in 1847. They had two children, Manly Bowie and Susan Lamar, whom I actually met once. He was elected to Congress in 1857 but resigned at the beginning of the Civil War in 1861. In the War, he served first in the Confederate Congress and then was on General Nathan Bedford Forrest's staff, attaining the rank of Lieutenant Colonel. Lamar tells me Grandpapa Curry fought in the 2nd Battle of Manassas. His wife died during the War and Jabez decided at the cessation of hostilities to move to Richmond, Virginia. He felt his children would have more opportunities for advancement someplace other than the deep South during those Reconstruction years. He became a Baptist preacher and was chosen President of Howard College in 1865 and had the reputation of being a fine orator.

Jabez was always interested in education. He taught at the University of Richmond and I believe there is a portrait of him in one of the University buildings today.

Young Manly, his son, earned a degree in Law at the University of Virginia. There is a Curry School there, which I am told was named for Jabez. Grandpapa Curry eventually married again, a Mary Connally, a rather wealthy woman from Richmond.

He was a good friend of Booker T. Washington. They were both intensely interested in educating the newly liberated Negroes. I was told by a relative that Mr. Washington said Mr.

Curry was so distinguished, he felt he should not sit in his presence.

Later in life, Jabez became the American Minister to Spain in 1885 and he and his wife were living there when Manly and Augusta were married. Mary, his wife, was a great hostess and they entertained most lavishly which is always a necessity in the life of a diplomat. He must have done well for he was recalled years later to Spain as a Special Envoy and Ambassador Extraordinary to be present when King Alphonso reached his coming of age in 1902.

During his early years in Virginia, he had handled the Peabody Fund, contributed by Mr. Peabody for educational purposes. On his return from Spain after two years, he continued in this capacity. After his death in 1905, the state of Alabama chose him to be one of two representatives from that state to have his statue in the Rotunda of the Capitol in Washington.

Enter now Grandpapa Bacon. His full name was Augustus Octavius Bacon. He was born in Midway, Georgia, in 1839. When very young, he was orphaned and sent to live with a relative, who had a large family. At an early age he showed promise of unusual intelligence by reading at age four, much sooner than his contemporaries. When grown, he studied Law and became a legislator in the Georgia Assembly. During the Civil War, he served with General Joseph E. Johnson as a Lieutenant. He was Adjutant of the Ninth Infantry Regiment and eventually attained the rank of Major. He married a Virginia Lamar and they had four children, two boys, Augustus and Lamar, and two girls, Mary Louise and Augusta Lamar. After the War, he became a U.S. Senator from Georgia and served in Washington for more than twenty years. In his latter years he was President pro tem of the Senate body. His home was in Macon, GA, where he built a home which he called Baconsfield. I am told he admired the British and was imitating the landed gentry. His father or grandfather was British and he was obsessed with the English concept of estate and posterity; the eldest son inheriting all the estate, insuring that it stayed intact. The name of Baconsfield for his home was chosen because he admired

Lord Beaconsfield's estate in England, which was well-known and very beautiful. The Senator lived in Washington most of the time but he always returned to his beloved Baconsfield for his vacations and to campaign. Political speeches were his forte as he was noted for his oratory.

Then tragedy struck. Both of his sons, who were in their teens, caught scarlet fever and were very ill. Miss Ginny, his wife, nursed the boys herself and on one occasion, opened a window when they complained of feeling so feverishly hot. They caught cold and their illness went into pneumonia and the two sons died within a week of one another. The Senator was so beside himself with grief that he accused his wife of causing their deaths. Miss Ginny, mourning herself, was hurt to the quick. When this outburst occurred, she rose to her full height of four feet ten inches and said, "Mr. Bacon, you will never spend another night under my roof as long as we both shall live."

And he never did. He had a small house built in the front garden, complete with kitchen and bath, and there he resided when his business brought him back to Macon. He was completely desolate as he had no sons to carry on his name.

Their two girls grew up and thrived. Mary Louise (Aunt Mamie to Lamar) was the elder and Lamar's mother, Augusta, was two years younger. She was called Gussie and was a pretty dark haired, black-eyed girl with a beautiful voice. She sang in public and Shirley, her daughter, told me her singing was the only thing she was truly conscientious about. I am told Aunt Mamie was a beauty too. When I met her she was quite elderly and although definitely a "Grande Dame," her beauty had faded. I have a picture of Gussie in her teens and she was very pretty.

There are several family stories about Gussie. One concerns a time when she was attending Wesleyan College and had come home for the weekend. When she returned to her academic studies on Sunday night, Grandpapa Bacon sent a carriage for her with orders that she come home immediately. When she did, her father told her to go upstairs and hang up her nightgown, which she had left lying on the floor. Then she could return to school. I imagine she carried out his orders.

Another family tale was about the time she went to her room after dinner to dress for an engagement she had with a young man. He arrived but Gussie was not there to greet him. Someone was dispatched to fetch her and found her sound asleep in bed. When she had started to undress, she must have forgotten about the date and had just gone to bed. The young man could not have been her most fascinating suitor. I seem to remember hearing that she did get up and get dressed. How long the young man had to wait, I haven't the slightest. She seems to have been a little "fey." I accuse my daughter Posy of having this characteristic.

Gussie and Manly were married in Macon in Christ Episcopal Church in the year of 1892 and I think it was in the Spring because the bride carried lilies of the valley and her veil was held with white lilacs. I am blessed to have an account from the Macon newspaper and I can't resist sharing it with you. I have not changed one punctuation mark or capital letter!

AT HYMEN'S ALTAR

Brilliant Marriage Wednesday Night Last

One of Georgia's Fairest Daughters United in Love and Matrimony to a Courtly Groom of the Far Northwest. Dazzling array of Costly Presents - Elegant Reception.

We do not remember ever having seen a larger assembly of the elite of Macon, than was gathered Wednesday night at Episcopal Church to witness the happy nuptials of Mr. Manly L. Curry and Miss Gussie Bacon. The event was one of the most brilliant and interesting in the social annals of the Central City.

The groom is blessed with great wealth, and conducts a most prosperous and extensive real estate business in St. Paul, Minn. He is a young gentleman of superior intelligence and polished manners; a man of much travel and general experience. He is the son of Hon. J. L. M. Curry, United States Minister to the court of Spain, and who was elected from Alabama to Congress before the war. At the time of his appointment to Spain by President Cleveland he was the general agent of the Peabody fund. The groom is an Alabamian by birth, but was raised in Richmond. He graduated at the Law School at the University of Virginia, but preferred the business in which he has become so successful.

The bride is the second daughter of Hon. A. O. Bacon, the distinguished lawyer, and prominent factor in the affairs of State. She is gifted with many personal graces, and mental attainments, which always made her a great social favorite, and ever commanded the homage of men and the praises of women.

Hence, it was not surprising that Christ Church should have been packed with a great mass of humanity to witness the marriage union of so prominent a couple. Eight o'clock was the hour announced for the ceremony, but nearly three hours before that time the anxious people began to assemble in a throng before the closed doors of the church seeking admission. Entrance was not given until after seven o'clock and when the doors opened steady streams of people poured into the edifice, and soon the pews and aisles were filled to overflowing, and when the bridal party arrived about half-past eight o'clock it was with the utmost difficulty that the attendants could gain sufficient passage to make their way to the chancel. Every available inch of space was occupied. The first floor and gallery was a huge tightly bound knot of humanity. The people were wedged to one another.

The Ushers

Messrs. Stewart Jones, J. P. Roosevelt, Ross White and O. G. Sparks were the duly appointed ushers, but their services were not needed. The people flowed past them in too strong a current. These young gentlemen also acted as attendants and awaited the arrival of the balance of the bridal party at the church.

Invited Guests

Those who were invited to the reception at the Bacon residence and near relatives of the bride, occupied reserved seats close to the chancel. The ladies were attired in most elegant toilettes, and the gentlemen appeared in rich full evening dress.

The expectant throng anxiously awaited the coming of the bridal party. The arrival of Mrs. A. O. Bacon, the mother of the bride, set the hum of conversation to louder tune, and the rustling of the congregation became greater, for it was the accepted signal that the bridal party was near.

The Wedding March

Under the artistic touch of Prof. Czurda, the organ pealed forth the glad notes of the wedding march, and to its inspiring and happy strains, the bridal party proceeded with graceful steps down the aisles of the church to the chancel railing behind which stood the Rev. J. R. Winchester, the officiating minister, who performed the service most beautifully.

The bridesmaids entered the church in couples, down the middle aisle, in the following order:

Miss Moore, of Mobile, and
Miss Jennie Rowland, of Augusta
Misses Estelle Chestney and
Birdie Coleman, of Macon.
Misses Emily Hines, of Macon, and
Miss Auerbach, of St. Paul.
Misses Leila Conner and
Mary Patterson, of Macon.
Misses Mamie Hunt and
Nanoline Holt, of Macon.
Miss Clara Dunlop, of Macon, and
Miss Olivia Cobb, of Atlanta.
Miss Nana Lamar, of Macon, and
Miss Mary Lou Bacon,
sister of the bride, of Macon.

On reaching the steps of the chancel, the bridesmaids separated, ascended the steps, one walking to the right and the other to the left, and took position on either side of the chancel, vis a vis, forming something of a semi-circle, about the groom and bride, immediately facing the preacher.

The picture thus presented was all that love and beauty, graceful womankind and gallant manhood, could possibly create. The eye was delighted by the sight, and the senses charmed.

The bridesmaids were beautifully attired in white tulle and silk; short tulle veils were held in place by half wreaths, some of forget-me-nots, pink rose buds, and others of daisies. Each bridesmaid carried a handsome bouquet of natural roses, the gift of the groom, ordered especially from Washington City. He also presented the groomsmen with their gloves.

The groomsmen headed by Mr. B. W. Branch, of Richmond, and Mr. Minter Wimberly, of Macon, walked in single file, down the aisles, each being opposite the bridesmaid in the middle aisle whom he would escort from the church. On reaching the chancel, each groomsman ascended the steps, walked and took position a little to the side of the respective bridesmaids.

The Bride

After the attendants had taken position in the chancel, the lovely bride, looking radiant in a most elaborate toilette of white moire antique silk, and Duchesse lace, with garnitures of white lilacs, gracefully arranged, entered the church leaning upon the arm of her distinguished father, and thousands of eyes gazed in admiration and love upon the fair being as she passed down the aisle. The long tulle veil which fell in graceful folds over the train, was held in place by a cluster of natural lilies of the valley, a lovely floral offering from the groom.

On reaching the chancel she was met at the altar by the groom, and his best man, Mr. Frank A. Davenport, of Richmond, Va., who entered from the vestry room. Major Bacon now stepped slightly back, and the groom and bride then locked arms, stood side by side before the preacher and spoke the words that united them in holy wedlock, and linked their future destinies together, so long as life lasts.

When the minister asked, 'Who giveth this woman in marriage?" Major Bacon advanced and placed the hand of his cherished daughter in that of the man of her choice.

The ceremony was performed with the ring, and all responses were audibly made by the happy couple.

Miss Mary Lou Bacon, who was standing near the bride, stepped forward and removed the bride's glove, and held her bouquet during the ceremony.

At the conclusion of the ceremony, the bridal party descended the steps, and proceeded out in this order:

The Bride and Groom
Mr. Frank Davenport, and Miss Mary Lou Bacon
Mr. W. H. Felton, and Miss Nana Lamar
Mr. Ross White and Miss Clara Dunlop
Mr. J. P. Roosevelt and Miss Olivia Cobb
Mr. Tracy Baxter and Miss Mamie Hunt
Mr. John Ogden and Miss Nanoline Holt
Mr. Stewart Jones and Miss Flew Reese
Mr. Thos. Cobb of Athens and Miss Fannie Hanson
Mr. Thomas Johnson of Baltimore and Miss Leila Conner
Mr. Monroe Ogden and Miss Mary Patterson
Mr. Lewis Pace of Covington and Miss Emily Hines
Mr. Roff Sims and Miss Auerbach
Mr. Handy of St. Paul and Miss Estelle Chesney
Mr. O. G. Sparks and Miss Birdie Coleman
Mr. Minter Wimberly and Miss Moore
Mr. B. W. Branch of St. Paul and Miss Minnie Rowland
Major Bacon and wife then followed the attendants.

Elegant Reception

From the church the bridal party, and invited guests repaired to the hospitable residence of Major Bacon, on College Street, where an elegant reception was held. The wedding feast consisted of the richest viands, topped with sparkling champagne, and rare wines. The wee sma"hours of the early morn were at hand, ere the delighted assembly would say good-bye to the joyous occasion.

An Incident

Connected with the reception, at one pleasant and remarkable, was the opening of a gallon of fine wine, in the supper room, that had been sealed 15 years ago by the bride, when she was only four years old, and the seal was stamped at the time with a gold seal ring now worn by Major Bacon on his finger. The bridal party quaffed of this wine, and with it the health and happiness of the bride and groom were drank! (great grammar, right?)

The presents

The guests at the reception found much delight and pleasure in viewing the dazzling and elegant array of magnificent bridal presents, which was the most elaborate and costly collection ever seen in Macon. A description in these columns could not do justice to the remembrances in jewels, gold and silver. They consisted of the richest gems, purest metals, and most exquisite workmanship.

It is impossible for us to give today a complete list of all the gifts, but, we append some to give you an idea of their quality and quantity. Many of the presents were from the relatives of the bride and groom.

The gift of the groom was a deed to $50,000 of real estate in St. Paul, Minn., which is constantly appreciating in value.

The parents of the groom sent from Europe elegant diamonds. (Posy has one and Linda Cox, another great-granddaughter, has the other. They were purchased in Spain, where Mr. Curry was serving as Minister at the Court of King Alphonso.) Solid silver tea service from Major A. O. Bacon, father of the bride. Set of solid silver forks, from Miss Mary Lou Bacon. Black Lynx boa and muff from Miss Mary Lou Lamar. (That's sort of strange.) Breast pin set with garnet from Mr. J. M. Ogden. White ostrich feather fan from Messrs. John and Monroe Ogden. End of newspaper account.

(Ann Shirley Pendleton who sent me this account, said the list went on for about 10 pages more. If I wanted the complete list, she would send it. I didn't! Please realize that all these remarks in parentheses are my additions.) Don't you feel as though you had been there? I do! Now we move on into Manly's and Gussie's married life.

The young couple went to St. Paul, MN to live, where Manly had that lucrative business. One year later a baby girl was born to them. She was named Shirley Holcombe Curry. She was beautiful at birth and at every age. We have snapshots of her when she was a child, as an adolescent and as a young married woman. In all of them she is lovely. She had her mother's dark hair and eyes. Their second daughter, Mary Louise, born two years later, had her father's coloring, blonde hair and blue eyes. She was pretty but she never attained the beauty that her sister had.

There was a third daughter born later. She died tragically in an accident when Shirley, aged six or thereabouts, was left to mind her. Shirley left her alone for a period of time and the baby, whom they called, "Baby Sister," crawled into the fire place and died of smoke inhalation. Poor Shirley. She told me about it once and she still felt guilty. I'm sure her parents tried to keep her from feeling responsible. Six is young to be given responsibility for a crawling baby.

In 1898 the Spanish-American War broke out and Manly became an officer in the U.S. Army, where he served in the Finance Department. He was sent to the Philippines as a paymaster. He took his family with him and Shirley told me that living there was very pleasant. They had servants galore and her descriptions of their quarters portray the house as large and very attractive.

After several years they returned to the States. Manly's new duty station was in New York. Gussie found herself pregnant again just about the time her husband was ordered back to the Philippines. She decided not to return with him but to stay in New York and have the baby there. The Tropics were not a good place to have a baby in those days. The next spring she gave birth to her first male child. On May 18th, 1905, my future husband was born. His birth certificate carries the name of Bacon Curry. We know that Grandpapa Bacon wanted to adopt him and make him his legal heir.

His two boys had died. Maybe Gussie wanted this too but the baby's father objected heartily. After all, he was the last Curry male too. Later, his baptismal certificate named the child, Manly Lamar Bacon Curry. This ended Gussie's child-bearing.

When Manly came home from the Philippines he was ordered to Fort MacPherson, in Atlanta, GA. Here, on Lamar's second birthday, Manly lost his life. He was in a carriage, going out in the country to get a kitten as a birthday present for his son, when the horse bolted, the carriage overturned and Manly was thrown out; the wheels ran over his chest and crushed him.

Years later, when Lamar was courting me, we went to Washington to see a fortuneteller named Mrs. McClaren. She was so well-known a psychic that having an appointment with her was the politically correct and fun thing to do in that capital city. Many people in the House and Senate visited her regularly. She told Lamar his father was in the Spirit world. She could see him. He had been killed in a carriage accident and he was crushed across the chest. Lamar told me later he never had known exactly where his father had been injured. He asked Shirley about the details of the accident and she told him the same thing Mrs. McClaren had. Did the psychic get this from his subconscious? Had he been told and just forgotten? Anyway, we thought it was interesting; maybe this woman did have psychic powers.

Now that Gussie was a widow, she took her three children and went home to live with her Mother. I don't believe she was in very good health at this time. Lamar says she was always overweight, took no exercise and developed gall bladder trouble. Lamar has just one memory of her. She died when he was seven years old and he remembers being taken to her room, where she was bedridden. He got up on the bed and she read something to him. A story? He can't remember. Evidently, it was important to her. Did she know she was dying? We'll never know. Because she was frightened by doctors, as many were in those days, she would never have surgery.

Lamar's memories are much more vivid about Baconsfield, his grandmother Bacon, whom the family called "Miss Ginny," his sisters, who were 10 and 12 years older than he was, his Grandfather Bacon and his Aunt Mamie Sparks and her children.

The big house that was called Baconsfield was a Victorian gingerbread structure. It was built on a large parcel of pasture land where Grandpapa had a dairy. Lamar said he used to say he had 100 cows and one bobtailed bull. The dairy proper was down close to the Ocmulgee River, which ran along that part of the property which was called River Bottom. Behind the big house, standing back from the river on higher ground, were three barns, one behind the other, which held farm equipment, hay and he remembers, three old carriages; a phaeton, a trap and a surrey. Automobiles were just becoming popular and Miss Ginny had a Buick that had a collapsible top that folded back, and the gear shift, a big heavy contraption, and the brake, were on the outside of the car. He said he never played in the old carriages as they were dirty and dusty. Lamar has always been fastidious; maybe he was told not to play in them.

Lamar's playmates were few and far between. A man named Custis Nottingham lived on the property and worked for Grandpapa. I think he was the overseer. This man had two daughters, Rose and Martha. The latter was sickly and Lamar says she didn't come out very much. The younger, Rose, was a couple of years older than he and bossed him around, which annoyed him but he wanted to play with her so much he put up with her bossiness. He had another friend, a little black boy who was much closer in age and they got along very well. What did they play? Papa says he had some toy soldiers and he and his friend would divide them into two armies; one, the good guys, and the other were "Lincoln's men." Lamar didn't know who Lincoln was but that's what the black boy called them. They were the Yankees, the bad guys.

Later, Custis Nottingham turned out to be a scoundrel. When Grandpapa died, this man was one of the executors and he was fired for dipping his finger in the till; stealing, in other words. Lamar says Grandpapa had always been very fond of this man and would have been horrified if he had known that he was not trustworthy.

Lamar remembers very little about the house, Baconsfield, and his life there. One thing that impressed him was the huge hand-carved mantel around the fireplace in the parlor. It had tiles that illustrated Walter Scott's novels. In front of the house, at one time there had been a pond with a fountain. Later, it had been drained and all that was left was the concrete depression. What happened? Were funds getting low?

Out beyond that was the Hut, Grandpapa's little house where he stayed when he was not in Washington. From there to the highway was a field of clover where Lamar played and picked wild cherry tomatoes in the summer.

Lamar remembers a vendetta between Miss Ginny and a young black female cook named Willie. His grandmother had a huge batch of keys on a chain around her waist. If Willie needed any supply such as flour, butter, sugar, eggs, or what have you, she had to ask Miss Ginny to unlock the larder. The lady of the house was sure Willie was "totin'," taking food home, which was probably true as that was the custom among darkies. She didn't trust Willie to go into the pantries by herself. I sometimes wonder if Mrs. Bacon was stingy with her money? Maybe she thought that fountain was an unnecessary expense. Most southerners expect their cooks to "tote." Perhaps Willie toted more than she was allotted.

About this time, Shirley and Louise were blooming and the young men were noticing. In those days, Southern gentlemen had the custom of calling on the young ladies in the area in packs. They would arrive say, on Sunday afternoon, ten or twelve strong, visit one young lady, eat and drink what was offered and then leave for the next belle's abode. This way the males and females got to look one another over and no one was compromised; nobody could say anyone was courting any girl in particular.

I forgot to tell you that Shirley and Louise went to Europe one winter with their mother, when Lamar was about four years old. (She was probably trying to get over her husband's untimely death.) She put her girls in a Swiss Boarding School where they learned to speak French, to not cross their legs, to balance books on their heads and to recite long passages of poetry. Gussie and Lamar stayed in Paris and took trips around Europe. All he remembers were the elevators!

When they returned to the States after a year, her grandfather invited Shirley to be his official hostess in Washington. I'm sure he hoped she'd make an advantageous marriage. Shirley was beautiful and strong-willed. She had been Grandpapa's official hostess in Washington for a while but she hated it. She was about eighteen years old and everyone she met in the capital seemed ancient to her! Some senators' wives took her under their wings and tried to teach her the proper way to do things in Washington but she was unhappy there and longed to get back to Macon.

When Gussie became very ill, Miss Ginny asked Mr. Bacon to let Shirley come home. She flew on wings! Back in Macon she made up for lost time and had beaux coming out of her ears. One young man especially caught her fancy. He was not suitable at all. He was the ticket collector at the Opera House. Grandpapa was infuriated that she would waste time on a man of his caliber; he had great hopes of her marrying well, at least a politician or a diplomat. He put his foot down about allowing her to encourage him. Shirley fought back, giving him as good as she received, shouting as loud as her grandfather. Lamar remembers one occasion when Shirley, Miss Ginny and he were all down at the Hut. Shirley and Grandpapa were yelling at each other. Miss Ginny turned and said to Lamar, "This is as good as going to the theater."

When Lamar was seven years old, Gussie died. He has no memory of going to her funeral which was held in the winter, a short time before Christmas. That was a sad holiday for the child. Grandpapa brought him a toy from Washington, some little wooden gadget he had bought from a street vendor, and no one could ever make it work. He remembers his Aunt Mamie had some presents for him at her house and he thinks he must have gone there for Christmas dinner. That had to have been a sad holiday for all of them.

Lamar always hated the color purple. I have a theory that his dislike is a result of his having so many relatives die and everyone going into mourning. People at that time wore black for a while after the death and later shifted into purple or lavender. They were naturally depressed when those they loved died and his childhood was so sad. Purple must evoke depressing memories even if he can't remember exactly what they were.

Shirley won out about marrying Walter, the unsuitable young man, in spite of the way Grandpapa Bacon felt about him. What a difference from her mother's wedding. The family was still in mourning, so that was one consideration, but the affair was simplicity itself; no wedding party, just witnesses. Grandpapa snubbed her and gave her a small silver card-case as a wedding present. She had inherited some money from her parents, which

Walter proceeded to invest in different things that all failed. Poor Shirley! She had just made a terrible mistake, one she would later regret for the rest of her life. Lamar says Walter was the poorest excuse for a man that he ever knew. He would say, "God made him; therefore let him pass for a man."

Since Miss Ginny was getting pretty old, Shirley said she would be pleased to raise Lamar. The Bacon Estate would pay for his clothes and board and she would be his legal guardian. No one objected except Louise, who later married also and wanted him to live with her half of the time.

Shirley didn't want that so Lamar lived with his older sister and her husband until he grew up and went to college. Walter was such a poor provider, Lamar thinks they lived some of the time on what the Bacon Estate paid them for his upkeep. He remembers often being hungry and having very little to eat. But he has nothing but praise for Shirley. She tried to be a mother to him and she raised him in a loving, Christian way. "If I do have character," he said, "it is mainly because she instilled in me all the right things."

Shirley had trouble producing babies. I know she had a miscarriage on a train early in her married life. Lamar says a lovely lady came to her aid and helped her through the ordeal. Can you imagine having a miscarriage in the toilet of a train with a stranger trying to help you? She, Miss Ginny and Lamar were all traveling somewhere for a holiday.

Walter and Shirley rented a house across the road from Baconsfield that first year. I was told he bought an automobile business with Shirley's inheritance. That failed. Then they later moved to a little town called Clinton, which was 17 miles from Macon. Going to town in a buggy took four hours if the horse walked and three and a half if he trotted some of the time. A trip to Macon and back home was an all-day affair.

Walter then decided to try his hand at farming. They rented a big old ante-bellum house which had no electricity or plumbing in Clinton, Georgia. There was a privy and each bedroom had a wash basin and pitcher of water to bathe with and a bucket into which to discard the dirty water. In cold weather chamber pots were utilized. All-over baths were probably in one of those tin tubs. "Lamps were 'better than kerosene,' maybe oil, but they gave good light, enough to read by," said Lamar. The front hall was spacious with a staircase that curved from the landing up both sides to the second floor. This was a common and attractive architectural detail in ante-bellum houses. Clinton had been overrun by the Yankees during the Civil War and nearly destroyed. Very few people lived there at that time. Lamar remembers the house had no closets so they used armoires to hold their clothes.

Lamar was then in second grade and attended a one room schoolhouse. He walked two miles to Gray, a town adjacent to Clinton, to attend school, took a lunch and walked home after school, along the country road, in good weather and bad. At school he shared a desk with a little girl who, he says, was all right. Somewhere I have a picture of him at that desk, his elbow resting on it to support his head and a resigned look on his eight-year-old face. He told me once he dipped that little girl's pigtail in his ink bottle.

Next to the big house was a fenced in yard where they raised chickens and hogs. He remembers vividly a hog killing. It was in the fall so it was chilly. The pigs had their throats cut and then ran around until they bled to death. That, he says, was the sad part. Then the hogs were cut up into hams, chops, bacon, hocks, spare ribs, etc. Some pieces were hung in the smoke house to cure, all the fat was rendered on the wood stove in the kitchen. Lamar doesn't remember what happened to the rest of the meat. I think it must have been canned as there was no refrigeration except maybe an icebox. The intestines were washed and stuffed with sausage meat. Now all of this happened in one day. Negroes were brought in to help and by nightfall, the operation was complete. Lamar remembers how good the cracklings tasted. Those were the crunchy pieces of rendered fat skin. Shirley made crackling cornbread with them. I think Lamar was always hungry; to have all that food made him happy. That made the killing of those hogs worthwhile. Killing chickens was a different matter. He had to kill them himself and to this day, he doesn't like to eat chicken or even smell them cooking.

Another memory he had was that Shirley encouraged him to read by getting him to read to her a chapter from the Oz books. His treat was she would read him a chapter from Treasure Island, a book he loved but found too difficult to read by himself.

One day Lamar went to the country store in Clinton. A young boy about ten years old came in and asked the proprietor if he had his tooth-pullers. The man said he did and went and fetched them. He took the lad out on the porch and sat him on the bench where the old men in town sat and whittled all day. The boy pointed out the offending molar and the man took his pliers and pulled it out. The kid spit out the blood in the dirt and went home. That really made an impression on Lamar.

Farming didn't pan out for Walter so the next year they moved back to Macon, to the same house they had occupied previously. Here Shirley gave birth to her son, Walter Junior, whom everyone calls "Cat." He was healthy and beautiful, inheriting her dark good looks. He was the nearest thing to a brother that Lamar ever had. He was exactly ten years Lamar's junior.

After a few years, Shirley built a house in Macon, on North Avenue. She was pregnant again. This time, it was a little girl.

She was one year old when she died of an ailment called "summer complaint," probably dysentery. Sometimes we forget how much progress we have made in refrigeration and medicine. That probably wouldn't happen very often today, even among the very poor.

I don't know what Walter was doing to feed his family at this time, but at one point, he collected manure from a circus that wintered in Macon. This he sold for fertilizer. I doubt if that bought much oatmeal.

A few years later Shirley was pregnant again. Before the expected day of delivery, she lost her water and went into premature labor. This must have been a terrible experience for her. She had a long, difficult labor and when the baby finally arrived, it was dead. She had lost her second son. I don't believe she was ever pregnant again. Lamar says that long labor frightened him of childbearing. He dreaded my going through anything like that. He was evidently home during Shirley's labor and the experience really "shook" him.

In the sixth or seventh grade, Lamar discovered the Boy Scouts. He became such an enthusiastic member, he stayed with the organization through High School.

On one occasion he and another boy were hiking through the woods when his companion was bitten by a copperhead. Lamar performed first aid, cutting the wound and sucking out the venom, applying a tourniquet and getting him to the highway by supporting him as they hobbled back to where a passing car helped them to the hospital. The boy lived, but Lamar always remembered the incident with horror; the boy was in such agony and the treatment was so painful.

When he was in high school, their Scout troop lost their leader so Lamar took over. They performed so well at the City Rally that his three patrols won first, second and third places. He never made Eagle Scout himself because he was so busy qualifying the other boys in his Troop.

His other interest was the ROTC program at Lanier High School, which he attended. This was during World War I and enthusiasm for the military was high. He loved the discipline and took to it like a duck to water. He told me in later years he thought his training there was a big factor in his winning the color company at the Naval Academy, which he attended several years later. He also became interested in Ham Radio. During this period, he made some crystal sets. Very elementary, he insisted.

When I asked him how he happened to go to the Naval Academy, he said there were two factors that made him interested in the Navy. One, he saw a midshipman in Macon and was impressed with the way he looked and conducted himself. Two, he went to a movie and watched the big battleships ploughing through the water in a newsreel and that scene stirred him tremendously.

There was really more than this although he may not have been aware of it himself. Growing up in Macon had never been satisfying to him. He knew he had come from an illustrious family with many military members, but his people had fallen on evil days. Living with Shirley and Walter in abject poverty was depressing and discouraging and he wanted to get away from it all and make a life for himself. Going to the Naval Academy seemed a good way to start.

Getting there was anything but easy. No one had ever taught him to study and the High School in Macon was not outstanding scholastically. Mathematics was his bugaboo and everyone at Annapolis was engaged in an engineering course. When he graduated from high school, he decided to go to Mercer College in Macon and polish up his math. The next spring he took the entrance exams for the Academy and *flunked!* He had been eligible for a presidential appointment because his father had been an Army officer but without the grades, the Academy would not accept him.

Not daunted, he attended Georgia Tech for a year and hired a tutor to boot. It paid off. The next spring he passed the math exams and was accepted as a plebe. He had never ever visited Annapolis before his day of admission but, when he finally arrived there, it fulfilled all of his expectations. He felt he was where he was supposed to be.

Plebe year at Annapolis is always tough but nothing discouraged this young man. He loved the discipline and especially the leveling of all the students. It was up to the individual man to produce his best and no one received anything he did not deserve. If Lamar did well he would be high-regarded; if he failed in some way, that was his responsibility. Early on as a young boy he had shown leadership qualities and this was confirmed at Annapolis; he did his best to keep his head above water scholastically, went out for sports and played inter-mural football, worked with the stage crew for the theater productions, took a cartooning course by mail and drew cartoons for the Academy magazine called "The Log," becoming the Art editor in his First Class year, was a member of the Rifle team, both indoor and out, and all this kept him busy. His social life was almost nonexistent. He taught Sunday School in the Chapel because his "First Classman" ordered him to do it. All of these traditions appealed to him and contributed to his development.

The second year at Annapolis, after the summer Midshipman Cruise, he went home for September leave, practically the only vacation those poor Middies ever had. It lasted a month. He ran into one of his old school buddies who introduced him to a girl named Sarah. Her father was a railroad engineer and the family definitely lived on the wrong side of the railroad tracks, literally as well as figuratively. Sally was attractive and her family's lack of blue blood didn't bother him at all. She was Lamar's first girl and way overdue. She was a needed adjunct to his life and when he returned to the Academy, they corresponded regularly. Now he had a girl. She wasn't around much but she was there when he went home for Christmas and subsequent September leaves. The relationship flourished and when he was chosen to pick a girl to "present the Colors" during June Week his first class year, he chose Sally. Lamar was the Company Commander of the winning company competition and because of this, he had the honor and distinction of taking a major part in a colorful parade which was usually national news. Many a newsreel have I watched and been properly impressed when the Color Ceremony was part of the news. Today I think the ceremony has been abandoned. What would they do if a woman is the Company Commander and her outfit wins??? Have some young man presented with roses and duly kissed by a female? Our new mores often pose some problems with tradition.

As Graduation neared, Lamar chose the Marine Corps over the Navy for a career. After two Midshipman cruises, he felt that shipboard life was a bit crowded so he opted for the Marines. In due time Sally played her part perfectly at the Color Ceremony and Lamar was proud of her. After graduation, Lamar, Sally, Cat and Shirley all piled into the Model A Ford coupe with a rumble seat that the young Lieutenant had purchased and they took off for New York. They had good weather, thank goodness, as all four could never have fit inside the car in case there had been a rain shower.

They planned to drive out to West Point in the afternoon to watch a Sunset Parade and come back for dinner and the theater. They left New York about two o'clock in the afternoon and two hours later our country bumpkins had traveled only about six miles, the traffic being what it is in those metropolitan parts. They crossed the river into New Jersey and returned to New York until they were on a parallel with New York downtown. They arrived at the theater a little late and dined at the conclusion of the play. It was a musical with Eddie Cantor in the starring role. They loved it.

Following their return home and at the conclusion of Lamar's leave, he went to Basic School in Philadelphia. This is an indoctrination into the Marine Corps where the freshly caught young lieutenants find out what the Military is all about. His roommate at U. S. N. A. for four years, Bill Coleman, also joined the Marines and his home town was Philadelphia. Knowing Bill's family was an advantage, Lamar automatically had a home away from home.

Dances were held at the Philadelphia Navy Yard and many of the attractive young ladies in the area that were available were invited to entertain the new officers. Here Lamar met a girl named Marie. He fell for her like a ton of bricks. She fascinated him; all thoughts of Sally went out of his head. That winter he courted Marie like mad. She was quite elusive, never kissing him goodnight but accepting all dinners, flowers and gifts that Lamar showered on her. Her mother, realizing that Lamar was a good catch, encouraged Marie to be nice to him.

After graduating from Basic School, he invited Marie and her mother to come to Shirley's mountain cabin for a house party. They came, but Shirley heard Marie's mother giving her daughter the devil for not making more of a play for this young lieutenant. She told Lamar and that discouraged him from any further involvement. But he was hurt and couldn't put her completely out of his mind. He was really in love for the first time in his life.

After Basic School, he received orders to Nicaragua to fight bandits. He was about to begin his military career.

He traveled by ship to Corinto and proceeded to Managua by train to receive his orders from the Marine Headquarters in Nicaragua. They assigned him to a little town called Ocatol. Sandino, a bandit, had his men operating all over the country and the Marines' job was to search out and kill them. Lamar was assigned to a tiny outpost called Apali. There were fifty enlisted men and he was one of two officers. Here he lived for six or eight months. Our government was phasing out the Marine involvement at this time. All military operations were being transferred to the Nicaraguan Guardia, who were considered sufficiently trained and equipped to handle any action instigated by the rebel forces. Lamar remembers only one incident when a bandit patrol fired on some of his men and the marines took one prisoner. This man told them they had nearly been ambushed a day or two previously. That was the only time he thinks he was in real danger during those months.

Lamar received orders to Managua. He flew into the city the day after the big earthquake in 1931. The volcano across the lake called Mombo-Tombo erupted and the city of Managua was almost totally destroyed. Remember I told you I had lived in the castle in the Marine Compound? Half of that building collapsed. The wooden buildings withstood the quake but all the native houses made of adobe were destroyed. The local hospital was gone so emergency medical shelters were set up in tents to care for the wounded. The Navy doctors were joined by a group of doctors from an Army battalion at Granada. When Lamar's plane set down, the heat from all the fires was intense and everything was in a state of chaos. The dead were being buried hurriedly in mass graves and the Marines were engaged in humanitarian endeavors. He was assigned to a food distribution point and there he worked without much rest until a few days later when he was feeling so bad he went to see a medico. The doctor stuck a thermometer in Lamar's mouth and subsequently told him he had a temperature of 105 degrees. It was the highest fever he had ever read on a person still on his feet. Lamar had malaria and was hospitalized for a couple of weeks.

When he recovered, most of the relief operations were complete and the Marines were just waiting for orders to come back to the States. He was given the job of planning activities to keep up the morale of the troops. They organized Smokers, during which there would be boxing matches. Lamar asked the men to volunteer to put on skits in the intervals between bouts. He was inundated with talent, so he decided to have one evening of pure theater. This went over so well, one of the participants asked if they couldn't do a real minstrel show. Lamar sent off to French's and bought the scripts for an authentic one. You probably never saw one as it has been politically incorrect to do anything in black face for quite a long while. Anyway, it was a great success and the theater group had a ball putting it on for their buddies.

Sometime in 1932 Lamar received his orders to Quantico. He requested duty with the 10th Marines as he was interested in artillery. This was in the depths of the Depression and the troops were doing almost nothing so Lamar was assigned to Guardhouse duty. He and two other officers took turns standing the watches. I think Lamar hated this assignment with a passion. He was nothing but a policeman and had to check on everyone who entered the Base, inspect the sentries three or four times night and day, take care of disciplinary actions that arose, inspect the Mess Hall every day he had the duty, which was every third day. He got very little sleep. To make matters worse, eventually he started courting me. I, of course, was sleeping in until about eleven o'clock every morning so I was bright-eyed and bushy-tailed in the evening. He told me once that he married me to get some sleep. I thought he was fooling but now I think he was serious.

One occasion I must relate. No soliciting was allowed on the Post. Salesmen were refused entry. One particular gentleman arrived at the Guardhouse, asking permission to sell his encyclopedias. He was dressed fit to kill and had some wonderful credentials, stating that high-ranking officers and politicians had nothing but praise for this man and the product he was hawking. He wanted to give away these valuable books to any officer who would give his product a personal recommendation so he could use it to sell his wares to others. It wouldn't cost anyone a penny. In spite of all of these advantages, he was refused permission to enter the Post to solicit. He asked if he could show them to the Officer of the Day, who was Lamar. Lamar said, "OK."

A short time later, the salesman got Lamar's signature on the dotted line. Then he said, "Another feature of this deal is the yearly supplement that keeps all the information up to date. Of course, we can't give this away so we will have to charge you ten dollars a year for each volume that you will receive in the future. That sounds fair enough, doesn't it?"

Lamar agreed and bought the twelve volumes of the encyclopedia, plus the Harvard Classics, bound in blue leatherette, plus a set of Kathleen Norris' novels, the two latter items a serendipity. After the gentleman left, Lamar wanted to kick himself. He had just bought $100.00 worth of books he didn't need. At that time he was making only $125.00 a month. This incident soured him on salesmen for life. As for the books, the encyclopedia was lousy. All the sketched portraits of famous people looked alike. I enjoyed the Harvard Classics when we lived in France. I was so starved for books in English, I became quite well educated. We gave the Kathleen Norris novels to the Quantico Library.

One more incident relating to this period of your Lamar's career. Lamar had a Navy doctor friend named Charlie Hatchett. Don't laugh! He was a surgeon but a frustrated one. His job was to inspect the maids' quarters on the base and disinfect them for lice. He yearned to cut on someone and told Lamar how he felt. Lamar said he was frustrated too, inspecting sentries and looking for parents of lost children. He thought he might have made a good surgeon but he had never seen an operation. Charlie said he would let him watch one if the opportunity ever arose.

One night Lamar received word that Dr. Hatchett wanted him in Surgery at the hospital. He had a patient who had been shot and he was going to operate. Lamar hurried over and was duly masked and gowned and guided into the operating room. Lamar thought this would be a delicate procedure and when he entered he saw Charlie with both hands, rummaging around in the buttock of a big Negro man. He looked like he was making bread except blood was all over the place. Lamar passed out cold. I think this helped convince him he was not cut out to be a surgeon.

Now that our two lives have begun to overlap and you already know all about our courtship, the time has come to tell about the first years of our marriage.

6

Early Marriage

When we left Quantico on our honeymoon, we headed for Mountain City, Georgia, where Shirley, Lamar's sister and Walter, her husband, lived in a log cabin that was 150 years old. At one time it had been a one room schoolhouse. Shirley had done quite a bit of remodeling during her ownership, adding a bathroom, a dining room and a kitchen. This had been home to Lamar when he attended the Naval Academy and he wanted to share that part of his life with me but it was not the most perfect place for a honeymoon. We were too naive to realize that. We chose it because we had very little money, it was up in the mountains and cooler than Virginia that time of year and Shirley had begged us to come. My husband had enjoyed house parties there when he was a midshipman and he wanted to share this place with me, his bride. We really didn't know each other very well and being thrown into such intimacy might have been easier if we had not been with other people at that time.

I don't have very happy memories of our honeymoon. The walls of the cabin were so thin we could hear the occupants in the bedroom next to us talking. We whispered but I was afraid those others could hear us so our sex was restrained.

I liked Shirley but I knew Lamar didn't like her husband Walter so I eyed him with suspicion and tried to stay out of his way. Walter Junior, called Cat, was seventeen years old and the usual brash teenager. He seemed immature to me and not very interesting, but he was always around and he thought he was pretty hot stuff.

Shirley was a good organizer and had set up a schedule of housekeeping duties everyone was supposed to follow. We took turns doing all the chores: hauling water from a spring for cooking and washing dishes, setting the table and fixing breakfast, food shopping and washing up. Shirley did all the cooking, thank goodness. In between these duties, we swept the floors, took out and buried garbage in the garden, dusted the furniture and did some laundry. This took all day. I was a confirmed hedonist who had habitually slept late in the mornings and whose mother always had a domestic to do those housekeeping chores at home, so I worried all the time that I was not doing my jobs to suit Shirley.

One day, I actually ironed a shirt for Lamar. What a disaster! I did such a bad job he never asked me to repeat the performance. In our home, shirts had always gone to the commercial laundry until wash-and-wear fabrics came into existence. When we later returned to Quantico, we always used the Base laundry and dry cleaner as all self-respecting people did. Once, before I was married, I had bought three yards of material for 10 cents a yard and made a tennis dress. I sent it to the laundry and they charged me 35 cents to wash it. I never did that again.

One day we all went to a lake to swim. There were no other people there. Lamar told me the lake was bottomless; if we drowned, our bodies would probably never be recovered. That's all I needed to know to scare me out of my wits. Our psychic friend, Mrs. McLaren, had told me to stay out of deep water as it was very dangerous for me, so this morning I just paddled around in the shallows where my feet could touch bottom. I was not relieved from worry though, as Lamar decided to swim across the lake to the other side alone. I was terribly concerned until he came ashore. I wasn't ready to die on my honeymoon or lose my bridegroom either.

I stood in the shallow water and sweated blood until Lamar returned safely. That was not a happy outing for me. The frequent Mountain City rain forestalled another trip to the lake, thank God!

Another day we climbed a mountain. The day was exceptionally hot. I was thirsty before we started our ascent and I noticed a thin trickle of water at a small spring at the foot of the mountain. When I remarked that I wanted to stop and drink, everyone said that I could have a drink when we reached the summit. We climbed and we climbed. At last we arrived at the top. With my mouth dry as a bone, I asked hoarsely, "Now may I have a drink?" Someone said, "Polly wants a drink. Who has the water?" Shirley said, "I brought a jug but I put coffee grounds in it as I am going to boil it and make coffee."

When we finally had lunch and I had some coffee, I was still thirsty; I remembered that tiny little trickle of water at the bottom of the mountain, coming out of that spring, and I could hardly contain myself to get through lunch and get back down that cursed mountain. There were a goodly number of rattlesnake skins around our picnic spot, which didn't seem to alarm anyone particularly except me. How I hated snakes, poisonous or not; I couldn't tell one from the other. But even the threat of meeting a live snake did not deter me from descending that mountain. I left all the members of our party and walked down alone. I found the little spring and managed to get some water in my two cupped hands. It was so wonderful; no drink in my life was ever sweeter, more appreciated. I don't believe I had ever been or ever have been again that thirsty in my whole life.

When we all arrived back at the cabin, Lamar said we had to take showers immediately, IN COLD MOUNTAIN WATER, (that's all we had) as the red bugs and chiggers were so bad, we would be a mass of bites if we didn't deal with them in short order. Not being a camper, I didn't realize they were part of any outdoor expedition; the nasty things burrowed under the skin and raised welts and itched you to death. Everyone else had swigs of "white lightning," (corn licker) to break the shock of the icy blast, but prissy old Me wouldn't even take a swallow of it. All my life, I have hated cold water. Ugh! That shower was pure torture. I don't believe I would have taken it if I had not been on my honeymoon; I would have washed around my middle and stayed dirty. I was proving to be such a tenderfoot, I knew Lamar would be ashamed of me if I didn't get under that cold water faucet. He was always a great camper and outdoorsman and I had never had even one day of camp experience. Marstons, females especially, didn't go to camp. I did get clean but my lips were blue.

Cat shot a rabbit one morning and Shirley cooked it for lunch. *That fast!* You know I didn't eat it. Cat gave me its bloody warm tail for a powder puff. I'm sure he had spotted me as a sissy and wanted to see me cringe. Another day we had pickled pigs' feet for lunch. Marstons don't eat pickled pigs' feet. I didn't eat those. Shirley was an excellent cook though, and I learned the Curry way to fix certain foods. For instance, she rolled grits in cornmeal, *not flour!* Marstons roll grits in flour but I learned cornmeal is better. Also, she made all her own bread and it was wonderful. Oh! Another thing! Leftover macaroni and cheese can be heated in spoonfuls if you have a skillet. Now we have microwaves, but in the 30's it was a jewel of wisdom for me.

Shirley had a friend who was a nurse. One day she came over to meet us. Shubby asked me to meet her at the door. I have faults but being socially gauche is not one of them. When I opened the door, I said, "You must be Shirley's friend. Come right in. I hear you are a nurse. You must get some interesting cases up here in the mountains."

This lady took the bait and started right in telling me she had just come off a very interesting case; the woman she had been nursing had an eye operation. She then proceeded to give me a blow-by blow account of the surgery. Guess what? Standing there in the doorway, trying to look interested, I passed out cold. She yelled for help and dragged me over to the sofa. When I revived, I heard her telling Shirley I was probably pregnant. I had been married *one week!* The fainting was a repeat of my experience in biology class in high school and the dissection of that frog's eye. I have learned now to just not listen when eyes are discussed.

One day we played bridge with Shirley's bridge group. Poor Lamar, dragged into this occasion, tried so hard to act interested. Cards are not "his thing" and he was bored to death. The ladies soon discovered that he knew absolutely nothing about the game and ceased to even call him by name. Someone would say, "Who bid?"

"He did."

"Whose play is it?"

"His."

Early Marriage

Finally, he actually trumped his partner's ace and the game came to an end. In the 66 years we were married, we never played cards as a diversion.

I was so glad to bid everyone at Mountain City farewell and start back to Quantico with Lamar all to myself. We spent a delightful evening at Blowing Rock, North Carolina, in a beautiful hotel where I had a hot bath and a wonderful dinner. When I entered our bedroom at the hotel, I was horrified to see we had twin beds. I was sure Lamar had become tired of me and sex and had specified that sleeping arrangement. Of course he hadn't and was as disappointed as I. We ended up sleeping in one bed. I was so relieved that he wasn't tired of me after all.

When we arrived back in Quantico, we went home immediately to see Boppie and Mother. It was about eight o'clock at night. We regaled them with all our adventures. Mother looked sleepy and my first thought was, "Maybe Lamar should leave and go home now." Then I realized that they expected me to leave with him. That really felt funny. Going back to his apartment seemed almost immoral. I ask you? How married was I?

Our real honeymoon started when we lived for six weeks in that teeny bachelor apartment. I finally realized it was my house too. Lamar put up with my youth and taught me to cook. We even invited people to dinner. He could roast a leg of lamb with potatoes around it. I could boil a vegetable, make a salad with "boughten" dressing, and serve store bought rolls and ice cream. I figured I could cook!

One mistake I made once when we had invited another couple to dine with us was using beer glasses for some peach parfaits. They were the right shape but the wrong size. Each one held at least a pint of ice cream and we and our guests had a hard time, getting to the bottom of those glasses before it all melted. Eating it all posed no problem because we were young and healthy. Naturally, it melted. Remember! No air conditioning, no refrigerator, just an icebox, and an August in Quantico is pretty close to hell in temperature.

I was learning to shop for food, too. The Commissary delivered telephone orders, which was convenient, and on one occasion, I remember ordering four lamb chops, two baking potatoes and fifty peas. That was the only way I could approximate the amount I wanted for two people. I swear I was not trying to be cute!

In September, Lamar received his orders to Fort Sill, Oklahoma, as he would be attending the Army Artillery School there. Friends that had served with that branch of the service warned us about the heavy drinking and wife-swapping that went on in the Army. We expected Gomorrah, but we found the Army no different from the Marine Corps. There was no wife-swapping that we were aware of and not everyone drank; Prohibition liquor didn't taste all that great. Our household effects were pretty skimpy but we did have all those one hundred and fifty-seven wedding presents to pack. Government Quarters were always furnished with furniture but we had to supply our own linens, kitchen utensils and china. And we had a few pictures, lamps and bric-a-brac. The day the Marine packers arrived I went upstairs to a neighbor's apartment to get out of their way and to drink coffee; our Quarters were so small they were called "four-in-a-boxes" and the packers needed every bit of room in it to do their job. I heard them leaving for lunch about eleven o'clock so I went downstairs to see what progress they had made.

They had packed quite a lot and I went out in the kitchen to make a sandwich. There I noticed some empty bottles sitting on the drain board. Lamar had made some liqueurs with straight alcohol (a gift from Dr. Charlie Hatchett, who had snitched it from the hospital!) and different flavorings purchased at the local drugstore. Also we had a bottle of dandelion wine that Shirley had made up in the mountains that she had given us. At first, I thought they had removed them from the cupboard to pack them. Then I noticed that all of the bottles were empty. There was nothing alcoholic left in the apartment.

When the packers failed to reappear after lunch, I called to find out where they were. I was told they had checked in sick, too sick to return to work. They were sorry but there were no other men available. Now I must tell you that during the Prohibition years it was a court-martial offense for an officer to be caught with alcoholic beverages in his Quarters or anywhere on the Base. A lot of people did have liquor but it was not flaunted openly. My father, for instance, never had a bottle of anything alcoholic in the house ever although he had been raised in a family of moderate drinkers. What should I do? I called Mother and she called Boppie. He decided that they and Betty and Lamar and I would do the rest of the packing; we didn't want those sick Marines confessing to drinking liquor found in our Quarters. There was no way we could complain to the authorities. Mother made us unpack everything they had packed because she was afraid they might have stolen something, we had to check the contents of the boxes and barrels with our wedding gift list. We worked up into the early morning hours packing. Time was of the essence. Our date of departure for Oklahoma was two days off and the place had to be thoroughly cleaned for the official inspection. (At that time, that was routinely done by an officer, who wore white gloves and ran his paddy-paws over the stove, icebox and all moldings; he missed nothing.) We had clean quarters in the Marine Corps; we found them that way and left them just as spotless. It was the Law!

The van came for our household effects, we cleaned our little cracker-box, passed inspection and spent the last night with my parents. Mother was sort of weepy the next morning when she saw us off. She begged me to make a lot of nutritious vegetable soups and to not get sick. I was 5'6" and weighed 115 pounds, I knew about birth control and no baby was anticipated during our first year of marriage. I didn't know how to make soup but I promised to learn. Since Lamar and I both think she had engineered this whole marriage, with Shirley's help, she must have felt responsible for its success. I doubt if I looked very promising as a wife at that point. Did her conscience hurt? Lamar was such a nice guy; how could she do this to him? Mother always said I wouldn't have stood a chance with him if she had been twenty years younger.

We arrived at Fort Sill after an uneventful three or four day trip. Our first night out we stayed in a hotel in Charleston, West Virginia. The garage stuck a horseshoe sticker on the bumper and we left it there as long as we owned the car. We were superstitious about scraping it off. (We never saw a motel until we drove to California in the 50's.) One night we stayed in our first tourist home.

Lawton, the town adjacent to Fort Sill, was a dinky little place with one hotel, where we spent the first night. Our room was as hot as the hinges of you-know-what but there was an electric fan that operated for an hour on a quarter. Lamar was up all night, putting money in the fool thing, as the room was unbearable without the breeze the fan generated. We ate Chinese food in the hotel restaurant and I was fascinated to watch a Chinaman put a bowl of rice up to his mouth and scoop it all in with his chopsticks.

The only celebrity I ever heard of who ever came from Lawton, Oklahoma, was Joan Crawford, who grew up there and went to the movies every chance she got. She was a famous movie star. The one theater in town boasted that she told the ticket collector her name would be up in lights one day. And it was.

The next day we found a boarding house, which was cleaner and cheaper than the hotel and had a lovely keeper who took an interest in us newlyweds. She cared for us like a mother. When we finally moved into an apartment, I called her every day for advice.

The apartment we rented for $43.50 a month was the downstairs of a two-story house. If it's still there, the address is 912 C Street. An Army lieutenant named Schindler, and his wife Ethel, lived upstairs. We wondered why they had preferred their place to ours. The downstairs was much roomier with a big kitchen, a large living-room with a grand piano, a real dining room, a porch to sit on in hot weather, plus an adequate bedroom and a bath and another little room that we called the den. The bath was off the kitchen, pretty far from the bedroom. The apartment upstairs was stuffy and the rooms were smaller, but our place had been available when the Schindlers moved in. Maybe it was because our apartment cost seven dollars more a month.

Early Marriage

We moved in the tenth of September and the weather was still scorching hot. One week later, we had our first "norther." It turned cold and the wind came roaring down from the North Pole, with nothing to stop it but a few flimsy snow fences, not even a good-sized hill to break its impact. We shivered in our place and turned up all the open gas burners that heated the apartment. There were no doors between the rooms except one swinging door between the dining room and the kitchen and a bathroom door, off the kitchen. The wind howled and we hovered in front of the heaters. Later, I bought yards of Monk's cloth and made draperies, which we hung between the rooms. In this way we could isolate some space and heat that only. The Schindlers told us they were quite cozy upstairs. Why not? All our heat was rising to their apartment. Now the light came on. Of course, they KNEW the weather was going to be so severe. No one told us. I had looked at those big rooms and visualized parties and that grand piano and dreamed of one of our many talented friends playing and entertaining guests. I don't remember anyone ever doing more than playing chopsticks on that lovely instrument. Maybe it wasn't even in tune. I draped a Spanish shawl over it and it looked very pretty. Movies of that era always had Spanish shawls draped over pianos. This particular one had been a gift from Earle, brought home from a midshipman cruise to Spain.

I usually undressed in front of one of those gas heaters at night and dressed there every morning. Eventually, I burned up all of my trousseau nightgowns. I stood so close to the open gas jets, I caught fire on numerous occasions. When most of them had been incinerated, I finally bought myself some flannel nightgowns for 98 cents a piece at the local Five and Dime store. To warm our bed at night, we heated bricks in the oven, then wrapped them in newspapers. Many a night we had frost on the inside of the window panes.

We had looked at one other place to rent. Arriving later than the other students at Fort Sill, we had poor pickings to choose from. In that other apartment the room that we first entered had a bed, an icebox and a sofa in it. I asked the agent what room this was and he said, "Well, you could call it a bedroom or a living room or even a kitchen." The "C" Street place we rented looked like heaven in comparison.

We hired a maid who came every day and cooked and cleaned and did the laundry. Lamar also had a "striker," a black Army private who cleaned his leather. The officers wore boots and Sam Browne leather belts, and Lamar had puttees and four or five pairs of shoes. All the officers had strikers so I guess they were considered a necessity. What second lieutenant can spend time cleaning leather?

Lamar's pay was $125.00 a month, a Second Lieutenant's pay, plus some housing and food allowances. Our food bill was $30.00 a month, which was very high as we always ate the best of everything. And we were feeding those two servants three meals a day. But remember, bread cost nine cents a loaf and coffee from the Commissary was seven cents a pound. The gas bill nearly put us in the poorhouse. Those heaters were on all day long as I was so cold. We paid the maid $4.00 a week. I found out later that she was a real thief. When I finally caught her stealing money, I fired her. Then I discovered she had stolen almost all of the forty-five pairs of hose that I had received at a stocking shower before I was married. She had rummaged through a trunk and found them. When I went looking for her in darky town, no one had ever heard of her. We discovered this was usual when you were trying to locate a Negro. If someone was looking for them, they were most generally in trouble. The Blacks stuck together; they never betrayed one another. We never saw her or my hose again.

Lamar loved Time magazine. He looked forward to reading it every weekend. His subscription ran out about the time we moved and he had not renewed. I'm sure we lived from month-to-month financially. Anyway, I felt so bad I went downtown and bought him a copy from a newsstand. We were so poor that month, I paid for it with 15 cents out of my penny collection.

The town was seething with Okies, impoverished Oklahoma farmers. The dust bowl had ruined their crops and they had nothing; they just wandered the streets, looking for work, and indigent Indians, who roamed around town, trying to sell five-cent items for a dime, and stealing anything that was not nailed down. We had a garage and our car was locked up, but someone broke the lock and drained our gas tank several times until we put a lock on it too.

Once I left the car motor running and ran into the house to get something, and when I returned, someone had stolen my silver cigarette case off the front seat. I saw no one on the street when I got out of the car, and there was no one around when I returned. Those poor people were poised for any opportunity that arose. In 1933 there was no national welfare, those people were in dire straits. Nothing saleable was safe. Someone stole my little Persian kitten the day before Christmas. I just hope they didn't eat her. I was so upset at losing her, I cried.

The Army-Navy game has always been *big* in Lamar's scheme of things. His loyalty to his Alma Mater was very intense. I decided to have a dinner party the night of the game as the Army people seemed just as excited as my husband. I think we expected Navy to win that year, so that would be nice. I decorated the buffet table with gray and gold and blue and gold ribbons, honoring both services, and made everything quite festive. Well, we lost and Lamar went into a deep depression. It would have been bearable if the Army officers had been gentlemen and soft-pedaled their victory but they didn't. They kept rubbing it in that the Army team was so much better. Lamar was very, very low but he had to be a good host, so he didn't murder any of them. I learned that night to never, never entertain the day of the Army-Navy game. It was serious business to this man I had married and it always remained so.

About this time one of my friends, Cary Luckey, who was a bride, too, and the wife of the only other Marine officer attending the Fort Sill school, called me in a panic. She was sure she was pregnant. We had both gone to the same family planning clinic back in Baltimore and we were told our little gadgets were trustworthy. I told Cary not to worry. Dr. Moses, the birth control guru, said in cases like this to take a hot tub bath and relax. This should take care of her problem. Later that evening, she called me and said my advice had worked; she was not pregnant.

Everyone was so horsey, Lamar insisted I be too. I went and ordered some custom-made "pink hunting" breeches, from Albert Moore, the country's finest tailor to the Cavalry. A representative was at Fort Sill taking orders. I would at least look like a good horsewoman even if I wasn't. A week after my first fitting, my "period" was late. I was as panicked as Cary had been. I called her and she gave me my own advice, "Take a hot bath, etc."

My period never arrived and a few weeks later I went to the hospital for a rabbit test. The results came back positive. I was pregnant and anything but thrilled. When I told Lamar, he said, "Well, there's nothing we can do about it so that's that." No string of pearls. Not even a single rose at my breakfast plate. (You can see my life was influenced by too many movies.) I found out real life was quite different. My husband was no more thrilled than I. I figured when next June came around, I would become a mother; vegetable soups were more important now than ever. I better learn to make them.

Christmas was coming. We decided to ask our Episcopalian minister for the name of a *small* family to whom we could play Santa Claus. There was a whole village of "packing crate" people in Lawton. They actually lived in wooden crates, originally used to ship heavy farm machinery. We knew poverty existed but we had never witnessed it. Our priest gave us the name of a family which supposedly consisted of a father, a mother and one child. We went out to see them and to find out what they needed most and found them, plus three more children no one had mentioned, in their crate. It was so awful to behold. We came back and spent everything we had, buying clothes, food and toys. I think we even borrowed money to get everything we did buy. Today we know the welfare in this country is badly managed and needs overhauling, but at least we don't see any one living in a packing crate, and children don't have to share their shoes and take turns going to school, as those poor moppets did. I hope! That Depression of the thirties was terrible.

Early Marriage

Remember I told you that Lamar was afraid of nothing? His horse riding had been mostly on Nicaraguan ponies in jungles, where style hadn't counted for much. Shortly after the Fort Sill school year opened, it was announced that there would be a Horse Show and it was open to all students. Lamar decided to enter. Then he found out that all of the other contestants were Equitation instructors or Advanced Equitation students. Nothing daunted, Lamar stayed entered. The appointed day arrived and Lamar went out to participate. I went along to sit in the bleachers and cheer on the contestants as they dashed to the finish line. It was a sort of race. The contestants were given slips of paper to decipher and present to a groom, who would then give them a mount. Then they would race their horses through the woods on a particular course to the finish line. Eventually, the first contestant appeared, his horse at a full gallop, taking some quite high hurdles. He knocked down a couple and disappeared towards the stables.

Soon another contestant appeared, and this time, his horse refused to jump one of the obstacles. The rider turned and made another attempt. The second time, he knocked it down. Riders kept appearing, some doing well, others not. But where was Lamar? I was terrified for him. He had never done any jumping and what would he do? Finally, I saw him walking out of the woods. He didn't have a horse. He had been disqualified by one of the stable grooms, who thought his piece of paper was the wrong color or had something wrong with it. Everyone sympathized with me because Lamar had been involved in a mix-up and didn't participate, but I know now the Good Lord was protecting him. He would certainly have bombed if he had been given a horse to compete that day.

The Artillery was horse-drawn in that era and it was as horsey as the Cavalry. Each student was required to train a green remount, a horse never ridden by man. When Lamar describes this procedure, it is quite amusing. Suffice it to say, it was a long, drawn out affair that took about three months to accomplish. He trained this beast to go forward when he clucked to it, stop when he said, "Whoa!" and allow him to bridle and saddle him. Finally the big day came when he tried to mount him. This was more easily said than done. This maneuver was the most interesting one of all. Not many of those animals liked being mounted and put up resistance. His horse was named Chief Buck and it took Lamar a while before this well-named animal allowed him to sit on his back. Eventually they became friends, although the wretched animal put my husband in the hospital with a twisted knee when he stepped in a gopher hole out in the field and fell, spilling his rider.

If a rider fell off a horse or was thrown off, he was required to have a "policing party." (The gopher-hole episode did not count as a policing because it was not the fault of the rider!) Everyone who witnessed the usual policing was invited to the party and it was always a "stag" affair. We wives had to do all the work of preparation and then we had to leave. I lived in fear that Lamar would "be policed" as we were so poor and a party with Prohibition liquor and food for all those men was expensive.

Lamar was also training a polo pony, which was part of the curriculum. Some of us wives were watching our husbands one day, shortly after the course started. The instructor told the riders to reach over and pat their mounts on the withers and then on their rumps to make the horses more amenable. Things were going swimmingly until Lamar reached back to pat his horse on its rear end. He bucked and sent Lamar flying over his neck. Lamar ended up with his arms and legs around the horse's neck. As he says, they were eyeball to eyeball. Everyone stopped and watched, expecting him to drop to the ground, which would have forced him to have that "policing party." Believe it or not, Lamar managed to get back in the saddle without any of his body touching the ground. A roar went up from the spectators, most loudly from his spouse who knew we couldn't have afforded a party. Eventually, later in the winter, he was policed but by that time, we had become better managers of our money and the event didn't crush us financially.

I shall brag on Lamar. He learned to ride and became an ardent, excellent horseman. Later in the school year, he entered another horse show. *Again?* This time he got himself a yellow ribbon by taking third place. This Fort Sill duty turned him quite horsey. A couple of years later, it led to his owning his own horse and entering horse shows at Fort Myer, VA and taking part in the Hunts in Quantico. He also taught Equitation to the teenagers in Quantico. But more of that later.

Early that spring, I started having some problems with my pregnancy; I was losing my waters. The doctor was not alarmed and put no restrictions on my activities. He told me many women had dry labor. I still walked to market and carried groceries home. I preferred letting Lamar have the car so I didn't have to take him to the Fort and retrieve him daily. I felt fine so I wasn't worried. I was too ignorant to know that a "dry" birth can be right rough.

I had a humongous appetite and learned to cook lots of new dishes. I learned about color on a plate and its importance. The meal that taught me that was a dinner of white fish, mashed potatoes and boiled cauliflower. Nothing I did improved its appearance. Paprika? Parsley? I had neither so I put food coloring in the potatoes, red, I think. Lamar was unimpressed.

A delicacy I learned to make was Black Bottom Pie. It had a gingersnap crust, a layer of rich chocolate custard, another layer of rum-flavored custard, then it was topped with a mountain of sweetened whipped cream with shavings of semisweet chocolate scattered over the whole thing. I invited the Schindlers upstairs to come down and share it with us. Ethel was pregnant too and like me, always hungry. I cut this 10 inch pie into four servings and we began to eat it. Both men finally quit as they were getting sick, but Ethel and I finished ours off and scraped our dishes clean. Such is pregnancy.

One night in March, I woke up with terrible stomach cramps. I was six months pregnant. We thought I had indigestion so I stayed in bed and Lamar went to school. He came home at noon. I was no better. He tried to fix me something to eat but, rare of rarities, I was not hungry. Finally, he called the doctor, who told Lamar to call the ambulance. It arrived about six o'clock and by then, I was miserable; I was sure I had ptomaine poisoning.

At the hospital I was put in a room with a woman who had come in for a rest cure. She had been living it up socially and she was worn out. She had a friend visiting her who had brought her some garden peas in a thermos because she had complained about the food in the hospital. She kept raving about how good the peas were and asking me if she could do anything for me. I was in a panic about now as the pains were much worse and in spite of all my efforts, I was beginning to moan. My roommate read my name on the foot of the bed and kept asking, "Mary, can I do anything for you?" No doctor appeared. I found out later he was out playing golf. Finally, a nurse came in and made the decision to take me to the delivery room. Dumb me! I still thought it was food poisoning. I thought the medico was going to pump out my stomach.

At last the doctor appeared, examined me and told me I was in premature labor. I was so ignorant about pregnancy and labor, I don't think I realized I had a fully formed baby inside me. The doctor soon educated me. In due course I was delivered of a 3 and a half pound baby boy. I heard the doctor tell the nurse to wrap it in cotton and the nurse said, "It's so tiny. I'm scared." Then I was put to sleep.

When I awoke I was back in a bed but in a different room. It was the maternity ward. I longed to see my baby but no one mentioned him. I figured he was too small to take out of the nursery. As the day wore on and nobody mentioned him, I really panicked. Lamar came in to see me but he didn't say anything either. I was too scared to ask if he had died. Someone might say, "Yes." As long as no one said he was dead, I could hope.

The next day Lamar arrived in dress blues. I knew there were social events that required that uniform, but this was in the morning so I was surprised. Then the doctor came in and handed him a paper. He looked so solemn I knew that it must be a death certificate. We still didn't talk about it and poor Lamar left to attend the funeral of his first-born. This was why he was in his dress blues. He told me weeks later that it was pretty awful. I had two baby garments. One was a little sweater Betty had knit for him and the other was a romper someone had given me as a baby present. That's all he had to be buried in. All of Lamar's fellow students and their wives attended the funeral and burial in Fort Sill Cemetery. But since I was still in the hospital, I could not.

There was no family there to console Lamar. He had to do that all alone. I was such a coward, I never went to the Fort Sill cemetery ever. I couldn't stand the thought of seeing my baby's grave. It was a long time before I could even talk to Lamar about it. I was sure God was punishing me for not wanting this child. Because this baby lived for forty minutes, he had a funeral. If he had been stillborn, he would have been considered a fetus and would have been discarded. I realize now that I have had four children, not three. Lamar named him "Monroe," one of Grandpapa Curry's surnames.

An Army chaplain, making the rounds at the hospital, stuck his head in my door one day and asked, "What brings you in here, little lady?"

I said, "I've just lost a baby."

He asked, "Was it baptized before it died?"

"I don't think so," I said. "It lived only forty minutes."

"What a shame," he said. "Now it will spend eternity in Hell's fire."

Whereupon I think I proceeded to have a case of hysterics. I know I told the nurse never to allow that man in my room again. I took a violent dislike to Roman Catholic priests, something I didn't overcome for years. What a cruel thing to say to anyone, especially a woman who had just lost a baby.

All of this happened pretty close to Easter, (Monroe was born on March 17th) and one of the bachelors brought me a huge Easter lily. I have hated them ever since as they always remind me of my baby's death.

I was pretty puny after my pregnancy and I was told to build myself up before I tried to have another baby. I took 18 pills a day, mostly iron and vitamins. The doctor thought I might be under-thyroid or was RH negative. He had no idea why I aborted. He thought I might have a weakness in this area. He led me to believe that I might never have children. If the hospital had owned an incubator, I think Monroe might have lived. A friend of mine who had a three pound baby that year back in Quantico birthed a future football star at the Naval Academy, and Monroe weighed six ounces more than he did. My care and facilities left a lot to be desired.

Oklahoma was not our favorite state. We had to get State tags for the car that January, and on the way east in June, going back to Quantico, we stopped for gas at a garage. The man at the pump grinned at us and said, "Hi there, Okies. Glad to see you." Lamar growled, "We're not Okies! We're from Virginia!"

When we arrived in Quantico, we were given a larger apartment than the one we had left a year ago; our address was 318-B. We were still in Guinea Pig Alley, so-called because junior officers lived there and it had the reputation of being an incubator.

Mother and Boppie lived in Washington as Boppie was on duty at Marine Corps Headquarters. Betty was enrolled in a secretarial course, which she hated but was conned into taking so she could support herself if worse came to worst, and she didn't find Mr. Right. She finally graduated and secured a position in the Iranian Embassy. There she was often sexually harassed by the head man. (No one called it sexual harassment in those days; it was called, "making passes.") Her boss would send her to the "stacks," then follow her there and try to kiss her. Since she was 5 feet, nine inches, and he was about five feet, one, he didn't have much luck.

Being a secretary was not her favorite occupation. She longed for a husband and home of her own. They were both right around the corner but she hadn't met HIM yet.

When John S. Letcher, 1st Lieutenant, USMC actually entered her life, it was on a blind date in Quantico. Lamar and I knew him and we thought he would make a good husband for Betty. They started dating and their romance was launched.

Jack, aged 17, was still in boarding school. This year he had a scholarship to St. Albans Episcopal Boys School in

Early Marriage

Washington, where he sang in the church choir. Because it was "politically correct" and it was Washington, D.C., he was invited to all the debutante parties. He told Boppie he needed a tuxedo. Boppie scorned the idea and refused to buy him one. Jack insisted he really did need one as all his friends were having a blast, and he couldn't join them without the proper wardrobe. Finally Boppie gave him $10.00 to buy a tuxedo as a joke.

Jack went to a funny little Jewish establishment and got one with *two* pairs of pants. It fit pretty well, too. Then he was off on a social whirl that wreaked havoc with his grades of course. He was so darned good-looking and personable, he was Mr. Popularity himself. The fact that he was young didn't seem to bother the girls, who were all older.

When we returned to Quantico, Jack came down to see us one weekend. We were going to the Club to a dinner party and I told him to fix himself something for supper if we had left by the time he got there. He always loved scrambled eggs and I knew he could cook them. I told him there was some deviled ham in an opened can in the icebox and that would give his eggs some flavor.

Later that evening, he appeared at the Club and cut in on me on the dance floor. I asked him if he had enough supper and he assured me he had but he felt a little queasy; he thought the canned ham tasted funny. I felt awful and wondered if it was tainted. When we arrived back at the apartment, I went to the kitchen to rummage through the garbage for the discarded can. It was not there so I looked in the icebox. There it was, just as I had left it. We had acquired a kitten and sitting on the kitchen counter was an empty can of cat food. Jack had added half a can of cat food to his eggs, thinking it was deviled ham. No wonder he was queasy. I didn't know whether to confess or not.

That Thanksgiving we invited my family for dinner. They all came from Washington and I pulled out all stops, cooking everything that was a tradition in the Marston family and setting the table with our lovely wedding presents. On the way to Quantico, Mother admonished Boppie to be quiet and let Lamar carve the bird HIS WAY. Boppie said he had no intention of interfering. He agreed with her, this was our party. When the turkey was brought in and Lamar made a stab at cutting it, Boppie winced. The performance worsened and finally Boppie said, "Lamar, let me show you one little thing." Mother frowned but Lamar was grateful. Boppie took over and sliced the bird with his usual aplomb, looking sheepishly at Mother. She was furious but Lamar was thrilled not to have to carve the bird!

We still habitually had a full-time maid. One named Irene worked for us part of that winter. She asked for a couple of days off before Christmas and we said that was all right with us. Christmas Eve I went to the hall closet to get down all the presents, still in postal wrappings, that I had stashed there, everything from Lamar's family and mine. The cupboard was bare. Irene had stolen every one of them. We didn't even know what the contents of the packages were. We contacted the Military Police but they never apprehended her and she never came back. They did tell us she had a previous record of theft. Why wasn't she barred from the Base? Maybe she changed her name every time she got a new job.

That Winter Lamar went on maneuvers on the island of Culebra. While he was gone, I went to Washington and stayed with my parents and Betty. I drove up there alone and parked on the street in front of their apartment. Every four days for six weeks, I moved the car about three feet so the tires wouldn't be ruined. No one ever drove it anywhere. I was cowed by the traffic. Boppie did all the driving when we went out. Betty was in Secretarial School and I don't remember that she drove my car either.

My father at that time was what was called in the Marines "the Detail Officer." He decided where officers would be assigned for duty. He thought Lamar might like to attend the French Artillery School in Fontainebleau, France. The French were considered the world's best artillerymen since World War I because they had built the Maginot Line between France and Germany, their traditional enemy, and it was considered impregnable against horse-drawn guns and tanks. Lamar thought France sounded pretty neat and said he would be delighted to attend. Although other American Marine officers were attending The Ecole de Guerre in Paris, which was the senior school for older officers, no American had been to Fontainebleau, which was a school for junior officers. Boppie decided to send Lamar to evaluate the course. We would be attached to the American Embassy, have the privilege of using their diplomatic pouch for our mail, be paid in gold as the monetary exchange was poor at that time for Americans abroad. We would live in the town of Fontainebleau with the other students, after six months in Paris, where we would first attend language school and polish up our French. Actually, Lamar's French; mine was nonexistent.

Lamar had a rough experience while on maneuvers. Another officer, Keith Williard, a friend of his, a very conscientious man, became emotionally upset because his commanding officer gave him a seemingly impossible task to perform. The poor man went out on a reconnoitering trip around the island and came back that night, hot and exhausted. Lamar slept in an upper bunk on board ship, with his head very close to a porthole. That night a loud noise awakened him and he heard a lot of commotion out on deck. He looked out the porthole and saw a figure in skivvy pants lying on the deck. He thought someone had slipped and cut his head because he could see a lot of blood. Some corpsmen were attending to him. Shortly thereafter an officer came into the cabin and asked if anyone knew a Lieutenant Willard. Lamar said that he did and he was asked to come and identify him in sick bay as he was injured. Lamar found him lying on the operating table, the top of his head blown off. Keith drew his last breath at that moment. Lamar says it was hard for him to identify him as the explosion had altered him so. This incident put a damper on the maneuvers. Lamar didn't admire that C.O. much either. After Keith's suicide, he couldn't abide him as he was sure he had caused it.

As soon as Lamar got home from Culebra, we started getting ready to go to Europe. After our six months in Paris, we would go to Fontainebleau for the nine months of Artillery School. We would be allowed to take our household effects so we would have a car, our radio and anything else we might need, such as books. (Example: the Harvard Classics which he had bought from that encyclopedia salesman when we were courting.) I was an avid reader and we were told books in English were expensive and hard to come by abroad. This was not true. We discovered British paperbacks and they were superior to ours in this country, just as cheap and more popular in Europe at that time. All our silver and china and bric-a-brac, pictures, etc., we would put in storage.

We had to find a home for our gorgeous cat, named Reuben. He was a fluffy, tiger-striped feline with a beautiful face. The folks to whom we gave him told me years later that he attained a weight of 30 pounds and was a wonder to behold.

We were excited. Neither one of us had been to Europe. What would it be like?

7

Innocents Abroad

In the spring of 1936, Lamar and I traveled to France on the City of Baltimore, a ship out of the port by that name. It carried 80 passengers and our voyage lasted ten days.

The day we left the United States, we had lunch at a wonderful seafood restaurant on the waterfront in Baltimore. Lamar ordered one of his favorite food, oysters on the half-shell. The waiter brought him a dozen Lynnhavens. He had expected Blue Points, much smaller in size. The Lynnhavens were so enormous, several waiters gathered to watch Lamar eat them. Since it is considered uncouth to cut an oyster, he had to stuff each one into his mouth whole and manage to chew it. Every time he swallowed, the waiters would nod approvingly.

Later in France, my seafood-lover husband often remembered those oysters with longing as the Continental varieties were very small in size and tasted like the inside of a copper kettle.

There was just one class aboard the ship. As there were so few passengers, eventually we met all of them and got to know most of them. I remember in particular one old ex-opera star who insisted on singing "Danny Boy" every night in the Lounge where we gathered for socializing after dining. I can't hear that song today without recalling her aging squawk.

A few days before we landed at Le Havre, France, a Swiss swimmer and his Hollywood wife asked us where we were going in Europe and said they would like to be helpful. We told them "Paris." They said they knew the city well and warned us that it was very easy to be taken advantage of by the French, especially as we didn't speak the language fluently. Why didn't we join them and they would help us find a moderately priced hotel? They were in the market for one also. Why not? That sounded pretty good to us; the man spoke excellent French and knew the city well.

Someone back in the States had given us the name of a hotel they said was not too expensive and was in a good district. When we mentioned this one, our Swiss friend's eyes rolled back in his head. "Very, very expensive!" he said. "We can do much better than that!"

When the ship docked and we had been through customs without them finding my beloved carton of Chesterfield cigarettes, which carried heavy duty, we boarded a train for Paris with our new friends.

When we arrived at the Paris station, we took a taxicab together and started out on our search for a hotel. After inquiring at several different ones about prices, we ended up on the Left Bank, in the Latin Quarter, an area so beloved by poverty-stricken artists and Bohemians.

Lamar and the swimmer would go into one of these rundown hovels and dicker for rooms. The swimmer had told us it would be cheaper for us all if the concierge rented to two parties. No place suited or was cheap enough for him. We had no idea what French francs were worth; the bargaining was so much Greek to Lamar.

Finally, the men came out of a hotel and seemed satisfied; they said they had made a deal.

We women got out of the cab and went to check our rooms. We went through a huge wooden door from the street into a filthy courtyard, where people were standing around, talking and smoking. Our men paid for our accommodations in the office. Then we carried our luggage up two flights of narrow stairs, down a dark hall to our rooms.

When Lamar opened the door of our room, we were assailed by flowers on the carpet, on the walls, on the bed, and, yes, also on an overstuffed chair. All designs were different; the effect was so awful it made me dizzy. To this day, I call interior decorating atrocities "French Latin Quarter!" There was also a screen, covered with another flowered chintz. Behind that was what I thought was a toilet. This was to be our home for a while?

The Swiss couple went to unpack and we did likewise. We planned to meet for dinner later for, of course, they knew all the good restaurants in Paris.

I decided to use the toilet but it turned out to be what the French call a bidet. I decided that wouldn't do at all. I went next door and asked our Swiss friends for directions to the bathroom.

The swimmer said, "You mean the toilet, don't you? Come, I'll show you." We went down the two flights of stairs, across the courtyard, up one flight more and he opened a door.

"Voila!" he said.

There was an empty room with a hole in the middle of the floor. I must have looked puzzled because he explained, "The occupant is to squat and the toilet tissue provided is that stack of old newspaper squares, stuck on a nail."

He left me there, I locked the door and accomplished my mission but I was shaken. I decided I couldn't live like that!! What would I do if I had to go to the bathroom during the night? I was ready to go back to the States.

For dinner, our friends took us to a little restaurant in the neighborhood where the food was very good and not too expensive. We later discovered that no restaurant in Paris can stay open if the food is not good.

Our friends wanted to take us sightseeing after dinner. There was a famous bar where tourists came to meet prostitutes. They would like to take us there. His plan was that we would sit at a table in the back of the room and watch the men who came in choosing their partners. Did we want to go? Of course we did! We didn't want to look like country bumpkins to these sophisticated Europeans.

After dinner, we took a taxi to this famous bar. It was early in the evening, about 8:45, when we arrived at the Crystal Palace. We found the "girls," about fifteen of them, naked as jay birds, dancing with each other to some canned music. This place was not as famous as the Sphinx, where, the swimmer told us, the members of the Chamber of Deputies hung out, but it was a house of prostitution well-known to tourists.

Some of the girls had Spanish shawls over their shoulders, not for modesty but because it was chilly in there.

At our entrance, ALL the females stopped dancing and ran in our direction. They pushed us women away and tried to get the full attention of our escorts. Which ones did the gentlemen want? The swimmer told them something and all but two wandered back to the dance floor. We went to a nearby table and the two "girls" joined us. Whatever made them think men escorting women, probably their wives, intended to have sex with them? I guess Frenchmen are different from other males or maybe American men are different from all others?

When I smoked a cigarette, one of the prostitutes asked me for one of my "Americains." Lamar gave her one and the creep took the whole pack. Since she was naked, I wonder now where she put it! I could have wrung my husband's neck. I had just gone to all the trouble to sneak them past customs. What nerve!

This was no dimly lit place. The lights were so bright, one could see every mole or pimple on the skin of the women. The evening wasn't turning out the way our friend had described it earlier. We were the center of attention. I realize now that it was much too early in the evening for us to be there as voyeurs as there was very little business. Perhaps at eleven or twelve o'clock at night, we could have faded into the background but not at eight o'clock.

We ordered some kind of drink and watched as a lone French sailor arrived. The female mob rushed him, he made a choice, went to the cashier's desk, where he paid a fee and was given a towel and a bar of soap. Then he and his "girl" disappeared upstairs, not to be seen again by us.

One of the girls who had attached herself to us told the swimmer that she could pick up a ten-franc piece without using her hands if he would put it on the table. He complied and she maneuvered the coin to the edge of the table with her knee and then picked it up between her legs! That was her parlor trick!

At last we left and went back to the hotel. We bade our friends good night and went into our room, where I mirrored such unhappiness, Lamar decided to go out and telephone the hotel that our friends back home had recommended. He wasn't too happy in this environment himself. He came back smiling. They had a vacancy! We packed our luggage and sneaked out without telling our friends farewell. A taxi took us to the Hotel de la Bourdonnais where we were given a nice room with a private bath. I felt better right away that we didn't have to stay in that sleazy place on the Left Bank.

We did some figuring and concluded this hotel's rates were on a par with those in the States. The one on the Left Bank charged us about $20.00 a week! No wonder it was awful. Innocents abroad.

The next morning, Lamar called the Swiss swimmer and told him I had become ill in the night and he had brought me closer to the American Embassy. Exit Swiss swimmer.

We became quite fond of the Hotel de la Bourdonnais. The food was delicious, which was always the criterion we used for any place we stayed.

Looking back, I realize we literally ate our way through Europe. In my letters to Mother, I wrote mostly about food, how good or bad or different it was. It took us some time but eventually we learned, with the help of a French dictionary, to decipher the Hotel Restaurant menus, written in purple ink on blotting paper.

Breakfast was always served to us in our room. I don't believe the dining room was even open for business. One day I had enough courage to call the dining room and order breakfast in French. They understood me!! My choice wasn't too complicated; "jus d'orange, café, croissants et mermelade." But the kitchen did not ask me to repeat it! What a victory!

We ate practically all our meals there for two weeks. I remember one wonderful dish on the dinner menu – a huge slice of eggplant, cut into fingers and French-fried. How I would have liked to cook that later when we returned to the States, but I never had a fryer big enough.

For All Our Days

We had been told in the States not to drink the tap water in France, so brushing our teeth was a daily problem; I think we added a few drops of Clorox to a glass of water. We became dehydrated, of course, and had insatiable thirsts. The answer? WINE! We drank juice and gallons of cafe-au-lait for breakfast and wine at lunch and dinner. I know we were usually a little drunk or hungover because we slept so much. We had planned to sightsee every afternoon after lunch, but we usually ended up taking long, long naps.

Five days a week we went to the Alliance Francaise, a school for foreigners studying the French language. Lamar had had two years of high school French and two more years at the Naval Academy; I knew no French except some words I remembered in Haitian Creole but my Spanish was good, which was no help in Paris; it just confused the issue. The French did not appreciate my substituting Spanish for their native tongue.

At the Alliance, Lamar was put in the high school level, where he did very well and I went to kindergarten.

My teacher disliked Americans. She continually made snide remarks about my beloved homeland.

The class I was in consisted of about ten men and women, each one from a different European country, and me. One day my teacher told us to translate a joke into French and to be prepared to present it to the class. I chose a very short joke because it was easy, about four cross-eyed men and a cross-eyed judge. In class the next day, the teacher called on a man from Lithuania. He told MY joke in atrocious French. When she called on me, I told her this man had just told my joke. She didn't believe me until I got to my feet and gave my version in equally bad French. Wasn't that an amazing coincidence?

Two other Marine families were in Paris, the officers attending the Ecole de Guerre, which is like our National War College, and we became good friends with them. One family, the Oliver P. Smiths, invited us to dinner one night and in so doing, educated us into drinking the water out of the tap.

I had offered to help set the table and my hostess asked me to fill the water glasses at the sink. I guess I looked surprised.

My hostess said it was perfectly safe to drink the water in Paris, but not in the outlying towns. That was a wonderful gift. We started drinking the water and sobered up.

After two weeks at the hotel, on the advice of the other American Military families, we moved into a School for young ladies where the teachers took a few boarders. We were told we would learn French much faster staying there. The school was run by two Mlles. Alix and Margot Chalafour; the first one was a lawyer and the other a full-time teacher. They were both in their forties and unmarried.

An American Naval Officer and his wife were boarding with them, and as we were being shown the apartment, I whispered to the American wife, "Do you like it here?"

"Oh yes," she said. "We love it."

"Is the food good?" (You know I would ask that; this was of utmost importance.)

"It's delicious," she said.

We made the decision to move from the hotel to the school. It would be a help if we would be forced to speak French with the Mademoiselles. Having another service couple there was a plus also.

We were given a nice room with a private bath, and we would eat all our meals with the Mlles., the Naval couple and the students, who numbered three or four. I can't remember exactly how many there were or much about them, except one girl was from South Africa and they were all in their late teens.

We soon discovered that Mlle. Margot was very frugal and she gouged us at every opportunity. No laundry was allowed in our bathroom; every stitch of clothing had to be done by a laundress that she hired. Since her prices were exorbitant, I would wash my underwear at night and hide it during the day so the maid wouldn't see it and report on me later.

After dinner every night, the students and boarders would gather for coffee in the drawing room. Mlle. Alix, would usually con Lamar into "lending" her one or two logs for the fireplace. He had bought some for the fireplace in our room. She would bat her eyes and say, "How chilly it is in here. Our load of wood hasn't come yet. Doesn't a fire make everything so much cozier?"

Lamar, the perfect Southern gentleman, would offer to get a few logs from our room. She conned him over and over and she never repaid him for one single piece of wood.

These two French women had a brother who was 40 years old. Their father didn't think he was old enough to own a car so he didn't have one. When do you suppose he would have been considered of the proper age?

Mlle. Margot was in a continual tizzy as she knew that we Americans spoke English in our bedrooms. I was 22 years old, close in age to her students, and we all had to speak French when we were in the presence of anyone living in the house. She treated me like one of them; I was served no food unless I asked for it in proper French.

One day, British royalty arrived in the area to see someone in an apartment across the Courtyard. We were eating lunch. One of the students ran in and told us Princess Marina was getting out of her car. I jumped up from the dining table and ran to the French window to see her. Mlle. clapped her hands and admonished me to come back to the table; it was bad manners to jump up like that. She never would have spoken to Mrs. Kniskern that way but she was 30 years old. Contrite and embarrassed, I returned to the table. And I never saw Marina!

When Lamar and I said goodnight to the group in the drawing room in the evening, Mlle. moped and shook her finger at me to remind me to speak French when I was alone with Lamar.

My French was pretty bad. One night, in the drawing room, as we rose to say goodnight, I said in French, "Good night, everybody. I am going to have a baby." Mlle. looked shocked but the others were roaring with glee. I, of course, didn't know why they were laughing. I meant to say, "I'm going to bed." My gauche mistake had to be explained to me. In the 30's, pregnancy was not a drawing room subject of conversation.

On another occasion, I was getting out of a taxi in the center of Paris. There was a huge crowd milling around, much larger than usual. I smiled at the taxi driver as I paid him and said, "What a crowd there is." He frowned as he drove away. I couldn't imagine why until I finally figured out that I had said to him, "What a fool you are."

The food was not good at the Chalafour table. One day I asked Mary Kniskern why she had given the school such a good recommendation. She confessed she had been so miserable, alone there with the Mlles. and their students that she longed to have another American couple come and share her misery. Our being there made it so much nicer for them. Looking back on that period, I'm glad we did decide to board there. It was an interesting experience and it did help us learn French.

There was another plus; Mlle. Alix, having been a teacher at one time, did take us on some cultural trips. One was to the Cathedral of Chartres, which is my favorite cathedral of all the ones we visited in Europe. Because Mlle. Alix had taken groups of girls there for years, she was known to the guides, who allowed her to take us places the usual tourists never see.

Once we went up into the bell tower of Chartres at noon to hear those huge bells pealing. It was a little frightening but exciting to see those enormous bells right over our heads, swinging from side to side, and to feel the vibrations that made the tower itself sway. The ropes looked old and frayed as if they might break at any moment; the noise was gloriously deafening and the tower was swaying. I will never forget it.

And the stained glass windows are my favorites too. The Cathedral is built of sandstone, which is soft, and it has worn down through the centuries, which make it appear much older than some of the other cathedrals which were built of harder stone. The stained glass windows were donated by artisans from different groups; the bakers, the winemakers, the cobblers, etc. Each group had financed its own window, a fact which I found sort of touching.

We stayed at the Chalafours for almost two months and attended The Alliance every weekday where we learned enough French to survive in stores and restaurants. We were not fluent by any means; reaching that plateau took us at least a year in Fontainebleau. We did a lot of sightseeing in Paris and traveled around the environs, visiting the numerous castles and historical places.

We found that Americans on the whole were very unpopular with the French but we were often taken for British citizens, which pleased us as the English were not as loud and didn't throw their money around as much as the American tourists we observed. This was during the period of the Ugly American, who tried to buy everything in Europe after World War I and bring it all back to America, even some castles and London Bridge itself.

While in France, we were officially attached to the American Embassy. One morning, the Embassy asked Lamar to represent our country at Notre Dame Cathedral. There would be a Celebration Mass on Joan of Arc Day and all the Embassies would be represented. Lamar asked me if I would accompany him. I wasn't dressed up but he said that didn't matter; no one would notice us and we could sit in the back of the church, if I liked. I said that was OK then, I'd go.

We took a taxi and when we approached the Cathedral, there was such a mob there that the cab could hardly move. One of the gendarmes spotted Lamar in his dress blues, complete with sword and white gloves. He stopped the cab, told the crowd to make a lane so he could pass, opened the door of the cab, saluted and led us through the mob, right up to the door of Notre Dame. From there we were escorted through the cathedral to a raised platform where dignitaries were assembled, facing the crowds already seated, waiting for the service to begin. I was seated next to a general who had more stars on his shoulder than any American general had ever received in our American history. Wow! Me in my dowdy tweed suit and loafers! All the other ladies surrounding us were wearing furs and jewels and spiked heels. After a bit, I got over being embarrassed and enjoyed the gorgeous music. I met the five-star general and he kissed my hand. Being 22 has its advantages.

In August of 1936, Lamar was ordered to a little town called Auxonne, where there was a detachment of French artillery, holding exercises in the field and our government and the French Army thought Lamar would profit from watching their Artillery at close range.

We were billeted in a little hotel in the town. Madame Au Petit was the owner and did all the cooking for the guests. To get to our bedroom, we had to go through the kitchen and up a flight of back stairs. There was no bathroom or shower. All bathing was done in the river. I'm sure we had a communal "cabinet de toilette" or I would have remembered the lack.

The first afternoon we walked down to the river in our bathing suits with a cake of soap and our towels to bathe. There were lots of people there, sunbathing, boating and paddling around in the shallows. No one was really bathing.

Suddenly the atmosphere changed. Everyone was excitedly pointing out into the middle of the river, where a man had disappeared under water. No one seemed to know what to do. Couldn't the French swim? Lamar immediately swam out to the boat and started diving for the victim. He brought him up and carried him to shore where he tried to revive him. It was too late; the man was dead. His body was taken away to the local mortuary and the town's church bells began tolling for him. This continued off and on during the night and into the next day. Everyone was so impressed and grateful to Lamar for trying to rescue the poor man. We had to go to the funeral the next day and the family made a great fuss over the "brave American officer" who had so gallantly tried to save their relative; Lamar was the man of the hour. He kept shaking his head and saying to me, 'Everyone should learn to swim. Why don't the French learn as we do?"

This experience ruined the river for me and during the rest of our stay, I bathed in the basin in our bedroom, just like the French people did in theirs.

Because we went through the kitchen to get to our room, we could see what was cooking for lunch and dinner. One day

I spied a grey, greasy calf's head floating in a bucket of water. Madame Au Petit said it was, "tete de veau" and we would have it for dinner. When Lamar came in from his morning in the field, not plowing but watching the Army maneuvers, I warned him about this gruesome dish being prepared for our delight. "Watch for it at dinner,' I said. "It shouldn't be hard to recognize." Well, we ate dinner and we never saw anything that remotely resembled that thing in the bucket. Innocents abroad!

We made some friends among the French officers and their wives. The commanding officer was a wonderful French gentleman who kissed my hand every time we met and once he gave me an insignia of the Mountain Battery he commanded, making me an honorary member of the outfit.

One couple we liked that lived at the hotel where we were staying, were Georges and Alix Font. One evening we were dining together and the entree was some small game, each bird cut in halves. The platter was decorated with a lot of parsley. Lamar was served first and saw that some of the portions had the head of the bird attached. Not wanting Alix or me to get a head, he took one and covered it with lots of parsley as he could hardly stand to look at it himself. Towards the end of the course, Alix said to Lamar, "I see you have the head."

"Ah yes," he replied.

"Are you going to eat it?"

"Oh no!" he said.

"Then may I have it?" asked Alix.

"Certainly," he said. It was transferred to her plate and she demolished it.

"There are some things in it." she said.

This was all in French, of course. Lamar told me later that he was afraid that there *were* things in it!

The Fonts invited us to a family picnic. We all drank too much wine and everyone lay around on the ground on blankets, trying to sober up. A young officer managed to change into his swimming trunks, sitting right next to me, chatting up a storm but he never exposed himself. I was a nervous wreck as I was sure he was going to do just that. The French are so open about nudity. Once a French woman showed me a picture of herself naked, nine months pregnant. As for that French officer, I think he was darn clever to change his pants so modestly, don't you?

In September we went to Fontainebleau so Lamar could start his classes at the Field Artillery School. We stayed in a "pension," a French boarding house, and went house hunting. All the other guests there were French except for one young English girl who had a two-year old baby boy. She told us she was a widow; her French husband had been killed and her insurance went so much further in France than it did in England, she decided to live on the continent. Her name was Peter Cederwell-Brown. She latched on to us but I took a dislike to her as she said nasty things in English to me about a Frenchman who sat next to her at dinner every night. I found that rude and unkind but I felt sorry for her because she was a widow so I tried to be nice to her.

We found a small house to rent at 11 Rue Carnot. It was a box, three stories high, right on the street, with a tiny walled-in garden in the back. The garden was so small, I trimmed the grass around the paths with scissors. The house was completely furnished, even to kitchen utensils, dishes and linens.

Downstairs there was a hall that went from the front to the back door. On one side of the hall was a tiny salon, filled with furniture, etchings and lithographs depicting gruesome moments in history, and heavy brass bric-a-brac, one very lifelike lion eating a lamb. The French antique furniture was formal, covered in red satin brocade, and there was a red Turkish carpet on the waxed floor. Across the hall were the dining room and kitchen. In the latter, was a "batterie de cuisine," without which no self-respecting French kitchen would be complete. It consisted of a set of copper pots, ranging from very small to very large, beautifully polished, hanging in perfect order. The stove was a two-burner affair with a tin box on top for an oven. There was no icebox so we rented one by the month and an ice truck brought me blocks of ice once or twice a week. None of our French friends had anything so modern. Before we attained the icebox, I had gone to market three times a day like the French did, and bought food daily; bread, butter, meat, vegetables and staples. Milk was delivered each morning in a metal jug and was immediately boiled since it was not pasteurized. Later, if I bought a whole chicken, I would take it down to the local bakery and they roasted it for me.

Upstairs were two bedrooms and a bath. We had what we thought was a double bed in the master bedroom until one of our friends from Paris came to see us and told me it was a three-quarter bed. We had thought it was sort of narrow but we didn't care; it was big enough for us; we just snuggled closer together.

There were no closets. We had armoires for our clothes. Our sheets were linen and felt wonderful but looked messy after one night's sleep. My idea of wealth would be to have linen sheets ironed and changed every day! The guest bedroom had a single bed. I have no memory of ever having an overnight guest.

On the third floor was a small bedroom and a bath, designed for a domestique (a maid.) We did get a maid but she preferred to sleep in town as she had a fifteen year old daughter and didn't want to leave her. Lamar used the maid's room as his study. The rest of the space was for storage.

We moved in and bought some silver plated tableware, as we had not brought our flatware, the only item missing to start instant housekeeping. Our effects arrived from the States eventually. We were glad to get our radio, although we had to pay a French tax yearly to keep it; some books; our car, (hardly anyone owned an automobile; everyone rode bicycles) and that's all we had shipped overseas besides clothes.

Because we were paid in gold Lamar made more money than the Commanding General at the French Artillery School;

we were the wealthy Americans. The exchange was fifteen francs to a dollar but we got 25 because we were "diplomatic." All our overseas mail was delivered to the American Embassy.

School started and Lamar diplomatically bought a bicycle and went off to class every morning, bouncing over the cobblestones and cursing in wet weather. He's like a cat; he hates to be wet. He didn't like to take the car as no one else had one.

My first job at 11 Rue Carnot was to take down 18 lithographs off the walls of my tiny salon and put them up on the third floor in the storage area. They were joined by the brass lion eating the lamb and other equally touching works of art. Now the room looked larger and less confining.

All the windows in the house were French. They were nearly as high as the ceilings and opened like French doors. No frugal housewife would open them as light might fade the upholstery or rugs. Besides, someone might peer in and see the furnishings and come back later and steal them. Being an American, I opened the two downstairs windows wide to let in the fresh air.

This resulted in my landlady, who lived in a big house next door, coming by and discovering the nude walls and absence of valuable *objets d'art*. The doorbell rang and I went to encounter a worried and frazzled Madame Reuss who could hardly get out the words to ask me what I had done with her valuable possessions. I told her I had put them in the attic for safekeeping. Not mollified, she demanded to see them. I honestly think she was convinced I had stolen and maybe sold them. We trekked to the third floor and I showed her all her things neatly stacked. She shook her head and I know she regretted renting to us. As she left, she admonished me to keep the windows closed when the sun was pouring in on that side of the house; even the wallpaper could be damaged. That was easy! The sun didn't shine much that winter nor the next either.

Another incident which arose as the result of my opening the windows occurred later in the year. Directly across the street lived the de Marnac family. The father was a colonel in the French Army and looked a lot like a polished Charlie Chaplin.

He had a timid wife and a slew of little girls, who wore black pinafores all day at school to save their dresses. They all looked pale and worked very hard at their homework, in spite of not getting home from school until four or four-thirty every day. They were a little standoffish, bowing to us but never acting very friendly.

One morning, I came from my bath and remembered my robe was in the guest armoire. Naked as a jaybird, I ran into the room to get it, forgetting I had left the long French windows open. To my horror, I spied Commandant de Marnac on the balcony opposite, leaning on the railing, smoking a cigarette. I hoped against hope that he hadn't seen me but he had been looking in my direction.

Later that morning as I was going to market, I heard a bicycle approaching from the rear, and looking back I soon recognized my neighbor. When he reached my side, he jumped off his bike, came up to me, grabbed my hand and kissed it. He tipped his kepi, smiled and said, "Bon jour, Madame Curry." Then off he biked. A few days later we were invited to tea with the family. Lamar said he definitely must have seen me in the buff and he must have liked what he saw!

At the tea party we had a strained moment. Lamar, in an effort to be nice, spoke to one of the littlest girls, "Bon jour, Mademoiselle," he said, "tu est tres jolie." (Good morning, little lady, you are very pretty.)

The Commandant blushed furiously and said, "Il est garcon!" (He's a boy!) Poor Lamar. How could he tell? The child was wearing the same black jumper as his sisters and he had a similar haircut. Since he was their only male child, his parents were insulted.

Going to market daily was a hassle. Everything was in a different store. There was a butcher shop, another for only pork items, another for horse meat, with a big gold shiny horse's head to identify it. Flour, sugar and canned things were in a special shop. The open market had fruits, vegetables, eggs, butter, poultry, cheese. Another shop had pastries, salted nuts and party fare. One store, a sort of Deli, had some prepared coquilles Saint Jacques, scallop shells filled with sliced scallops, mushrooms and cheese in a cream sauce. We loved them and I bought them frequently. I hate to think how much butter was in them.

The market was my Waterloo. I was spotted as a foreigner and all prices were elevated. I couldn't even pick out my own fruit; they gave me bad oranges, mushy apples and half-rotten vegetables.

My friends told me we needed a maid so we put an ad in the paper and our first prospect was a middle-aged French woman named Annie Bayles. She spoke English and had worked in the States for many years. She told us she had been housekeeper for one of the Vanderbilts. She had become ill and thought she was going to die so she returned to France to do just that. After an operation, she took a new lease on life and decided to go back to America, but she needed a family to sponsor her as immigration was tight. She wanted to work for us, hoping we would take her home when we returned to the States.

We were surprised that Annie accepted the pittance we offered her; working for a Vanderbilt had to have been very different from being a maid of all work. Her wages must have been quite good in the States if she had been the housekeeper. We hired her and life was much less hectic than it had been before. Annie moved in. Lamar relinquished his study. Annie cleaned, shopped and cooked very well. We were satisfied until we decided to invite our English friends, the Pelham-Burns, to dinner. They had entertained us several times and we wanted to reciprocate their hospitality. Now that we had a maid it would be so much nicer. They had a cook, a maid, a nanny for their children, and several gardeners.

When we told Annie that we would have a couple to dinner the next Friday, she looked horrified. "I can cook for four people but you will have to get someone to serve. I certainly can't cook and serve FOUR people!"

I said, "That's ridiculous. I cook and serve for six or eight people all the time." Annie fumed and said she would try but I shouldn't expect too much. She did very well but I knew I had a high-powered thoroughbred in my stable, not a percheron.

After a month, Lamar said our food bills were getting pretty high. Maybe we could eat something besides steak, shrimp, lamb chops or quail. I asked Annie if we could have meatballs one night or spaghetti or something cheaper. She rose to her full height and said, "You can eat stuff like that if you like. I shall get a little steak for myself."

We decided this arrangement was not going to work. Always terrified of hired help, I lied through my teeth and told her we had had some financial reverses and couldn't afford a maid. We paid her off and she left in a huff, to search for a wealthier American, a needle in a haystack in Fontainebleau.

A newspaper ad led us to another maid. She turned out to be a small woman, terrified of her own shadow, about thirty-five years old with bad teeth and stooped shoulders. Her name was Blanche and she was the one who had a fifteen-year-old daughter. There was never any mention of a husband. Did she have a love-child? I never asked her. We offered her less money than we had given Annie and she took it. Three hundred fifty francs a month, Sundays off. That was about $18.50 American money a month with room and board. She seemed frail and we thought she might have T.B.; half the people we knew had pulmonary trouble of some kind.

Blanche arrived at six o'clock every morning, brought in the milk which was sitting on our doorstep, boiled it, and set it aside to cool. Breakfast was cafe-au-lait, toast and marmalade, and because we were strange foreigners, we had orange juice. Some days we would have croissants or brioches, both delicious. Lamar had butter, of course. How I survived two and a half years in France with my butter obsession, I'll never know. If I couldn't see it, I pretended it wasn't there. I must have consumed pounds and pounds of it as everything in France had butter in it!

Blanche was a good cook and saved us a lot of money. I gave her two dollars worth of francs every day. She went to market and came home with wonderful food; no rotten oranges or wilted lettuce were sold to her. We ate well and I loved the homemade soup we had twice a day with our lunch and dinner. The French are big on soups. What she used to make it was and is a mystery.

Innocents Abroad

I had been taught that meat stock was the important ingredient for any soup but she never seemed to have any. Maybe she used bouillon cubes! I remember clear tomato soup, bean, potato, onion, cream of vegetable, bouillon with rice or veggies, cream of pea, carrot, watercress, mushroom, etc. Every item we ate was always a separate course; soup, omelet, fish, meat entree, veggie, salad, cheese, dessert, fruit. We didn't have all those things at every meal, but every item we did have was served solo. Think of the dishwashing involved in an operation like that.

Blanche seemed to enjoy working for us and began to smile a little. As I said earlier, she would not live with us as she wanted to be with her daughter. She put on some weight and looked better too. Every cook or maid I ever had gained weight, working for me. She became a permanent fixture and stayed with us until we left France. She spoke the "language of the people," which was not the same French used by the military Officers and their wives. I learned dreadful expressions from her and used them at soirees and receptions, where I shocked my hearers. I was usually unaware I had done so unless I was told. We were learning the language, but we were a long way from being fluent. Because I talked so much with Blanche, I was getting quite proficient in "street" French. When we went to Paris to see a French play once, the only actress I could understand was the prostitute.

In the early part of our life in Fountainebleau, our social life was nil. In order to call on our instructors and superior officers, we had to wait until they had an "At Home." Finally, one did and we dressed in our best finery and attended, Lamar in dress blues and white gloves, I also dressed to the teeth. Out we went to conquer the hearts of the French Army personnel. When we arrived at the residence, we entered and were seated on chairs, placed in a circle. On our arrival, one couple left. As new people came in, we moved up into chairs closer to our hosts. Finally, we were next to them and we chatted until another couple arrived and it was time for us to depart. This was so formal we didn't have a chance to get to know anybody. How different from American military custom where you had to call on your superior officer within twenty-four hours of arrival on a Base.

Lamar's head instructor, a Capitaine du Rosemont, and his wife finally invited us to an evening reception because we heckled them so much about calling on them. The appointed hour was 9:00 p.m. We arrived at 9:05 and they were not even dressed. No one else came so we waited alone in their salon until about 9:45 when our hosts descended to greet us and a few others began to arrive. Most of the guests arrived around 10:00 o'clock. We were introduced to no one else and it was a strange evening. Every man there danced with me and not one woman acknowledged my presence. The de Rosemonts didn't seem to understand anything we said. If Lamar or I made a remark, all they could say was, "Comment?" which meant, "What did you say?" This was usually followed with a slight frown. Repetition didn't seem to clear up the situation at all.

At midnight we decided to take our departure, a decision that seemed to confound our hosts, who said we were soon to have a midnight breakfast. So we stayed and at 1:00 a.m., a very fancy and heavy meal was served. We got home at about 2:30 and Lamar had a class at 8:00 a.m. Now I am convinced the de Rosemonts didn't like us and invited us to embarrass us. Lamar was the only student invited.

Finally, after a few months, in desperation, we decided to have a party ourselves. We would invite the student officers and their wives, and some of the instructors that Lamar liked and their spouses. What to serve? I asked one of the wives I had met and she said, "By all means, give us American cocktails. That will be a wonderful change for us."

The French we met at that time drank very little hard liquor. The usual party fare was wine of some sort, usually champagne. We decided to have martinis; nothing was more American. The big day arrived. Blanche and I had slaved to make this a success. We had all the usual food that is served with cocktails: ham rolls, cheese spreads, dips with vegetables, salted nuts, etc. We served champagne but everyone wanted "the American cocktail!" Unaccustomed as they were to such strong drink, they were soon drunk as hoot-owls. One woman went outside the house to have a tete-a-tete with a young bachelor she had been flirting with and her husband locked her out and wouldn't let them back in. Another couple was running upstairs, slamming doors and yelling like children. The noise tempo rose and Blanche, in her new cap and apron, stood in the kitchen with her mouth hanging open. She had never seen French ladies and gentlemen acting like this.

Finally we stopped serving cocktails and our guests slowly took their leave. Lamar and I looked at each another and wondered what we had done. Would we ever see them again?

Some of the bachelor students came back later that night to serenade us and they threw their kepis (a cap with a flat circular top and a visor) through our open bedroom window where they landed on our bed. We decided to not pay them any attention. They were out of hand! We did throw their kepis back but since we didn't appear, they finally went home.

Lo and behold, the next morning there were lots of little notes slipped under the front door, thanking us for the lovely party, and in the next day or two, there were others, inviting us to parties they were giving. The Currys had arrived socially! Since Lamar was the same age as many of his instructors, some of them became our friends. So many of the students were bachelors, too poor to do much but look for a girl with a dowry to marry. They entertained very little.

I could play bridge and was soon invited to be a member of a foursome. We played in French and I am sorry to report, some of those ladies cheated.

One day I was in Paris and I picked up a book called "Brighter French" in one of those little outdoor stalls along the Seine. The book was a collection of cute jokes. I decided to be scintillating at my next bridge game. I memorized some of the jokes, which I thought were sort of funny.

The next week the first time I was dummy, I said *in French*, "I heard a cute story the other day." Then I proceeded to tell it. There was a thick silence. I thought maybe I hadn't told it right. Later I tried again. I said, "Have you heard this one?" And I recounted another.

This was met with blank stares. No one commented. When I tried a third joke, one of the ladies said, "Paulie! Where did you hear these filthy stories? They are awful!"

"They are not dirty to me." I said, "What makes them so awful?"

"They employ words that have a double meaning, and you evidently don't know the off-color one!"

I got rid of that book and humbly realized how little I knew about the French language.

Remember the young English widow, Peter Cederwell-Brown, who was at the pension. I took her under my wing and introduced her to my French military friends. With my endorsement, she was accepted and invited to some of the parties. She moved into a larger apartment and began buying a lot of new clothes. I was worried that she couldn't afford this new way of life but she didn't seem concerned. She was dating one of the officers and having a ball!

One day she called and said some friends from Alsace were spending the night with her, a Baron and Baroness. They all wanted to go to Paris the next day, and she knew Lamar and I were driving there in the morning. Could they all drive up with us? I told her that was fine and we would pick them up the next day. When we arrived at her door, she appeared with just the Baron. Peter said the Baroness had been indisposed and had decided not to come on the trip.

As we drove to Paris, I kept looking at the Baron, trying to decide where I had seen him before; his face was so familiar. Then the light came on! He was the spitting image of Peter's two-year-old son! I mentally reconstructed the whole story: the baby was illegitimate and the Baron was supporting them. His wife probably didn't even know about this affair. Peter was demanding more and more money to keep up her social life and the Baron had come to investigate. I felt like a twerp. My first impressions are usually right and Peter had been no one I wanted as a friend.

I felt that I had been used. We left them in Paris and from then on our relationship cooled. I'm sure she realized she had made a mistake, introducing us to the Baron. Did she think we were so dumb that we wouldn't notice the resemblance? Maybe she wanted us to know so she could be honest with us. I guess we were naive, but I was mortified that I had launched her among my friends. After we came home from France, one of my French friends wrote me that Peter had another illegitimate baby and one of the bachelors we knew and her friend from Alsace both were at the Clinic when she gave birth; they were not sure which of them was the father.

At Christmas, 1936, Lester and Mary Dessez, an American Marine Colonel, attending the Ecole de Guerre in Paris and his wife plus their eight-year-old daughter named Duffy, and Captain Louis Marie and his wife Lucy and the Currys went to St. Moritz, Switzerland. The three men were the only Marines attending French military schools at that time.

We bought clothes for skiing at a big department store in Paris. What a difference from the skiing clothes today. Everything was wool; jacket, pants, underwear, socks and gloves. Nothing was waterproofed. All skiers get wet so once we were on the slopes, we were drenched and had to wait hours for our clothes to dry on the radiators before we could go out again.

We did not invest in ski shoes; they cost a mint. We bought lumberjack shoes that came up to our ankles. Skis we rented in Switzerland.

The trip by car to Switzerland with the Dessezswas uneventful except the eight-year-old sang the Twelve Days of Christmas all the way to St. Moritz and nearly drove us nuts. We were sitting in the rear seat with her all the way from Paris to St. Moritz.

St. Moritz was beautiful when we arrived about 11: 00 p.m. It looked like a Christmas card with the enormous snow covered mountains, the hotels lit up for the holidays and the crisp dark blue sky, studded with stars you felt you could reach out and touch. The hotel was luxurious. The beds had mountainous down quilts that smothered you, and a maid brought us plates of delicious sandwiches and pots of hot chocolate to our rooms to consume before going to bed. At midnight the bells began to toll. What a lovely sound. It was Christmas Day and we sleepily separated and went to our own rooms, tired but excited by all we were experiencing.

We stayed until January 3rd and tried to learn to ski, not an easy accomplishment. The skis were so long then, about six feet in length and quite cumbersome to get around on. We skied everyday and some of us improved. I spent the whole time learning to go uphill. I have no memory of attacking a slope and attempting a real descent. Lamar climbed to the highest point he could reach and descended in atrocious style but safely. The fearless one!

We were told the Protestant church was holding its annual service to bless the skis. That sounded interesting so we all decided to attend, good church people that we were. We skied over to the Service through the snow covered streets, found the little church, removed our skis and carried them in to be blessed. We thought we had made a mistake as we were the only people there. Soon an Anglican minister came out and invited us to be seated. The seven of us sat in about the middle of the church, in a solemn row, bundled up like stuffed bears. We weren't quite sure what was going to happen and we didn't want to sit too far forward. We all hoped someone would come in and sit in front of us. No one else arrived and the service of Vespers began.

When the Offertory was upon us, the minister asked Lamar, who was on the end of the row, to be the usher. He took the plate and after getting our pittances, extracted after much effort from voluminous clothing, went to the back of the church, waiting for a signal from the minister to approach the altar. Finally the priest nodded and Lamar started forward. As he was abreast of us, the cleric said in a loud voice, "Let us pray!" Lamar dropped to his knees in the middle of the aisle like he had been shot, and the prayers went on and on. By now, we were all hysterical and nearly exploded trying not to burst into laughter. Eventually, the Minister motioned to Lamar to get up and bring him the plate of offerings and the service continued to its conclusion. No one ever blessed the skis or explained to us if they had been.

None of us broke or dislocated any bones so we considered our Swiss trip a success. When we had arrived and gone upstairs in the elevator, it held several passengers on crutches and in casts. We felt lucky that all of us returned to France unscathed.

At St. Moritz on New Year's Eve, I encountered my first lesbians. The hotel held a dinner-dance that we all attended. At midnight the orchestra started playing "Auld Lang Syne" and all the lights were dimmed. People started hugging and kissing one another. At the table right in front of us were two rather middle-aged women, grey-haired and mature looking. As the lights returned, we noticed these two locked in a passionate embrace, their lips sealed in a fierce kiss. I just couldn't believe what I was witnessing. I'm not sure I even knew at that time that lesbians existed.

When Lamar and I returned to Fontainebleau, we found out the school was going to put on a variety show and people were asked to do skits. I was invited to sing a song in French to the tune of The Lullaby of Broadway. Everyone in the cast was named for a horse in the School stables and mine was Palm Beach. In the skit I wore a big floppy hat and beach pajamas. I could never remember the words to the second verse of my song so I wrote them on the palm of my hand and tried to remember not to turn it towards the audience. I was nervous when I started singing but soon got over that and began to enjoy myself. I waved my hands around and some people could see the words on my hand and started to laugh. That didn't bother this ham. Anything for success. Lamar said the French found me charming. That was all I wanted to know! I might be comique but I was charmante!

Lamar was "Uncle Sam," named for another horse and he had a bit part in a skit, about which I remember nothing.

Lamar wanted me to take riding lessons because everyone at the school was so horsey. He himself rode two hours every day. A riding instructor, a civilian named Andre Portais, consented to give me lessons twice a week. My horse was enormous! Sixteen hands high. I had to climb up on a platform to mount him. He was an ex-race horse and liked to go. If I leaned over to adjust my stirrups, he would take off like a rabbit.

We always rode in the beautiful forest of Fontainebleau, which was on the edge of the town. I learned to ride in French, all directions being given in that language. Once my horse ran away with me and I couldn't stop him. Portais, galloping madly behind, yelled to me, "Ralentisez les reines!" Did that mean to tighten the reins or loosen them? Nothing I did seemed to work. Finally, we came to a macadam road and that intelligent animal automatically stopped; he knew he was not supposed to run on hard surfaces.

Portais would trot along in the forest, humming to himself, looking for fallen trees. The forest was so well manicured, they were few and far between. When he spotted one, he would kick his horse into a gallop and jump the trunk, giving me no advance notice. My horse would immediately follow, being herdbound as the species is. Often I came close to being thrown until I learned to anticipate my teacher's sneaky ways.

One day, in the forest, we came upon a group of officers jumping their horses over some hurdles. Portais barged in on them and asked if Mme. Curry could take some jumps. The only jumping I had done was over those fallen trunks. They said I could, and to my horror, Portais urged me into a three and a half foot jump. I approached the hurdle uncertainly and the horse felt it and started to refuse. Portais swatted him over the rump with his whip and the horse took a standing jump, right up in the air. We made it but I was thrown up onto his neck and was hanging on by his ears. Everyone laughed and Portais said he was training me for the Concours Hippique, the International Horse Show in Paris. That paralyzed me and I feared for his sanity. He would *never* talk me in to that!

The first rainy day I had a scheduled lesson, I rejoiced. No riding lesson. I went back to sleep. Then Blanche came up and awakened me. Mr. Portais' groom was at the door. Where was I? My instructor awaited. I had to get up, get dressed and go out in a downpour. I discovered rain would not save me from a riding class.

It rains a lot in the winter in France. One morning I told Lamar it had snowed in the night. I was looking at it out our bedroom window. He must come and see the white pavement. He came to the window and shook his head. "You poor thing," he said. "There is no snow; the sidewalk is dry for the first time in three months."

Rue Carnot, where we lived, led into the entrance to the cemetery, which was at the end of our street. All funerals came by our house were the dreariest things you have ever seen. First came the black-frocked priest, carrying a cross and saying prayers. He was followed by a horse-drawn hearse, which had glass sides so one could see the coffin. The carriage was black and draped with swags of some dull, black material. The horses were draped also and had high black feather plumes on their heads. Behind the hearse came the mourners, some weeping copiously in full mourning dress, some veiled. Everyone walked; no cars followed the procession.

I told you how I hated anything to do with death. Every time a funeral came by, which was often, believe you me, I had to watch and then I would get depressed. My landlady's lovely 24-year-old daughter died of childbirth fever the first winter we were there. I was horrified. No one in the States died of things like that! I was terrified that I would get pregnant in France and die over there.

Well, I didn't get pregnant but I did get sick once with a "tired stomach" from eating in so many four star restaurants. The food was so rich, even my cast-iron Marston stomach couldn't take it. The doctor "bled" me and put suction cups on my back to bring out the poison. He put me on a diet of boiled ham, rice and charcoal. Later, when I was better, he prescribed horsemeat to "build me up" but I cheated and ate cow steak. Happily, I did recover but I was sure I would die in France.

We had been told the Field Artillery Course would be for one academic year but we discovered it was a two-year course, so we would be in France for a second year. This was a mixed blessing. The good news was we would have time to travel around Europe during the vacations and, after two years, our French would be much better. The bad news was Betty was getting married and we would miss that, since we couldn't afford to go home until we were ordered back by Uncle Sam. Then we heard that Mother and Boppie were going to China for two years. The umbilical cord was still hanging by a thread and this meant I wouldn't see my parents for four years in all! I could hardly bear it! Nevertheless, we never complained verbally; that was just the way the cookie crumbled. We would have to take it like good Marines. We settled in for the long haul.

That spring we made a trip to Belgium, The Netherlands and part of Germany. The tulips were superb and the Dutch costumes were so colorful, I bought one for myself. In Brussels, we bought some lace and I fell in love with some little porcelain figures I spotted in a store window on a Sunday. The shop was closed, of course, for the Sabbath, so we stayed over an extra day. I bought a couple; they were expensive but I couldn't resist them. We left for Germany and found the same figures in all the stores we visited in that country. They were Hummels and we had paid the duty on them in Belgium. Innocents abroad again!

We loved the toy stores in Germany. Lamar bought enough toy soldiers to make a display of a whole Artillery battery, about a hundred. He had soldiers cooking, shaving, cleaning rifles, doing everything soldiers do in the field. He trimmed the German helmets on the figures to look like Marines and painted each and every one in Marine green. Back in Fontainebleau, he worked on his display and dyed sponges to make bushes. He loved his new hobby. That display was really pretty impressive. Years later, he gave it to Culver Military Academy when he was on the faculty there.

I fell in love with the little wooden angels in Germany. We bought as many as we could afford. They became part of our Christmas ritual; we put them out on display every year and agreed that the German toys had it all over the American ones.

My little angels came to a sad end. I always packed them in cotton and put them in a metal box in-between Christmases. In Evanston in '58, we had a flood in our basement and my toys got damp. The trunk they were in was floating. When we examined the contents, we found the angels destroyed. The cotton was wet, the paint was gone and the wooden pieces were all unglued. There was nothing recognizable. I trashed the whole mess.

In 1937, we were in pre-WWII Europe although I don't remember being alarmed. The German food we had on our trip there was heavy and salads and vegetables were scarce. Nazi soldiers were in evidence but they were not considered a threat at that time, at least, not to us Americans. Lieutenant Louis and Lucy Marie, who had gone to Switzerland with us, met us in Germany that spring. Louis took a picture of a haystack and was surprised to have his camera seized by the police, who confiscated his film. Inadvertently, he had taken a picture near something the Nazis considered secret. His having a French name was no help; the Germans and French were long-standing enemies. He was furious at losing his film and amazed at the animosity shown him.

We thought Germany was pretty; we thought it was so much cleaner than France. We especially loved going to the little walled towns of Dinkelsbuhl and Rothenburg. Sightseeing was OK, but eating was more important to us. Since we were eating our way through Europe and the food in Germany was not the best, we didn't give it any stars.

In June, at the end of that first year, Lamar was promoted to Captain and we traveled to England, where an American warship had docked. I guess an American ship is considered America. He could have his required physical exam on the ship. We flew from Paris to London, the first flight of my life. I was scared and wrote letters to everyone I knew, the week before we left. I had seen an Imperial Airways plane the day we bought our tickets and it was not a shiny bird like the ones that Lamar usually traveled on in the States. Shades of Cornelia Otis Skinner! I was sure the plane would crash in the ocean and it was not a sea plane. I had a mental picture of Mother reading my letter and saying, between sobs, "Just think! She wrote this the night before she died."

When I saw our plane at the airport, I was sure we were doomed. It was dirty, and looked old and needed a coat of paint. Visibility that morning was so bad we flew very low over the Channel and I could see the whitecaps on the waves. Amazingly, we arrived in England safe and sound and the ocean grey was displaced beneath us by beautiful green hedgerows and a landscaped countryside.

We landed at the London airport and went into the city to the Regent Palace Hotel. It was very nice and it was such fun, hearing English spoken again, even if it wasn't American. There were several restaurants in the hotel and the first night, we tried to eat in a bar but found out ladies were not allowed; it was for men only. That was sure different and would never have happened in America. The waiter directed us to another room where women were welcome.

The next day, Lamar went to the coast to Portsmouth to have his physical exam and when he returned, we did some shopping. He had a fitting on some Maxwell riding boots made to order. I went to the Army-Navy Store and was fitted for a Harris tweed suit. Then we rented a car and went to Sussex to visit my Great-aunt Anna Marston, who had married an Englishman named Goodwin Green. They lived at Hampstead Heath in a charming English Tudor cottage with a beautiful garden. They were elderly but Uncle Goodie, as we called him, was very spry and took us sightseeing. We spent one day at the beach. I think it was Brighton. We just walked around as June in England is usually chilly. There were not many people on the beach.

Aunt Anna was fragile and concentrated on stuffing us with food every time we walked into the house. The routine started at breakfast. Eggs, bacon, chops, kidneys, creamed fish, crumpets, scones were served from a buffet. Then lunch was announced at about one o'clock. That was a huge dinner-type meal. Afterwards, everyone took a nap. Around four o'clock, there was tea, complete with sandwiches and cake. Dinner was at eight, with soup, entree, salad, dessert and always, a savoury, usually with cheese melted somewhere in it. I'm not through! At eleven, we always gathered for a light repast so we wouldn't die of starvation in our sleep. Aunt Anne was overweight while Uncle Goodie was wiry and spare.

When we left "Wayside," as the Greens called their place, we went to Stratford-on-Avon and visited Shakespeare's bailiwick and his wife's cottage. That evening we attended a play in the Shakespearean theater.

The next morning, Lamar and I separated. I had another fitting on my suit in London quite early so I had to take the train to the city, and Lamar drove back to London more leisurely to turn in the rented car. We planned to meet at a hotel called the Lancaster Arms. Our favorite hotel, the Regent Palace, was full and our hosts in Stratford recommended the other and secured us reservations.

I arrived in London, took a taxi to the Army-Navy Store, had my fitting, all on schedule. Lamar would meet me for lunch at the hotel so I took a taxi there. When I arrived, I noticed it was on the small side, being part of a long row of houses. I entered and asked at the desk if a Captain Curry had arrived yet. I was told he had not so I booked a room and went upstairs to wait for him. One o'clock came and no husband. Two o'clock, ditto. I was getting nervous and began to wonder what I should do. Had he been in an accident? No one would know I existed, and if they did, where would they find me? Should I call the American Embassy? Would a hospital contact them if they had a wounded or dead American citizen on their hands? Three o'clock came; I was in a cold sweat. Where was he? Four o'clock, five o'clock, no Lamar. I did not know one soul in London and I had two pounds in my purse, about ten dollars at that time. Credit cards were unknown. At six o'clock, the phone rang. I dashed to answer it. It was *Lamar!* He had been next door in the Lancaster Arms since 1:30, waiting for me to arrive. I had taken a room in the Lancaster Gate, which was next door. He was as frantic as I was. He was sure I was dead or lost or had amnesia. I went downstairs and paid for my room and Lamar appeared at the front door. Relief flooded our faces. Thank God we were reunited.

When we left the hotel I had been in, we looked up the street and saw the whole block was a series of small hotels: The Lancaster Gate; The Lancaster Arms; The Lancaster House. Who would have anticipated anything like that? Of course, we were starved and wanted to dine right away. To add insult to injury, these were all Temperance Hotels. They sold no alcoholic beverages. We couldn't even get a drink to steady our nerves.

How had all of this happened? The cabby had let me out in front of the wrong hotel. All I saw was the word Lancaster in lights and deduced that I was where I was supposed to be. From this night on Lamar and I did not separate; we stuck together every moment.

I must tell you that the tweed suit that caused all the trouble about the hotels was a mess. The first time I wore it in France, a British lady said to me, "I can tell by looking at you that you just love horses and dogs!"

Moi? I hate dogs and just do tolerate horses. The second time I wore it, when I went to my dressmaker in Paris, she said, "Madame, I think I can improve your suit; it is so heavy and bulky. Look, Madame! You have eight thicknesses of tweed around your waist!" I brought it back to her on my next trip to Paris and she did fix it somewhat. Lamar remembers my wearing it in Italy, where I was pinched on the fanny by some strange man, but the tweed was so thick, I didn't even feel it. Lamar saw him in the act or I would never have known.

One night in England we took a couple from the Embassy out for an Indian curry dinner; I don't remember who they were but we must have been indebted to them. The waiters there wore turbans and Indian dress and it was all quite elaborate. We ordered the "real thing." Having eaten home style curry all our lives, we wanted to see what we had been missing. When it arrived, it was so hot and spicy none of us could eat it. They served something like raw potato with the condiments, to "cool the throat" and that's all we ate. Our guests told us later that they never ate highly seasoned food, even pickles!

We returned to France with all of our goodies. My most treasured gift was a zippered teddy bear Lamar bought me. I named him Picadilly and he graced my bed from then on; my nightie reposed in him in the daytime. Lamar wore his Maxwell boots through customs, hoping not to pay duty on them. Of course, the boot-trees were in the suitcase so no one was duped but he did not have to pay duty on them. The fun came that night in the hotel in France when he had trouble getting the boots off. His feet had swollen and I had to hold his feet while he kicked me in the fanny. Well, he couldn't sleep in them, could he? We finally got them off.

That summer, Lamar was scheduled to go on maneuvers with the French Army again. Lucy Marie, Louis' wife, and I decided to go on a cruise for a month if we could find one we liked and could afford. We went to a travel agency in Paris to find out what was available. The agent mentioned a ship that was going to Spitzenbergen and Norway. The only accommodations left were two first class ones and the price of each was 5000 francs. We shook our heads; they were too expensive. We couldn't afford more than 3000 francs each. The agent thought a minute and then he said, "Very well, Mesdames, you may have the stateroom for 3000 francs a piece." We couldn't believe it. So fast and almost half his asking price? We took his offer. Coming out of the office, Lucy said, "Won't it be fun to be with some English and American people! I get so tired of trying to speak French. I'm sure there will be Americans on board!"

The cruise would last a month and when we returned, we would join our husbands in the towns where they were stationed that summer. I forget where Louis was going to be, but Lamar would be at Montpellier with a French battalion of Mountain Artillery.

In due time, Lucy and I took the train to Le Havre in France and joined our cruise ship. As we went aboard, I asked the purser how many Americans were aboard. He said, "Mademoiselle, there are two American ladies."

"How many English?"

"There are no English people aboard; there are two hundred French people and two American ladies." He didn't recognize me as one of those two Americans. My French was getting better?

Thus began our trip to the Land of the Midnight Sun with 199 French and Polish Jews and one Roman Catholic Archbishop. We didn't mind their being Jewish but we wanted to talk with English speaking people. We were homesick! We had dreamed of lovely English tourists.

The next day we looked the passengers over and decided they were a scruffy-looking group. They looked better as the week wore on and after two weeks, they looked fine. We had some celebrities aboard; one was the Archbishop, quite elderly, and the lone Catholic. Another was a French movie director, the brother of Rene Clair, France's outstanding movie mogul; his name was Henri Chomette and the passengers called him "Clair Obscure," a play on his name which meant, "light." His light was obscure as he was not as well-known as his brother. He continually took movies of us all. I wonder if he had any film in the camera?

Chomette was a handsome devil with coal black hair and deep, penetrating blue eyes. He had two friends traveling with him. One was a lawyer and the other an engineer. All three were bachelors and they soon attached themselves to Lucy and me. I had to have been the attraction as Lucy was fortyish, overly plump and matronly. I was 23, skinny and a terrible flirt. We ate together, the five of us, went on excursions as a group, did things as a fivesome on board ship and in port. I was having the time of my life. Lucy was my chaperone and protected me when I led these men on in my youthful fashion. Looking back, I realize my flirting was dangerous and not very smart.

My female friends in Fontainebleau did not dare to flirt; liaisons were a serious business in France and usually led to some legal action. In my day a lot of American women flirted outrageously and it meant absolutely nothing. Look at an old movie of the period; banal and harmless! Today I wonder what Henri thought I was doing; was I as interested in a relationship as he was? He probably wondered why I was so slow getting to the point.

One afternoon during the "tea" hour, we were all sitting at a table, eating pastries and planning the next excursion when we landed in Bergen. I realized I had forgotten my cigarettes so I excused myself and went up on deck to our cabin to get them. I had locked the door to our stateroom when I had entered as I thought I might go to the bathroom while I was there. I heard a knock at the door, not very loud. I didn't answer. Then I heard a voice in a whisper ask, "Paulie, Are you there?" It was Henri's voice. He had followed me up and I was terrified. Did he really think I would let him in? He knocked several times and then went away. I waited until the coast was clear before I opened the door. There was no one in the passageway. I went and rejoined the table. Henri was seated there and when I sat down he brazenly said, "Where have you been? I went to your cabin to give you your dark glasses but no one answered when I knocked."

One night Lucy was talking to me in the dark before we went to sleep. My bunk was under the porthole which opened onto the deck. Suddenly Lucy said in a stage whisper, "I saw a man's hand come through the porthole and feel around your bunk!"

I said, "Lucy, that's your imagination. Why would anyone do that?"

"Well, I saw it," she said. "I know what I saw!"

The next morning, Henri asked me where my bunk was in the cabin. I asked him why he wanted to know? He said he had come up on deck the night before and figured out which was our cabin. He stuck his arm through the porthole, hoping he would grab me! I said that Lucy slept there and she would be terrified if he tried that again.

We habitually put our shoes outside the cabins at night and the stewards polished them. One morning my shoes were not there. Someone had taken them and put them outside the Archbishop's door. The French are great on silly things like that. Everyone teased the Monsigneur at breakfast and he enjoyed it too; to think he might have had an affair with the young American!

The trip was one of spectacular beauty. The narrow fjords were dramatic with the high mountain peaks on each side. I remember one sunset that was breathtaking. We were sailing through a narrow passage, the afterglow having painted everything in dramatic colors, even the sea gulls were a luscious pink. I sensed that I would always remember that moment. Every object, the water, the trees, the clouds looked artificial, but most of all those rosy seagulls were unbelievable.

We kept going farther and farther north. We saw Lapps in their native costume, with their beautiful fluffy white dogs, pulling carts and even sleds over the snowy terrain. We had no more night. I remember dancing in dark glasses at midnight in bright sunlight. Our inner clocks got fouled up. We slept the night through in sunlight. For some reason, we found this very tiring.

Our ship maneuvered successfully around the ice glaciers and we saw seals, polar bears and sea birds. We crossed into the Arctic circle and had an initiation of ice cubes put down the front of our dresses for the women, or down the front of the trousers of the men.

Everyday was an excuse for a party or banquet. Once we had a fancy dress ball. We improvised our costumes, dressing up only our heads and shoulders. Lucy was a pirate and I was a Bretonne, my coif and collar made from paper doilies. By now we were on intimate terms with everyone aboard; we even borrowed clothes from one another.

One day we visited a Viking village. I had read Kristin Lavransdatter, a prizewinning trilogy by Sigrid Unset, the summer before so I was fascinated with the replica of the house she could have lived in, back in 1200 A.D. The Viking ship didn't look capable of traversing Lake Michigan, much less the Atlantic Ocean. But it did! That book came alive for me. It is still one of my favorite books, after all these years.

One day we all went ashore and took a train to Sweden, just to say we had been to Sweden. It seemed much like Norway but not as spectacular.

Nearing the end of our cruise, we landed in Denmark where we visited Copenhagen. My memory of that city is vague except I think we saw Hamlet's castle. And we made a trip to a huge amusement park called Tivoli Gardens. It was nothing like the ones in our country; it was very clean, manicured and in much better taste. We had dinner at an outside restaurant which was built in tiers and carpeted in red. There was a full symphonic orchestra, playing musical comedy and popular light opera tunes. It was like fairyland and the food was wonderful. I'm sure anyone who has been to Copenhagen knows it, but that was back in the late thirties and it might be different today. We rode on a roller-coaster and danced until early morning and then returned to the ship for our final hours aboard.

When we said farewell to our cruise mates, we swore undying friendship. We would get together for a reunion soon! Little did I know that we would see some of them on the streets of Paris in a couple of months and they would look so scruffy again, we wouldn't bother to hail them across the street. This is a mystery of shipboard friendships. Don't ask me why but it's a fact. Henri's parting quip to me when we landed was, "You will be sorry when you are an old woman that you didn't sleep with me!" Am I? Never! Maybe?

Lucy and I parted. She went back to Paris. I was on my way to Montpellier, in the south of France. I would go to Marseilles on the coast and then cut across the southern part of France to the Cote d'Azur. I found myself on the train in a compartment with seven French people. They were friendly and very helpful. After a couple of hours they were so friendly, they demanded to see my ticket and discovered I was on the wrong train. The one we were on was a slow one and I had a ticket for the Express, which was more expensive. The conductor was called to our compartment and he agreed; I would have to get off at the next station and wait for the next Express. I had already lost a lot of time. I would get to Marseilles at midnight instead of three o'clock in the afternoon and I would have to sleep in the station Hotel. The next morning, I was told, I could take a train for Montpellier. Sound simple? I didn't think so but I did what they told me to do. They waved me goodbye and there I was, standing on the platform with my luggage, wondering if I'd ever see Lamar again.

The ticket master was kind and handed me on the right train when it finally appeared. I shared my compartment with a traveling salesman who politely offered to carry my luggage to the hotel in the station. (How *gallant* can we get?) It was 12:30

a.m. and he saw that I got a room and a wake-up call for 6:00 a.m. Then he tipped his hat, kissed my hand and disappeared into the night. He was a true gentleman!

The trip to Monpellier from Marseilles was uneventful and I was met by my wonderful husband who had champagne and flowers in our room in celebration of our reunion. He had enjoyed his duty with the mountain battalion. His commanding officer was a dear and they had hit it off famously. Commandante Bricka was such a gentleman, he came to the hotel to call on me. He gave me the insignia of his outfit, which I still have. I think he really loved Lamar. We were beginning to love the French people.

Lamar had the car and we were going to Italy for a few days. We left Montpellier and drove the Grand Corniche, a beautiful, winding, scenic road along the coast. We stopped in Monte Carlo but didn't stay there very long; just long enough to go and inspect the gaming tables where people made and lost fortunes. We went to Pisa to watch the Tower lean, then on to Genoa, because Columbus came from there. Next we continued on to Florence where we admired all the art and did what tourists do there. I remember the cemeteries were art museums, filled with statuary. I was so impressed with the photographs of the people who were buried beneath the tombstones; I had never seen that before. Venice was next and we found that city fascinating. I doubt if it has changed much since those days, although there might be a Wendy's or a Hardee's there now, unfortunately. We left our car and took a boat over to the city. I remember one trip in a gondola, when we went under the Bridge of Sighs. (Doesn't everybody?) We fed the pigeons in the square and saw everything tourists see. What impressed me most was the size of the bathroom in our hotel; it was bigger than some of the living rooms in the houses we had lived in.

The food was so-so but Italy was being ruled by Mussolini and austerity reigned. Spaghetti was plentiful, but the sauce was skimpy; hardly enough to color the pasta.

Mussolini, Il Duce, had cleaned up the country in another way. We went to a theater where we saw all these characters posing in long winter underwear. We finally realized they were supposed to be statues; Mussolini's purity laws did not allow the actors to be painted with theatrical make-up; nudity was definitely out. After living in France, where naked bodies were displayed without shame on the stage and quite often elsewhere, we were amused at Mussolini's prudishness. As I narrated earlier, one of my friends in Fontainebleau once showed me a picture of herself, naked and nine months pregnant. It was the first photo in her baby's album and she wasn't embarrassed a bit. I was uncomfortable just looking at it in her presence. I told you I am a Victorian. I don't think women are at their height of attractiveness at that stage of their lives.

We returned to Fontainebleau without seeing Rome or Naples. No time. Lamar's second school year was about to begin. We always expected and hoped to get back to Italy but we never had the opportunity. Now I am resigned to never getting back to Europe. I'm glad we saw it when we did though, without fast food joints and hordes of tourists, looking like they never washed themselves or their clothes. Now, a large portion of the population of the Western world is sloppily dressed and all Western nationalities look alike. In the Thirties you never saw a woman on the street in Paris that she was not dressed in what we called, "street clothes." No one ever wore jeans in those days except farmers and they didn't wear them when they went to the city.

That next winter we hosted some parties. Two that I remember especially were held at a lovely hotel in Fontainebleau called Le Hotel de la Poste et de l'Angleterre. (Translation: Hotel of the Mail and of England. Weird, huh?) Maybe the mail stage coach stopped there in the 1800s before going to the coast to send people and mail to England.

Once we had a big cocktail party. Monsieur Richard, the maitre d'hotel, had firm ideas about what we would drink and serve in the way of food. I was completely cowed by him and did exactly as he suggested. I'm glad I did, as everything was just about perfect. The room was beautiful; it had white walls, covered with etchings in black frames and there was a deep red carpet throughout; the tables were covered with spotless white linen and the champagne punch had fresh fruit floating on top. Everything was so elegant and our French friends were as impressed as we were.

The other party was a seated dinner at the same place. We had about twenty people and there were many courses. The week before the dinner, I asked Monsieur Richard if I should order flowers for the table. He shrugged his shoulders and said, "Of what significance are flowers? I will just throw some on the table." I really didn't know what to expect but I didn't dare argue with him.

And that's exactly what he did. We arrived to find he had scattered fresh flowers all along the length of the table. And they looked gorgeous!

We started dinner with Oysters Rockefeller, a first for me, and I fell in love with them. The dinner was superb, from beginning to end. It was a fitting end to two years of interesting experiences. We were paying back all the parties we had enjoyed with our French friends that winter. We had been very social that second year, as the military personnel had decided we were OK. This dinner was our unofficial farewell, so we had pulled out all stops.

That was the winter that the King of England, Edward, renounced his throne in order to marry Wallis Simpson Warfield, a twice-divorced American. Our magazines were full of the scandal but the British papers and periodicals were almost silent on the subject. Our English friend, Ian Pelham-Burn, would come to our house every week to read our Time magazine, as the British edition said little about the royal scandal. How times have changed! Today, every detail of their courtship would be plastered on the front pages of every European newspaper. The British were saddened and unbelieving that their monarch would give up his throne for any woman.

The night that King Edward spoke on the radio to his subjects, saying he could not face life without the woman he loved, we were at a dinner party. When a servant told our host that the King of England was making a speech, we left the table abruptly to go and listen to him, as our hosts had a short-wave radio. We all were saddened for our English friends. I never told Ian that Mrs. Simpson was some relation to me; I was ashamed to claim her as a relative. Still am.

What a difference technology has made in communications. Today news is instantaneous around the world. Even radio was not as prevalent then. The British people were unprepared for the shocker when it came, although the affair had been going on for months. Their press had stayed mum on the subject

That Christmas we returned to Switzerland but not to St. Moritz. We went to a charming hotel in a little town called Pontresina, which was across the mountain from where we had stayed the year before. Our train arrived at midnight and we descended from our railway car into fairyland again. We rode in horse-drawn sleighs, under fur coverlets to the hotel where we found wonderful accommodations and the usual sandwiches and chocolate awaiting us. It was Christmas Eve and we opened silly presents before going to our separate rooms. The bells were tolling for Christmas and the crisp mountain air felt like ice on our faces. Snuggling under our eiderdown was pure bliss.

The day after Christmas, Lamar and Louis Marie decided they were expert enough on skis to take a train to St. Moritz and ski home over the mountain. The rest of us were impressed with their courage but opted to stay on the local slopes.

As the day progressed, we began watching the run for our intrepid men. It began getting dark, and we started to worry as they had not returned. Suddenly, on the porch of the hotel appeared Lamar and Louis, grinning sheepishly. They told us their story.

They had taken the train as planned and when they arrived, they had lunch to fortify themselves for their great skiing expedition. Then they carried their skis to the base of the run and paid an exorbitant amount to ride the funicular railway to the top. When they got off the car they noticed there was a brisk wind blowing. It was strong enough to blow the snow away from the ski tracks, so instead of being concave, they were convex. Just about then a young female skier came flying by and attempted to come to a halt near them. She didn't stop but skidded sideways and disappeared over the crest of the hill, not to be seen again. Louis and Lamar watched the few people around who were struggling to stay upright and decided this was not a good day to descend the slope to Pontresina. Embarrassed, they returned to the funicular station and asked the conductor how much it would cost them to descend. He told them, "Nothing!" Mortified but relieved, too, because their funds were low, they got on the empty car and returned the way they had come.

We thought they showed great sense to act the way they did, but Lamar was haunted by the memory of that cute young girl who skied past them when they first arrived, up on the crest flying on the wings of the wind, not even using any poles; she just switched her body around to keep her balance. The fact that she was female made it worse. He had not been raised with athletic women. When he was a boy, he told me once, he didn't think women were capable of running or playing ball; he thought it was because of the way they were built. Victorian women were not encouraged to be active in sports. His sisters were very sedentary, and they looked awkward when they participated in any sporting activity.

One of my most vivid memories of this trip to Switzerland was the baggage routine the three men, Lamar, Louis Marie and Lester Dessez, underwent on the train trip to Pontresina. We had left from Paris and had to change cars many times and each time we did, they had this harrowing experience of getting thirteen pieces of baggage off one train onto another, all in excited French. How we ever arrived with everything intact was a miracle. Of course, our return trip was a repeat but by then they had their routine down pat.

Back in Fontainebleau we resumed our pleasant friendships with our military friends. One young officer paid me a lot of attention. He sought me out at parties and always danced with me at soirees. I can't even remember what he looked like or what his name was. One morning about ten o'clock, I was down in the basement, taking clinkers out of our furnace. How I happened to be assigned this job with a man in the house and a full-time maid, I can't imagine. My guess is I liked doing it. Otherwise, I'm sure I could have escaped this chore.

Blanche came downstairs and informed me there was a gentleman to see me, one of the Lieutenants. She did not look very happy. I said he couldn't want to see me; it must be one of my husband's friends. Blanche said he had expressly asked if Madame Curry was at home. Blanche was acting awfully funny and I asked her what she was worried about. She said, "Madame, this gentleman should not come to see you when he knows Monsieur Curry is not here, and he knows very well he is in class."

I agreed. "Tell him, Blanche, that I am in the basement and he can come down here."

Blanche looked shocked. "But, Madame, you are in your apron and not dressed for company."

"That's OK, Blanche. I shall receive him here."

Pretty soon the lieutenant who had been paying me so much attention all winter appeared on the staircase. "Come on down," I said. "You can help me with these clinkers. It's a messy job and I could use some help."

We worked for about ten minutes, and then he said that he had to go. He made no passes at me and nothing unpleasant happened, but at the next soiree, he was much less attentive. I think he must have misinterpreted something I said or did on some previous occasion and expected to be received very differently. Anyway, I think I handled the whole thing rather well. A woman in old clothes and an apron does not expect to be seduced.

Even if I had wanted to have an affair, which I didn't, such liaisons were considered by the French ladies to be extremely dangerous. Women in France were second-class citizens. A married man could have all the affairs he cared to indulge in, but a woman who was unfaithful would be divorced and lose her dowry. I met such a person in Cannes when I was on the beach one day. I told her my husband was at Fontainebleau, and she wistfully told me she had been there several years before. Her husband fell in love with the wife of one of his military friends. She was so mad at him, she began flirting with one of the Lieutenants. One thing led to another, and her husband surprised them in bed. He immediately sued for divorce, and she lost everything she had brought to the marriage.

When I returned home I asked some of my friends about this sad case and several of them remembered her. They shook their heads and said she had been so foolish; they would never have become so involved. A little flirtation, yes, but not too serious. I remembered our party when they were all running around, going outside for a tete-a-tete, and running upstairs and closing the doors. That was OK. Getting caught in bed was not OK.

Speaking of women being low-regarded, when we first arrived in Paris, I had tried to open a charge account at one of the big department stores. I went to the office and was told that only two women in France had accounts with them; one was the wife of the President of France and the other the wife of a multimillionaire. I left properly chastened and glad, as I so often was, that I was an American.

The longer I stayed in France, the more patriotic I became. The sight of the Stars and Stripes in a Pathe Newsreel would move me to tears. I told Lamar I was going to kiss the ground when we returned to America. (I changed my mind when we docked in Norfolk. It was so ugly!)

Having a car abroad was a great advantage. When we had time off we would make trips to other parts of France. We toured the Chateau country once, visiting all of those fabulous castles. Another time we went to Brittany and stayed at Mont Saint Michel. There we indulged in their famous Madame Poulard Omelet, which is cooked over an open fire in a large black skillet. I watched carefully as it was being prepared but I could never reproduce it. The Mont was one of my favorite places in Europe. At high tide the entire town is surrounded by water; at low tide you may come and go on a causeway. On the top of the mountain is a lovely monastery. The narrow streets wind down into a quaint town filled with shops and restaurants. It's a charming and romantic spot.

One more incident in France to relate; one night at the end of the school year, we attended a dance in a castle, which was either rented or owned by a wealthy American. The ball was on the evening before the big parade in Paris on July 14th, Bastille Day. The castle was out in the country, not far from Paris, and I remember it was so isolated we needed maps to find the place. As we approached our destination, we saw it from afar. It was illumined on the exterior, and looked fairylike. As we came nearer we heard music from the orchestra. It was quite a soiree, everyone dressed to the teeth. I remember I wore a white brocade ball gown, designed by Agnes Drecoll, silver shoes and long white gloves; Lamar was in his evening dress uniform. Everyone looked gorgeous. We danced and dined and didn't leave until about three o'clock in the morning.

Afterward we drive to Paris to our favorite hotel de la Bourdonnais, arriving at about four a.m. We asked for a room and the sleepy clerk took us upstairs in the elevator, down the corridor and opened a door. There was no bed! A sofa, yes, but no bed and we were exhausted. We complained, and the clerk took us to another room. He apologized; I guess he thought we were having an affair and they had special suites for such couples.

After a very short night, we went to the parade on the Champs-Ellyses. Someone at the American Embassy had an apartment with a balcony there so we had a great view. The French pull out all stops on such holidays and the display of armaments went on forever. When we told our friends about our experience at the hotel the night before, they were not surprised. Now I wonder, do hotels in this country have special rooms for couples who are not interested in sleeping?

By this time, we were short timers so we dashed around, doing all the things we had put off, hoping somebody in the family would come over and visit us before we returned home. No one did, so some places we missed like the Tour d'Argent, a famous restaurant that served nothing but duck, cooked in myriad ways. It was so expensive, we knew we could go only once and we wanted our kin to share the experience with us. Ah me! Well, life has its little disappointments.

We went to England before we returned home to the States. Ian Pelham-Burn tried to plan our trip for us around all his relatives. He said we could stay with different members of his family every night we were in his country. Lamar told him we would visit ONE relative, spend ONE night with him and that was all!

He chose his half-brother, Sir Arthur Hazelrigg of Noseby Hall, who was the King's Lieutenant for Leistershire and lived in an old chateau which had been in the family for centuries. That sounded different and sort of like an English novel, so we chose that relative and made our plans. We were going to Scotland to watch the salmon leap, something someone, probably Ian, told us we had to do, for some reason. We took the boat to cross the Channel. Before we left, we remembered our projected visit to Noseby Hall and went into a liquor store to buy an ordinary bottle of French wine as a house gift. We traveled the Channel at night, so we had booked a stateroom with bunk beds, No one else on board seemed to have accommodations so the trip was noisy with people streaming by our open port hole until we docked in the morning.

Upon our arrival in England, we drove our car to London. Lamar was buying some Peale boots, and he wanted a black tie to wear with his tux when he got to Noseby Hall. We had been alerted that we would be expected to dress for dinner. We didn't have to be told; we read lots of British literature.

None of the shops we went into carried anything as loathsome as a pre-tied black tie, and in desperation, Lamar bought an untied one, telling me I could tie it for him. I didn't have the faintest idea how to tie a tie. "You could practice," he said.

We left London and proceeded to Noseby Hall, arriving at teatime. Lady Hazelrigg met us as we came up the driveway of this gorgeous place. She had been gardening and wore a big floppy hat and a sweater that was more holes than wool. We gave the butler our car keys so he could park the vehicle and went inside to the drawing room. There we had a sumptuous tea while I stewed internally. Poor Lady Hazelrigg. Her clothes were a mess. I was embarrassed to contemplate her reaction to my French Couturier gown when we dined that evening. What would she have on?

Sir Arthur arrived with a young woman named Rose, who was his secretary-companion. He was heavy in build and had a florid face, I was sure he was going to have apoplexy any moment. He wanted to show us the chapel. He was very proud as it was hundreds of years old and all his ancestors were buried there. We accompanied him outside and across the manicured lawn, while he regaled us with stories about his antecedents, who had been in the Crusades and the War of the Roses. We approached a stone, vine-covered little church and entered. It was dark and dank. Sir Arthur pointed out some tombs and plaques, telling us a little about each one. Suddenly he reached down to the stone floor and grabbed a heavy rope. He hauled on it and with many screeches, the stone was raised. Now, I thought, he is going to have that stroke. But no, he survived, and taking a flashlight, he pointed it down into the depths and there were lots of coffins. The floor had water on it and it was a horrible-looking place. After we had duly admired the broken and caved-in stone sepulchers, we were allowed to leave and get back into the open air. I wasn't wild about sleeping so close to all those bones. You all remember how I felt about death.

When we returned from our tour, Lady Hazelrigg said one of the maids would show us to our rooms. I wanted to unpack and hang up that dinner dress, so we excused ourselves. Dinner would be at eight, and some of the country squires and their wives were coming in to meet us. We followed the little maid in her starched uniform up the long staircase, down innumerable hallways and finally came to a huge room with a bed that would have slept six girls at a house party. Then she said she would take the gentleman to his room!! Where was she going to take him? Next door, maybe. They left and I looked around for our baggage. It was nowhere to be seen. Then I opened an armoire. All my clothes were neatly stashed in drawers, my dresses hung on hangers, pressed, everything that had been in my suitcase there but nothing of Lamar's.

There was a knock at the door. I thought it was Lamar, but it turned out to be the maid again. I asked her where my husband was and she replied that he was in a different WING! She would draw my bath for me at six o'clock and the bath was across the hall from my room. Did I wish her to help me bathe? Good Lord, no! She left and I stewed alone until time to bathe and dress for dinner.

Meanwhile, Lamar was discovering his clothes neatly unpacked and distributed in HIS armoire. To this day, I'll never know why we were separated. I forgot to mention that he had found his pre-tied black tie in his suitcase when he was packing the newly purchased untied one. The clothes he would wear to dinner were laid out ready to be donned. There was the English tie but the American one was nowhere to be found. Knowing he couldn't tie that one, he started searching everywhere for the other. He found his suitcase and went through that with a fine-toothed comb but with no success. Then he sleuthed every nook and cranny of the armoire and finally found it stuffed back in the recesses of a very deep drawer. Relieved, he managed to dress for dinner.

We met in the drawing room at five minutes to eight. I was amazed and relieved to see Lady Hazelrigg gowned in a lovely, becoming blue chiffon dress. She was nearly unrecognizable from the disheveled woman in torn and ratty clothes who had greeted us that afternoon. There were quite a few guests there but Sir Arthur was rattled. One couple had not yet arrived. We met the squires and their ladies, and at eight o'clock on the dot, Sir Arthur announced we would repair to the dining hall; we would not wait for the tardy neighbors. We were seated, about twenty of us, and the waiters began bringing in the first course. A wine steward leaned over my shoulder and whispered, "Les Caves de Chateau-Armagnac, 1930."

The soup course was followed by the arrival of the late comers who were breathless and effusive in their apologies. Sir Arthur hardly acknowledged their presence. They seated themselves at the empty places and dinner continued.

Each time a new course was set in front of me, the steward would bring a new bottle of wine and as he poured it, would give me the name and year. I remembered the dumb everyday bottle we had brought as a gift, and was embarrassed.

As you know, the English use their eating utensils differently than we do. When we cut our meat, we put down the knife and spear the morsel with a fork. They never relinquish the knife. It is held like grim death in one hand and the back of the fork is piled high with food, until it is brought up to the mouth. This takes a little practice, but I was determined to eat that way and not look like an American boor. Eventually, I got tired and reverted unconsciously to my habitual eating style. Was it the copious glasses of wine? Anyway, I looked up to see many eyes on me. The British were watching us like hawks. I quickly changed back, but the damage was done. The Americans were barbarians!

After dinner, Sir Arthur asked me to play bridge. He said Ian had written him that I was an excellent player; I knew Culbertson! He was the "horse's mouth" for anyone who played contract bridge back in the thirties. I joined the table and said I would enjoy a game. Rose, his secretary, was one of the foursome, Sir Arthur's partner. One of the squires was mine.

I picked up my cards, and I had a wonderful hand. I bid way up there and in playing, I made a small slam. I was so pleased with myself. Sir Arthur said nothing. The next hand was pretty good also. With a little help from my partner, I could make game, probably. I bid and then I caught Rose's eye. She indicated disapproval, and I realized Sir Arthur didn't like to lose. He bid some suit and when it came around to me, I passed. Rose smiled at me. I was doing the right thing. He made his bid and looked pleased with himself.

The next hand was a winner but I passed, thinking what a childish creature that apoplectic nobleman was. The whole evening was spent passing up on good cards and trying to smile as Sir Arthur played hand after hand. What a boring night.

The next day was Sunday and Sir Arthur announced, as we retired for the night, that "family prayers would be in the dining room at eight o'clock sharp." I bid Lamar good night, forlorn that he would not be with me, returned to my room and made a conscious decision to not oversleep. I undressed, got into bed and turned off the light. Through the open window I could see the chapel in the moonlight, and I began to think about all those dead people buried over there, wondering if many of them had slept in the bed I was crawling into. I noticed an eerie light hovering over the bedside table. "Oh my God," I thought, "One of those ghosts is coming to haunt me!"

I lay there unable to go to sleep. If I could have found Lamar's room, I would have bolted there in a minute. I watched the light and it moved slowly every once in a while. I turned the light on. It disappeared. When I turned the light off, it reappeared. Finally, I went to sleep.

When I woke up, my watch said seven-forty. I jumped out of bed, washed my face, and threw on some clothes. I hurried downstairs and into the dining room. There sat Sir Arthur in regal solitude at the head of the table with an open Anglican prayer book before him. Lined up against the sideboard were about ten servants, the men in livery and the maids and cooks in starched caps and aprons. Everyone turned as I entered. Sir Arthur rose and asked me to come and sit with him. I obeyed, wondering where Lady Hazelrigg, Lamar, Rose and some house guests were. Sir Arthur read the prayers and asked me to read the "morning lesson." As I did, I glanced at the hired help and read consternation on their faces; they didn't understand a word I was reading; the barbarian accent was too much for them. With the last amen, the servants drifted away and Sir Arthur and I helped ourselves to the sumptuous breakfast hidden under silver covers, over hot water, on the sideboard; eggs, bacon, sausages, kidneys, toast and crumpets. What a spread! The others began arriving, surprised to see me there so early. They said no one ever came to family prayers. As usual, I hadn't gotten the word, but Sir Arthur seemed pleased that I had joined him, so I didn't care. I was sort of glad that I had witnessed that little bit of British custom.

After breakfast, I excused myself to pack. Lady Hazelrigg just smiled. When I got back to my room, I found every garment gone. My clothes were packed in the suitcase and the bag was in the car!! We were ready to roll. I had asked my hostess if she had ever heard of a light that glowed in my room. She said that it must have been the luminescent bulb that was on the cord that turned on the night light. My ghost was explained.

We were glad to leave and continued on our journey to the tip of Scotland to watch the salmon leap. It seems that was the thing to do so we were following someone's suggestion, maybe Ian's. We drove and drove and the landscape became more and more bleak and barren. Towns were few and far between, gas stations more so. About five o'clock we passed a "bed and breakfast" so we thought we'd better stop. Our landlady said she could give us a "high tea," whatever that was, and showed us our room. Our bed was hard as a rock. We investigated and found there were no springs, just a hard mattress on ropes! A first and I must confess the only time we ever slept on such a contraption, thank God.

While we were waiting for our "meal," the landlady suggested we go across the road and "watch the salmon leap!" We did. They were leaping upstream a mile a minute and we saw them!! Having accomplished our mission, we decided to go back to London the next day and see some stage shows and get some good food. Our "high tea" turned out to be a salmon casserole with some bread and salad. It was ample, and we didn't complain.

Returning to London, we went to Edinburgh to sightsee, but the fog was so thick, we walked up to the Castle and patted it but couldn't see one stone of it. Back to London we went and, oh happy day, the Regent's Palace had a vacancy. We spent all our money on food and shows before we left. Such plebeian tastes we had. We did our share of sightseeing, but restaurants and theater were our first loves.

Our European tour was over. The next morning we drove to the coast, had our car hoisted aboard the "City of Baltimore" and started our trek home to the U.S.A.

We had been abroad for two and a half years without ever hearing any family member's voice or seeing anyone we had known before we left. My parents had just departed for Peking, China, and it would be two more years before I would see them or hear their voices. Such was the situation in those days but we didn't even feel sorry for ourselves. That was the world of 1936-39, and we were part of it.

When the War exploded two years later, we lost contact with all of our friends in France, and I'm sure some of them were killed or wounded. The Atlantic Ocean was a great separator, and Europe was very far away.

Today with people flying to and from Europe in less than a day, it seems strange to think our crossings took 11 days. But that was seventy years ago and I can remember it as though it had all happened last week.

8

Parenthood

Back in the States, we returned to Quantico for duty. Lamar was ordered to the Marine Corps Schools to teach Artillery, for which he was certainly well-qualified after his training at Fort Sill and the School in France. He discovered he loved teaching and he was happy to have this job, which he held for three years. He bought himself a mare, a good jumper that he named "Stardust." He also trained a remount named "Gracious," a grey horse that turned out to be a wonderful jumper with a marvelous disposition. I am told there is a marker in Quantico today in her memory. Lamar would loved to have owned her or have had complete control over who rode her but that was impossible; she was in the pool of mounts and very popular with adults and children alike. He bought "Stardust" so he could train her for himself alone. He also volunteered to teach equitation to the Base teenagers. He loved doing this and those kids were soon participating with him in the Horse Shows at Fort Myer and elsewhere in Virginia.

He especially enjoyed the young girls and one was completely enamored of him. She was Phyllis Atkinson, fifteen years old and cute as a button. One day, she asked her mother if Captain Curry was married. Her mother said he was and his wife was very nice. There was a pause and then Phyllis asked, "Do they have any children?"

"I don't think so," her mother said.

"Well, thank goodness there are no children to complicate matters!"

Lamar's horsey activities became quite lucrative for us as he won a lot of events and the prizes were usually silver platters, pitchers, trays, or bowls.

Meanwhile, I was concentrating on starting a family. We had been married six years and our tour in France had kept me from even thinking about having a baby. America was far ahead of the rest of the world in medical matters in those days.

I consulted a specialist in Washington, a Doctor Mundell. He was a famous gynecologist and had served in the Navy at one time. Now he was in private practice but he was still in the Reserves and did his compulsory service by giving a few days a month to the Navy and taking care of some of the more complicated pregnancies of their dependents. No one had ever really explained to me why I had lost that baby at Fort Sill. My case was considered complicated enough to warrant Dr. Mundell taking me on as a patient. His usual fee was in the thousands but because I was a Service wife, I would be paying very little more than the usual Navy doctor would charge, which was minimal. On my first visit, he pronounced me fit for motherhood. One month later, I was pregnant and as excited as anyone who wanted a baby could be.

There was one drawback; we lived in a third floor apartment and everything I bought had to be carried up two flights of steps. Sometimes these objects were heavy. After my second appointment with Dr. Mundell, I started bleeding. He told me via the telephone to go to bed and he instructed the local OB Doctor to come and give me shots of morphine. A Dr. Clarke was the Navy doctor assigned to the Obstetrics Department at the family hospital on the Base. He came daily and gave me shots. I lay on that bed like a dope addict all day and night almost completely unconscious for a week and then my body aborted the fetus.

When Dr. Mundell was informed of my miscarriage, he decided I needed building up again and I swallowed so many pills, I rattled. I took all kinds of vitamins, thyroid, iron, cod liver oil pills. You name it! I remember the number. I took 18 pills daily.

He also insisted that we be moved into a cottage from the third floor apartment because of the steps I had to use. This was accomplished and that summer we moved.

Parenthood

I was again pronounced fit so we tried once more. One month later, I was pregnant again and Dr. Mundell told me he anticipated no problems.

At two months, I started bleeding. Dr. Mundell talked to Dr. Clarke and told him I was never going to carry this baby. That made the good country doctor furious. His mother had died in childbirth and her death was the reason he had specialized in obstetrics. He came to see me, told me he was determined that I was going to have this baby, had me transported to the hospital by ambulance, given uterine sedatives and not allowed to put my feet to the floor. There I stayed until I reached my seventh month of pregnancy. When I was seven months pregnant, he allowed me to go home.

Most of the day I rested on the bed or in a chair with my feet elevated. He said he wouldn't be alarmed if the baby came any day but he was shooting for a nine month's pregnancy. He told me my baby was viable and lots of seven-month babies lived. I was a nervous wreck the whole time I was pregnant, remembering my experience at Fort Sill. I surely didn't want a repeat of that. It seemed to me and everyone else in Quantico the longest pregnancy on record.

Because of my lengthy stay in the hospital, bedridden, I owned just one maternity dress which Lamar and one of his cherished equitation girl students, Peggy Erskine, had picked out for me on a day of shopping in Washington. I think the only mail order catalogue in those days was the Sears and Roebuck one. Peggy's mother also was in danger of losing a baby and had to stay in bed just as I did so Lamar and Peggy, an unlikely pair, went shopping together for our wardrobes. When a fifteen-year-old and a 33-year-old man went to the maternity section of Woodward and Lothrop department store, the clerks thought they were a couple and disapproved heartily. Their relief was great when they asked for dresses two different sizes, neither of which would fit the young girl standing before them. The dress they bought me was a green-blue paisley and, to this day, I hate that color and paisley prints too. My face was covered with what they call, "the mask of pregnancy," blotchy dark areas that looked like a peeling sunburn. Probably all those uterine injections caused them. Anyway, that blue-green was not becoming and I got very tired of looking at myself in the mirror and *seeing that*. I had to wear it as it was the only thing I could get into.

My baby was due on Easter and he arrived one week early. On Palm Sunday, we had had a dinner guest and he and Lamar sat talking after dinner while I sat there and squirmed, not knowing what my complaint was. Finally the guest went home and I told Lamar I had pains. I never have I seen a man move so fast. He said, "We're off to the hospital!"

I was never given any anesthetic because John came so quickly. I remember Dr. Clarke saying I had a fine boy and feeling his little body being propped up on my stomach, right after he was born. Lamar says Dr. Clarke called him in to meet his son as soon as he had been cleaned up. I don't know which man was more pleased. Clarke was so proud of this baby and with good reason; he wanted Lamar to see him right now! In those days, fathers seldom witnessed the births of their offspring.

The next morning, Helen, the head nurse, brought me my baby. That was the most wonderful moment of my life; he was so beautiful with his golden fuzz and his peach-colored skin. He had everything he was supposed to have, even eyelashes and fingernails. For some reason, I didn't expect him to be so complete. Successfully giving birth to this baby was the greatest thing I had ever accomplished and I reveled in motherhood. I stayed sixteen days in the hospital (fourteen days was the usual in that era) for Lamar had a horse show in progress and the house was overrun with out-of-town guests. When I did leave, my bill was $33.50. The Navy charges you only for the food you eat when you are hospitalized. Even this amount sounds very small but our entire food bill usually ran only into the forties for a whole month.

At that time, we had a wonderful full-time maid named Rose, She was married to a Marine and was Polish. In addition to her, we hired a practical nurse for six weeks to take care of the baby. Rose's feelings were hurt, but we were not sure she was capable of caring for this remarkable infant. I sure knew I wasn't!

Parenthood

My dear friend, Mary Dessez, who had been in Europe with us, was John's godmother. She lived a few houses away and I was in complete bondage to her advice. She told me what to put on this child, how often to feed him, when to put him down for his nap, etc. All the wisdom she had accumulated raising Duffy, her ten-year-old, she passed on to me. I obeyed every direction she gave me. She rightly thought I knew nothing and also she was just naturally bossy. Once she drove by our quarters, saw John out in the yard in his playpen, not wearing a hat. She called me on the phone and ordered me to put one on him right away. Naturally, I did.

The first time the practical nurse had a night off, I panicked. Rose always went home after dinner every night. What should I do? I couldn't hear the baby if he snuffled in the next room. Mary had told me to bring the kiddie-coop, his bed, into our room so we could hear him. We did and I didn't sleep all night. If he snuffled, I worried. If he didn't, I thought he was dead. Mary said that was better than not hearing him at all and suspecting he was dead all night long. The next time the nurse had a night off, I disobeyed her and used ear plugs and slept fine, in between four-hour feedings.

Lamar weighed this baby before and after every feeding. He kept a chart and when he wasn't there, the nurse or I had orders to do it. He didn't gain weight very fast and that worried us. Dr. Clarke didn't approve of formulae. My milk was not very rich and finally, when John was five months old, he let me give him a supplemental feeding because he was verging on rickets. Part of his new diet was ox blood, squeezed out of very rare steak with a press and fed him from a bottle. He loved it! Soon he was plumping out and putting on weight. We called him "Ducky," short for Bombay Duck, which, as we all know, goes with curry.

We had him christened John Lamar Curry when he was six weeks old. The same Rev. Heaton who had married us did the honors. This time Lamar crossed his palm with quite a bit of silver, trying to make up for not giving him anything when we were married.

There was never a child to equal this one; he was the smartest, he walked the soonest, he did everything three months earlier than the baby books said he should. We weren't prejudiced, were we? Well, he rolled off the bed at four months!! He walked at nine months! He had a vocabulary then, too. We read him books and sang to him, pointed out objects for him to recognize. Oh, he was so smart! Unfortunately, he slept very little every day and the rest of the time, he kept us on the move. No wonder he was skinny. Other babies with their rolls of fat and Buddha-like figures seemed pudgy and dull to us; our son was slender and definitely overactive but we didn't know what that was in those days.

Mother and Boppie came back from Peking in 1939 and went to Chicago for duty. Betty and Buzz had been in China with them and had a one-year-old daughter named Katherine Paul, nicknamed Chickie. They returned about the same time from the Orient to duty in San Diego. I had not seen or spoken to my family for five years. My parents arrived for a visit to see their first grandson, and on the same day, some workmen came and removed our one bathroom. Instead of a week, their visit was curtailed to one day. If you lived in Government quarters, you had no control over the actions of the people under the command of someone senior to you. When a decision was made to paint your quarters, they painted! When they decided to change your plumbing, they did so. There were no motels or nice Inns in that area in those days so they returned to Chicago.

That Christmas, we went to Chicago on the train to visit them. Remember, I had seen my parents one day in five years. Ducky was eight months old and it was a complicated trip for us because we had so much paraphernalia to lug with us. We took a drawing room on the train which was expensive but roomy.

That visit to Chicago wasn't easy on my parents either. I remember Boppie had some very handsome military brushes, which Ducky managed to get hold of and push out an opening in the bathroom. Their apartment was on the 14th floor. Of course, the brushes were never retrieved. Ducky's parents thought that was funny; I don't think the owner agreed. Mother and Daddy must have been glad to see us leave.

Parenthood

The new year was 1940. Things in Europe were getting scary and we were worried about our French and British friends. We didn't get mail from them that Christmas as we usually did for they were involved in the French war build-up brought on by Hitler's advance in Europe. They were being assigned to war units, the wives going home to parents or digging in for the duration. Some of our American officers expected the United States to get drawn into the fray but that didn't seem likely to us; Europe was so far away in those days that we couldn't conceive of war actually touching us.

In the spring of 1940 Lamar received orders to sea duty on the battleship U.S.S. Colorado, which was docked in Long Beach, California. We bought a new Dodge, and paid $600.00 for it. It cost $900.00 but our trade-in for "Muggins," our Chevrolet coupe was $300.00 so our old car must have been in good condition. Lamar's policy was to buy a new car every two years. That is, he did that as a bachelor. He felt a car began to cost you money after that length of time.

We planned to drive to California and my brother, Jack, would go with us. He had left college after two years for a career in show business. He had been singing in nightclubs, but he felt his beautiful upturned nose went in the wrong direction, (he thought the entertainment business was controlled by Jews) He decided to go back to college and had been accepted at the University of Oregon. He planned to take some summer courses there before registering in the fall.

In June we started off, Ducky, 14 months old, in the back seat with a mattress to play and sleep on, all the equipment a child that age requires, and, in this case, an adult to share the space. That ten minute nap became the best time of the day to whomever it happened to be. The rest of the time was completely monopolized by caring for that highly charged toddler.

There were no interstate highways at that time and dual highways were rare. Most of the "good" roads were three-lane, which were dangerous because everyone used the center one to pass. Motels were almost nonexistent in the east so the roads took you through cities, towns and hamlets. We had to stop at hotels at night which involved carrying suitcases, baby equipment, anything needed overnight, through the lobbies and up elevators. We fed Duck in our hotel room and the three of us took turns going to a restaurant for dinner.

One night in Wyoming, Lamar and Jack went out to eat and I fed Ducky. We were in a small town, full of cowboys. My men ate in a local eatery and found the steaks were delicious. When they returned, Lamar said he would go back to the restaurant with me while I ate my steak.

It was chilly, so I wore a navy blue suit and spectator pumps. I remember I was wearing a rhinestone lapel pin. Lamar used to say I looked like I could take one hundred words a minute when I wore that suit. When we entered the restaurant and seated ourselves, Lamar remembered the waitress. He grinned at her in recognition but she was very distant in her manner. I ordered a steak with all the fixings and Lamar asked for a cup of coffee.

There was a long counter on the opposite side of the room and every stool was occupied by a cowboy in boots, jeans and ten-gallon hats. While I was eating, every single one of those men left his seat, strolled the length of the restaurant and gave me the "once-over." The waitress ignored me and wouldn't even look me in the eye. We knew we looked like city folk; every other woman in there was in a cotton dress and wearing sandals. Some of the cowboys got bolder and deliberately smiled at me as they sauntered by. Then the light came on! They thought I was a prostitute! They were sizing me up and wondering what my fee was. Lamar was furious, but I was tickled to be taken for a woman of ill repute. I thought I looked too young and naive; to the hicks I must have looked sophisticated.

It took us ten days to reach San Diego. We bade Jack farewell and good luck as he left for Oregon by train. Betty and Buzz were living in San Diego and were renting a house there and it was great to see Betty again after five years and meet Buzz. And get to know their little girl who was adorable, just one year older than Ducky. Lamar was getting ready to join his ship so I would stay in San Diego until he decided where we should live;

if the ship went to the Far East, I would stay where I was. Betty and Buzz would look after me.

I found a very nice apartment but it soon gave me the willies. It was so well furnished, even to toaster and waffle-iron, I asked the agent why it was for rent. He said the occupant, an old lady, had just died and her heirs hadn't decided yet just what to do with the property. Let me tell you, that old lady resented my using her things; I felt her disapproving presence so strongly, I was even a little scared sometimes. Once, my cousin Tootie Wood, came to see me. We were sitting in the living room, where there was a large wall hanging mounted over a table. Tootie said, "This place makes me feel weird. Do you have a ghost?"

I told her I sometimes thought I did and I explained about the old lady. She asked, "Polly, what's behind that curtain?"

"Nothing," I said. And I showed her the blank wall.

Tootie said, "It moves sometimes. I saw it flutter just now. I think your ghost lives there. I couldn't stay here one night!"

Well, the ghost and I battled it out until I left for the Islands.

While Lamar was in Long Beach, waiting for the USS Colorado to return from sea maneuvers, he went to the YMCA and waited for orders. They gave him a beautiful apartment with two bedrooms, a kitchen, a dining room and the whole place was completely furnished with china and kitchen utensils. It cost him only a couple of dollars a day. He phoned me and invited me to come for a honeymoon. I bundled up Ducky, packed a bag and drove to Long Beach, losing no time taking him up on his offer. We had a lovely time. The last night I was there, Lamar wanted us to go out on a date, so I went to the desk and asked how I could find a baby sitter. The girl said she would call and get me someone reliable. I heard her speaking on the phone and she said, "Chaplain Curry needs a sitter for this evening."

She had mistaken Captain for Chaplain and had given him the suite reserved for missionaries and men of the cloth. All the furnishings had been donated by goodhearted Christian people. I told Lamar about this and we both felt awful; we were there under false pretenses. I don't remember confessing the mistake to the management though, and besides, I was going back to San Diego the next day for Lamar had received orders to join his ship in Honolulu.

I returned to San Diego where I saw Betty every day. Now that we both were married and mothers, we had more in common. We really enjoyed one another. We went on picnics with our offspring, to the zoo and the beach. It was fun being with her and we had a wonderful relationship. Since then we have been best friends all our lives.

My trunk never arrived from Quantico. Buzz, Betty's husband, put a tracer on it for me. Finally, he tracked it down. It had been shipped to the aircraft carrier, the Enterprise, which was at that time on its way to Hong Kong. I went out and bought some clothes for Ducky and myself as I couldn't stand those few garments we had been wearing for six weeks. Eventually, the Enterprise came home and I got my trunk back.

Lamar wrote that the ship's home port was now officially Pearl Harbor, Hawaii, so I could join him there if I could get passage on one of the Matson Cruise ships. The Marine Corps would pay my way first class minimum. I applied and waited and waited for a couple of months.

At that time, my parents had duty in San Francisco. Boppie had been made a general and this was his new billet. One day Boppie asked me by telephone why I didn't join Lamar in Hawaii. I explained to him that I was on a long list of people, waiting for passage. Boppie used his influence. He was Head of the Department of the Pacific Theater. He knew Mr. Matson personally, so he called him and explained my predicament; I was soon issued my ticket.

Parenthood

The ship I traveled to Hawaii on was the SS Lurline, named for Mr. Matson's daughter. I embarked in San Diego and was the sole passenger for one night on the ship. That was a strange feeling. It was almost dreamlike; the big ship cutting through the water, no passengers anywhere, all of our lights blazing, I ate a solitary dinner in the large dining room and went to bed.

The next day I saw Mother and Boppie, and then we re-embarked for Hawaii. In those days it was a four-day trip to Hawaii. My plans were to get a good suntan and keep Ducky from running overboard. I certainly didn't expect to travel like a hedonist. I had packed in my suitcase one evening dress for the last night aboard, the Captain's dinner, which was always a gala affair on any cruise. I had barely unpacked my things in the cabin when I received a formal note from the Captain, telling me I was expected to dine at his table throughout the voyage. I was floored! Of course this was the result of my father pulling strings to get me passage. Instantly, I was a VIP. I asked the steward, who was waiting for my reply, what I should do? I had a small child. He said that was no problem. He would assign a steward to stay with Ducky while I was dining. I told him I would accept since I didn't know how to refuse. I knew you didn't say no to "rank!"

When he left, I had my wardrobe trunk (Yes! We actually used those things!) brought up out of the hold, all my nice clothes and evening dresses pressed (which cost me a mint!) and accepted my roles as nursemaid and cruise passenger.

That evening, after I had fed Ducky and put him to bed, the steward came and I, dressed to the teeth went to dine with the Captain. When I arrived in the salon, there was no one at the table. The Captain was on the bridge, getting us out of the harbor and all the other guests were having cocktails in the bar. Soon they came trooping in, drunk as hoot owls. We were told the Captain would have a tray on the bridge, but he expected us to be prompt the following day at lunch. We ate our dinner, everyone trying to sleuth out why the others were invited to sit at the Captain's table. I was wearing my three-carat diamond which was duly noticed by the others. They thought I must have money! Weird for a Marine officer! The group decided I should sit next to the Captain, on his right, as I could talk seagoing lingo, being married to a Marine. They had heard this Captain was difficult and humorless and no one wanted to be forced to talk to him at every meal.

As a group, we planned to meet in the bar and fortify ourselves with alcohol before lunch the next day since he was irritated with us. One of the men invited us to be his guests. That meant each of us would take turns being host or hostess. I hoped drinks were not expensive as my turn would come.

The next noon we met in the bar, had a drink and began to "develop community." Finally, someone looked at his watch and said, "Good Lord, it's nearly one o'clock. We'd better hurry."

We dashed down to the dining room and the waiter told us the Captain had eaten and left. We could tell by his expression that we were in the doghouse. We decided to be more circumspect and get to dinner early. And we did. We finally met the Captain and I did my gracious guest routine and kept him talking throughout the meal. He was a nice man and pretty bored with all the social amenities that were demanded of him. He told us to order anything we wanted for dinner or luncheon. He would not always be able to join us but would be there when he could.

There was one gentleman at the table who wanted nothing but filet of beef every lunch and dinner. He became quite annoyed if we wanted some variety. It seems that we all had to have the same thing if we ordered anything not on the menu. Loud were the arguments daily about what our entree would be. The rest of the time on board I got my exercise, walking Ducky on a leash. He ran everywhere like a wild Indian; he was never known to walk!

The four days came to an end and we arrived in Hawaii. My newfound friends were all going to the Royal Hawaiian Hotel for the weekend and then on to Samoa and then another ship would take them back to San Francisco. Remember, this was a cruise ship. I had no idea where I would be staying but I knew it wasn't the Royal Hawaiian which was the most expensive hotel at Waikiki.

When the boat docked, I saw my beloved Lamar waiting at the end of the gangway. He was so glad to see us, he was grinning from ear to ear for we had been separated for four months. In the taxi, he said we had reservations at the Royal Hawaiian for two nights as a honeymoon and then we would move to a family hotel until we found an apartment. I was gleeful because all my shipboard friends would be there only two nights also.

Arriving at The Royal, we found our accommodations were superb: a large room overlooking the ocean with a balcony. There was a crib for Ducky and on the table was a huge platter of fruit, containing slices of papaya, mango, pineapple and other tropical fruits. We had a sitter that evening and dined in the gorgeous dining room where the food was fabulous. That night Ava Gardener and Mickey Rooney were honeymooning at the hotel and everyone was staring at the two movie stars who were so poorly matched: she so tall and beautiful, he such a tough-looking little shrimp. She was a full head taller than he. We saw all the people from the Captain's table. They seemed thrilled to meet Lamar. I continued my unuttered role of being wealthy; our hotel choice matched my diamond.

The next day we swam off the private beach in front of the hotel and, in the dining room, ate our way through three more fabulous meals. I don't know what the Royal looks like today but in 1940, it was the TOPS. In the lobby there was a famous hibiscus tree; It was leafless but every morning the bellboys would gather and place on the tree 1500 fresh hibiscus blooms. By nightfall they were wilted but were replaced before morning. That, to me, was the height of elegance.

We moved after two days to the Pleasanton Hotel, a family type place, where we had a bedroom, bath, and living room. We ate all meals in the dining room. There was a garden filled with tropical plants and the hotel lived up to its name. I have one special memory of that place where we lived for at least three weeks; I had bought a new straw pocketbook and a new lipstick. The next morning I awoke and found Ducky had discovered both of them on the bureau, reached over and taken them, had opened the lipstick and drawn pictures all over the new bag. They were both ruined.

We eventually rented an apartment out near Diamond Head that belonged to an artist. The living room was on two levels, the dining area one step down from the main living room. It was attractive but small. In addition to the living-dining area, we had a bedroom, a tiny bath and a small kitchen. The beach, which was private because no one else ever went there, was behind the house and a block from my back door.

Lamar was out at sea a lot but did come in from time to time. Life was leisurely and very pleasant; I had lots of friends with small children and we all lived on the beach, played tennis on the public courts. We all loved being in Hawaii. When the ship was in, we got sitters and went to parties, restaurants and the country club together. Ducky had his second birthday party there with all his little friends. We had a movie camera and were happy to have a record of those times. Unfortunately, all of those films were ruined by being stored in excessive heat in later years.

One night we had a dinner party and among the guests was the Captain of the Colorado. In honor of him, I hired a little Japanese cateress named Ishi. She arrived at four o'clock, dressed in her robe and obi. She brought dessert which was usually papaya ice and homemade sponge cake, and homemade rolls, and then she proceeded to finish cooking the dinner. The main course that night was Chicken Coconut Curry and rice with all the "boys," the things you serve with it. Her price for doing all this and serving and cleaning up was $5.00. Of course, I had to pay her for the rolls and dessert.

That night, the cocktail hour was a little long. In the service, people don't like to be hurried over their drinks. Finally, I told Ishi to start serving dinner. The table was set and she came tiptoeing in with a huge platter of chicken curry, surrounded by rice. She forgot the step down and went head over teacup and the food went flying all over the floor. The Captain blanched as he observed this and he said, "Oh, my God, I hope there's more in the kitchen. I'm so hungry I don't think I can last much longer!"

I'm glad to relate that there was ample food on the stove and we all had plenty after the mess had been cleaned up.

Being a service brat (brought up in the Corps) I thought I knew everything about the military and I was never unsure of myself socially. The first time I went out to the USS Colorado for dinner, I really bombed. The ship had sent a motor launch to pick up passengers for the battleship. There were older women waiting with me, so remembering my manners, when it came time to go aboard, I held back so the older ladies could get on first. They insisted that I precede them. I insisted they board first. We Alphonsed and Gastoned until someone whispered in my ear that "rank boards last." I was the junior woman present. So I at last admitted defeat and boarded the launch. As we approached the ship, I jumped to my feet to be the first to disembark. To my amazement, I was pushed aside and not allowed to get off until every other woman had preceded me. One of the seamen, seeing my consternation, said, "Rank disembarks first!" I didn't know anything about Navy protocol, but I was learning the hard way. Standing aside, I was the last to disembark.

Eating in the wardroom of a warship was an experience. The officers have stewards that serve them and the tablecloths and napkins are linen and the members have silver napkin rings. Service is wonderful and there are rules and regulations about how everything is done. No wonder Navy wives have trouble keeping up the service when their husbands have shore duty. Lamar was so spoiled by this fancy living, that forever after this duty, we were never allowed at home to put any commercial containers on the dining table. Everything had to be put in decent receptacles made for that purpose. Once, when she was very young, Posy told me that John, or Ducky, as we called him then, had put a "mercer attainer" on the table! (her effort to say, "commercial container.")

There were very strict rules about driving a motor vehicle in Pearl Harbor; one speeding ticket and your permit would be revoked for months. One night, coming back from dinner on board the Colorado, it was late and I had to drive back home through Honolulu, through all the deserted pineapple fields. There had been some holdups and I decided to step on the gas. I was barreling along when I heard a police whistle. I froze because I knew I would lose my license to drive on the base. I pulled over and a young Marine approached me with a flashlight. I was terrified. He shone the light on my license plate and then approached the front seat. "Ma'am, do you realize how fast you were going?" From his drawl, I knew he was southern as spoon bread.

"My land," I said, my accent thicker than his. "It sho sounds good, hearing someone from home. Where ah you all from?"

"From Savannah, Ma'am. We're sho fah from home, ain't we?"

"We sho are. I'll be glad to get back South."

"Me too, Ma'am. Well, you be careful on this road. After you cross the railroad track, you can just fly along but until then, be careful. These regulations are sho tough to deal with."

"Oh, thank you. Talking to you has made me much less homesick."

"Me too, Ma'am. Goodnight, Ma'am."

This was one of my better moments in Little Theater. From then on, I followed the young man's advice and didn't speed until or after I came to the railroad track. One day, the phone rang and the caller was my old sweetheart, Earle, who was on an aircraft carrier, stationed at Pearl Harbor. He wanted to come and call on us. This surprised me as I had not seen him since the night I swore undying love for him, back in Quantico, nine years before. Once he had written me at Fort Sill and wanted to stop by to see us but he had changed his mind. He had said he was afraid he might kill Lamar! Lamar thought he was a kook and was very relieved that he didn't have to meet him.

Here he had surfaced again. He said he was married and had twin girls. I invited him to dinner the following weekend as Lamar's ship would be in, and I preferred seeing this old beau in the presence of my husband. Earle accepted my invitation. Being a female animal, I planned to impress my first love with my beauty and hospitality. I engaged Ishi and planned a super meal; I went to the beach daily and got myself a terrific tan. I filled the house with exotic flowers and wore a sophisticated evening pajama outfit. Everything was in readiness to snow this old flame.

The hour approached. I was getting sort of nervous. How would we all react to one another? The first call came from Lamar. He couldn't make dinner; the Colorado was putting out to sea for maneuvers and he would see me in about ten days. He was sorry he couldn't be there to meet Earle. When he hung up, I felt a little sick. How would Earle act after nine years? He had always been so volatile.

The next call came from Earle. His Carrier was going to sea and he would be unable to dine with us. He was desolate as their next port of call was San Diego. He would not be in Honolulu again anytime soon.

I sat there in my decorated, attractive apartment, with my Japanese catered dinner, awaiting my pleasure. I was all dressed up and had no place to go. Finally, I called one of my close friends, Kay Sherman, and asked her if she could get a sitter and come and have dinner with me. She accepted, and, about an hour later, arrived. I had made a pitcher of daiquiris for the three of us which we two consumed as I told her why everything was so fancy and formal. We found the whole thing hilarious and nearly died laughing as Ishi served us this gorgeous meal.

One little aside: When Ishi had arrived at four o'clock, she seemed surprised that I hadn't called her and canceled. She was not surprised when I told her neither officer would be there that evening. This was a few months before Pearl Harbor. How did Ishi know so much sooner than I did? We thought later she might have been involved in a big Japanese spy network. There was one in the Islands and what better way to keep tabs on ship movements than by working for American officers' families? Many Japanese were loyal but not all, by a long shot. After Pearl Harbor, they were rounded up in detention camps, which seemed a smart move to us at that time. Today they are suing the U.S. government for so doing. I'm sure some good citizens of Japanese heritage suffered, but the Japanese were held in poor regard by everyone I knew after December 7th.

When Lamar came ashore again, he couldn't wait to find out how the evening had progressed with Earle. I made up a beautiful story how he had tried to seduce me and I had told him to leave; every fear I had held about this reunion had materialized. Then I burst out laughing at myself and my horrible pride. I told Lamar I was just joking.

It's very strange that I never ever saw Earle again. After all, service people run into each other all their lives, it seems, over and over again. Once, in the 50's, Lamar had duty at Maxwell Field, Alabama. We were hosting a cocktail party and one of our guests called and asked if she could bring along a couple of "visiting firemen." I said, "Of course."

When she and her husband arrived later, they had no extra guests with them. I inquired as to their whereabouts. She explained there had been a change in their orders and they had just flown back to Washington. She said one of them said he knew me. He was a Captain Gallaher. Did I remember him?

Did I remember him? That was Earle, surfacing again and for the last time. Some years later, I read his obituary in the Naval Academy magazine, *Shipmate*. He had had a distinguished war record; he was what they called, "an ace." All of his decorations were listed and they were formidable.

Back to my Hawaiian adventures. Not long after the dinner party that wasn't, I was having dinner with my godfather, Admiral Theobald, at the Waialai Country Club. While we were dancing, he casually asked, "Tillie, why don't you go and visit your parents in San Francisco?"

"Why should I do that?" I asked. I knew Lamar had been at sea for quite a while. This meant usually that the ship would be putting into Pearl very soon. Besides, it was very expensive to go back to the Mainland. Fuzzy, as I called him, said, "I just think this might be a good time to go and see them. No other reason." I knew Fuzzy couldn't tell me in words that Lamar's ship was not coming back to the Islands, but I took the hint.

Monday morning I was in the Matson Office, making reservations on the cruise ship, Mariposa, scheduled to sail in ten days. A week later, we were informed the Colorado was in Long Beach, its new home port. All the wives were scrambling around, trying to get ship accommodations back to the Coast. One of the Navy wives came to me in tears and asked me to share a second-class cabin with her on the Matsonia, another ship in the Matson fleet. Unless I did, she would not be able to occupy it herself. Someone else would get it. Dumb me! Always accommodating Polly. This gal had a little boy who was five years old and I felt sorry for her. I canceled my lovely stateroom, first-class, to be nice to a Navy wife and said I would share her accommodations and leave a week later.

We went aboard and our small stateroom had four bunks and no porthole. The first night, her son cried and cried. By morning, she called the ship's doctor and he told her the little boy had measles; she would be quarantined immediately and Ducky and I would be given another cabin. Our new cabin was smaller and no nicer. The doctor's news was worse. He told me that it was just a question of time before my son would come down with the same disease because he had been in that enclosed cabin all night with this other child. The incubation period was ten days to two weeks. When I arrived in San Diego, I was to find a dark apartment because measles are hard on the eyes. There my Ducky would get sick. It was inevitable, he assured me.

I remember that trip as the roughest ocean voyage in my life. The Matsonia pitched and then rolled from side to side. Once in a while, she shook herself like a wet dog. My poor friend was stuck in that cabin of hers and couldn't get out. Going second-class was as unlike my first-class trip out as it was possible to be. The food was lousy, the dining hours were horrendous, there was no entertainment and I realized no one went second class except servants and workers. We were treated like second-class citizens and all of us were so glad to land and get off the "finest freighter in the Matson Fleet."

When I saw Lamar, who was waiting for me on shore, he told me his ship was going into overhaul in Bremerton Navy Yard in the state of Washington. I informed him we were going to stay where we were and wait out the measles. So we started looking for a dark apartment. We found one, very dark, in a basement. And there we waited for the dreaded illness to break out on our beloved son. Each day we searched him for symptoms and finally decided he was going to make medical history and not get measles at all. The very last day of incubation, the fourteenth, at 11:00 p.m., we were awakened by whimpers and cries; Ducky had a high temperature and was nauseated. We were ready with baby aspirin and when he could keep that down, we fed him teaspoons of ginger ale all night. When the fever broke, he was covered with spots, in his scalp, his ears, nose, everywhere, you name it; he had a severe case and we just had to ride it out.

When he finally recovered, and our blue Dodge arrived by freighter from Hawaii, we drove up the coast to Bremerton. I had written Alice Shell, one of my bridesmaids, whose husband's ship was stationed there, to find me an apartment. The place smelled of cabbage and the stairwells were obstacle courses because the numerous small children kept their riding toys there.

All the Colorado people were scattered around the town and we kept up our social life of dinners and get-togethers. The ship would leave for Pearl Harbor early in December. Ducky and I had reservations on the Lurline to return to Hawaii on the third of December, first class! We planned to have Christmas in the Islands.

Then there was a fire on the Colorado. The overhaul would take much longer than the authorities had anticipated, so we canceled our Matson reservations and bemoaned the fact we would be in that shabby apartment at Christmas. Lamar and I decided as usual to make the best of it.

One Sunday morning in early December, I was outside with Ducky as he rode his tricycle down the sloping sidewalk. He didn't sit on it like any normal child; he stood on the back, hands on the handlebars, and, with one foot pushing the pavement, got up enough steam to go flying down the hill like a bat out of you know where. Each trip was torture for his Mother, who watched in terror, expecting him to go head over heels into the street. He always managed to keep his balance and not have an accident. As we returned for another go, Lamar stuck his head out the window, and yelled, "The Japanese have bombed Pearl Harbor!" He had been listening to the radio and had heard the report.

Other people were around and no one could think what to do. We went in and Lamar had his ear glued to the radio and gave me the few details he had heard. He was reporting for duty immediately to the ship and he would call me as soon as he knew anything definite. The truth was everyone expected the Japs to bomb the Coast next and that's where we were. As the day wore on, the reports from Hawaii were devastating: thousands were dead, ships were sunk and the rest were "out of commission."

There was an order for a blackout in Bremerton. No street lights after dark and blankets were to be hung over the windows if the lights were on in the apartment. We all put buckets of sand in the trunks of our cars, along with containers of water, in case there was a general exodus away from the coast. The ship was on a 24-hour alert and Lamar came home for a few hours every day. The Lurline, the ship we were supposed to be on, arrived at Honolulu the day after the attack. No one was allowed to land and she took on a slew of passengers who were being evacuated and immediately returned to the States.

Days went by and the Japs did not attack the Coast. We were still scared but were getting used to the situation. Christmas Day arrived and Lamar managed to have his time at home early in the morning so he could watch Ducky open his stocking. We have movies of that morning. Ducky enjoyed all the excitement of the tree, stocking and presents. Then Lamar had to leave to give one of the other officers time with his family.

Lamar was promoted to Major immediately. He had too much rank to hold the job he had on the Colorado so he was ordered to a Marine Regiment in California. My father had been in Iceland, in command of the 1st Marine Brigade. When the U.S. declared war on the combined countries of Japan, Germany and Italy, Army troops were sent to Iceland and Boppie brought his Marines back to San Diego. Mother and Boppie had rented a house there so we went to stay with them.

I failed to mention that we had decided to have another baby. I'm sure the war had something to do with our decision. We knew Lamar would be going into action somewhere and maybe wouldn't come home. I don't think we consciously said this, even to ourselves, but there was an underlying fear that he could get wounded, even killed. I wanted another child, whether he came home or not. I never had any trouble getting pregnant, but staying that way was always the problem.

We left Bremerton and drove to San Diego. A few days after arriving at Mother's, I felt awful, like I was coming down with the flu. I had a headache, my bones ached and I felt sick. Mother got tired of my complaining and told me to go out in the patio and soak up some sun so I would feel better. I went. I lay there baking for an hour but I didn't feel better at all. Mother came out and took one look at me. "Tillie," she said, "you are covered with spots! It can't be measles. You had them when you were a child!"

But I did. I had the three-day variety, not serious except for pregnant women. It could cause trouble for the fetus in that case. I was pregnant but didn't know it, although I soon found out.

We moved to a hotel while we hunted for a house. You can't stay with your parents forever and they were very busy as Boppie was a general. We found a cute oceanfront cottage in La Jolla, completely furnished, even to sheets and bed linen, kitchen utensils and china. We were just waiting for the place to be cleaned and made ready for occupancy. I suspected that I was pregnant and wasn't surprised when I did my usual, I started to miscarry. The doctor told me to stay in bed and he would send me a practical nurse to take care of Ducky and me. The next day I met Victoria Pache, the most unusual and unforgettable person I had ever met in my life.

Pache, as everyone called her, was a short, plump, dark Mexican about 50 years old, very quick and energetic. She told me that she had been married and had a son who was a Lieutenant in the U.S. Army. Her marriage had been a failure so she had divorced her husband. Her son was married but she couldn't stand her daughter-in-law. There was *nothing* that she couldn't do and do well. Lamar knew he would be shipping out at any moment and he persuaded her to stay with me until the baby was born. She finally assented and moved me out to the house we had found in La Jolla when it was ready. I have never been so spoiled in all my life, before or since. I did nothing but loll around and Pache cleaned, cooked, shopped, mended, built shelves, entertained Ducky by taking him to the beach and making saltwater aquariums, building a toy box *with* him, teaching him songs and Spanish. She made my bed and turned down the sheets every night. Wow! Was I spoiled!

Lamar was training a battalion of artillery and came home when he could. I held on to my fetus and found a good gynecologist named J. T. Lipe, who became a personal friend too. Mother and Boppie bought a house in La Jolla Hermosa, down the road a piece. We all settled in for the "Duration." The Japs didn't seem interested in bombing the West Coast of California and people stopped evacuating the area.

Four months after we moved to La Jolla, Lamar, Boppie and Buzz all went to the South Pacific. Buzz made Betty promise to take herself and his two children back to Virginia; he hated California and didn't want them raised there. She left us for Lexington, Virginia, where Buzz's parents lived and he had been raised. That was God's country, according to Buffy, that had a fine history and heritage: not this Godforsaken state, full of Mexicans, Orientals and the dregs of all the other states. (His words.)

Before Boppie left Camp Elliot, which was under his command, he managed to get Lamar's sister, Shirley Cheatham, a job as hostess at the Hospitality House on the Base. She had finally left Walter and needed some employment. She was great in that job because she loved people and became Mom to all the Marines she worked with. I think that period was one of the happiest times of her life. She had a lovely apartment, got a nice salary, knew all the "brass" and had a social life too. She loved to have Ducky come out to spend the night. Pache made him a uniform and put three stars on the shoulders because Boppie had two and she wanted Ducky to outrank his grandfather.

We were soon living in a manless world, except for teen-agers and white haired grandfathers. We were contending with the rationing coupons for meat, milk, butter, sugar, coffee, shoes, oil, shortening, gasoline. Other things were scarce such as children's clothes and all luxuries. No one complained. That was the way it was and our fighting men rated the best of everything; we wanted them to have the things we were going without.

My doctor was called up for duty in the military. He told me he had contacted a specialist in San Diego, who would take me as a patient. I think his name was Belford. I went for a checkup and he was nice and said he would come to La Jolla to deliver my baby, which was due in six weeks. I think he was expensive but I never asked him his fee.

One month later, I was playing bridge out at Shirley's apartment when she was having a bridge-luncheon. I started losing my waters and I was embarrassed to death. Shirley poo-poohed my concern. She said it was nothing to worry about. I sat on bath towels and continued to play bridge and gush like a geyser.

When I got home, Pache was furious and insisted that I call Dr. Belford. When I did the nurse told me the Doctor was ill and couldn't take any calls. I explained why I was calling, and she told me to call another doctor, one to whom Dr. Belford had referred his cases. His name? I've forgotten. I called him and he told me to check into Scripps Hospital the following morning at seven o'clock and he would induce labor. I was terrified. Who was this man? Why would he induce labor? Pache didn't look very happy about it either. I didn't sleep very well and Pache had me up early. "What did I want for breakfast?" she asked. "Everything!!" Then I had a pain. I called to Pache in the kitchen and said, "Skip the eggs. Just coffee." Then I had another pain. "Skip the coffee! I'm going to the hospital now!"

I drove the four blocks to Scripps and went to the desk and identified myself. The girl started to ask me to fill out all these forms but I refused. "I'm having a baby and you can ask me later." I went upstairs and found the OB nurse. She put me in a room with a timer and told me to time my pains. When they were three minutes apart, I was to buzz her. She left the room and I buzzed. When she stuck her head around the door, I said, "This is one long continuous pain. It never stops!"

She came over and examined me. "We're going to the delivery room now!"

When I was wheeled in, I saw a strange doctor. "I'm so glad you got here in time, Dr. ????"

"I'm not he," he said, "my name is Dr. Chambers. I was just going off duty here at the hospital and I was called to come here."

Well, he did fine and I soon delivered my darling baby girl. I had been in labor for one hour. Again, no anesthetic! Posy made her entry so fast, I had a lot of repairing done and my baby was so pretty. She had long black lashes, dark hair and a beautiful nose and mouth.

I stayed in the hospital two weeks. She was born on November 13th, two weeks early. That was the night of the Battle of Midway and the radio reports were so bad, the nurse took the radio out of my room so I wouldn't hear them. The outfits involved were mentioned and Lamar's Regiment was there.

Pache brought Ducky to see "Mariposita," the little butterfly, as she called my baby. I was big Butterfly because I flitted around so much. Ducky couldn't say, "mariposita;" it was too long. The best he could say was Posy and that's what she has been ever since. It would be 18 months before her father came home from the South Pacific and met her.

Incidentally, having a pregnancy so disjointed was pretty cheap. I paid Dr. Lipe for two or three office visits, then Dr. Belford for one visit. Dr.??? never sent me a bill. By the time he arrived at Scripps, Posy had been born. Dr. Chambers billed me for the delivery, which was peanuts, maybe $30? I think the delivery room charge was $20. That included the anesthetist who never did anything. Dr. Lipe, released later from the Army because of poor health, came home. He couldn't believe how cheap Posy's entrance into the world had been. Of course, room and board at the hospital cost the usual and I was there for two weeks. But the doctors' fees were very little.

After I returned home, Pache told me her son, Robert, needed her. She would stay until Posy was three months old but then she had to go to Arizona to take care of her own grandchild. If someone had threatened to cut off both of my arms, I couldn't have been more desolate. When she finally left as scheduled, one of my friends sent me a black-bordered note of condolence. Everyone knew what a jewel I had in that wonderful woman.

An Army wife, Mrs. Mallonee, whose husband had been taken prisoner on Corregidor, bought the house I was occupying and the one behind me on the same lot. She wanted my house to live in but she would rent me the other one. It wasn't as nice as the oceanfront but it would suffice. Pache and I moved. How that woman longed for me to buy a house. She would watch the ads in the paper and then go on her own and look the properties over. Finally, she found the perfect bargain. It was the Presbyterian Manse, well-built and in excellent shape. She knew because she had crawled all over it, even under the house on her hands and knees. "All the plumbing is copper," she related to me in great excitement, "the floors are hardwood, and we wouldn't have to spend a penny making it liveable. We could move right in."

I talked to Mother about it but I didn't have power of attorney to sell stock in order to buy it. The price was $9500. Today it would go for at least $500,000. Ah well, remember I told you no one in our family ever made any money. I could probably have rounded up enough for a down payment from Lamar's holdings, but getting his permission would take months. We moved to the "Back House," as we called it. No real estate venture for us.

Our second Christmas in La Jolla was in the Back House. By then, toys for the children were scarce and very cheesy looking. Months before Christmas I had bought a wagon for Ducky. It was not assembled and I hid it at my friend Alice Williams' house. Her husband was serving somewhere in the South Pacific; she had lost a baby about the time Posy was born. She was one of my dearest friends and when Pache left, she would take Posy home with her if I had a cold or flu or something. She would march in and take her bed, clothes, food, potty seat, all her requisites. When I was well, she would reluctantly bring her home.

I invited her to spend the night with me at Christmas. We couldn't do a thing until the children were asleep. Then we decorated the tree, filled the stockings, arranged the toys under the tree, put milk and cookies on a plate for Santa Claus and then, we could go to bed. We opened the box that held the red wagon and it was completely disassembled!! What to do? In desperation, I called a male neighbor, who lived nearby, whom I hardly knew, and he came and assembled it for us. Then we went to midnight church. We had a babysitter, a young girl that we had to both pick up and take home. Allie picked her up and we went to the Midnight Mass. It took forever and we got home at one-thirty in the morning. I took the sitter home and we hit the sack at two-forty-five a.m. At three o'clock Ducky appeared at the door in his pink Dr. Dentons and announced in an excited voice, "Santa Claus has come!!"

I had fallen asleep but I heard Allie, who was never known to swear, exclaim, "Jesus, what a short night!"

We gave Ducky his stocking and lured him back to his bed. Happily he complied and later fell asleep again. Posy woke us at about six and our Christmas began. I remember Allie's mother in Iowa had sent her three pounds of bacon, (a cherished scarcity) and there was a trail of ants leading to that parcel. The cardboard carousel I had so lovingly assembled, fell apart right away. As a gift, it was a washout. The wagon was a winner!

Lamar was very impressed with women in uniform. He was so proud of the women with whom he served. He had been raised with the impression that women sat on soft poufs and ate curds and whey. To observe them in danger and discomfort was a new experience for him. He talked constantly about the ones he met. I was determined to be in uniform when he came home from the War, so I joined the Motor Corps which was part of the Red Cross. I took a course in Motor Mechanics, (not very hard or extensive.) I wore a uniform and did errands for my superiors and drove patients with battle fatigue to people's houses for refreshments. They were usually garbed in pajamas and robes and were not allowed to get out of the station wagon. Pache decided that battle fatigue meant they were unhinged mentally and worried to death every time I had the duty.

Once I had no designated place to take them so I brought them home for watermelon and cake. We served them out in my front yard for I had a picnic table and benches. I sent one of them to the kitchen for a knife to cut the melon and when he appeared at Pache's elbow and asked for a big knife, she nearly fainted. She came out, carrying the weapon and scowling at me. She cut the melon and took the knife back in with her. Pache did not think I was the smartest.

Once a strange young man came to the front door at 11:30 at night and asked if he could have some water to make coffee. He was carrying a small saucepan. I invited him in and took him to the kitchen. Pache woke up and came to see what was going on. I told her this stranger needed some water; he had just moved in and his water had not been turned on. She glowered but didn't say anything until he had filled the pan with water and left. Then she lit into me and said she would leave if I ever let a strange person in the house again. "Mamacita, you know NOTHING about the world. We could all have had our throats slashed, Ducky and Mariposita too. You know nothing about people!!"

I admitted I knew little about the world and I would be more careful. About a week later, I was going to church to serve doughnuts and coffee to servicemen. When I got into the car, I realized I had left my cigarettes on the mantel. I went back to retrieve them. I entered the house and I heard Pache say, "Is that you, Mamacita?"

I didn't reply and she repeated her question, this time with panic in her voice. Then I stuck my head around the door and she saw me. She gasped and pulled down her suitcase from her closet and started to pack. She was furious and I had to talk to her for twenty minutes before she relented and started unpacking. Never again did I tease her.

Once Pache bought me a canary. She thought everyone should have at least one canary in a lifetime. She bought one in San Diego on her next day off. We invested in a cage, food, paper for the cage bottom, a few playthings and, last of all, a birdbath. We could never entice the bird into the bath which infuriated Pache, and thus he got his name, "Lou," which was her ex-husband's name. She said he had the same problem; he never took a bath. Was this why she left him? I consider this a perfectly valid reason. Lou never sang although it was supposed to be a male so we surmised he was a she. I guess singing is a male canary trait.

Pache was a wonderful cook and on occasion would fix us Mexican food. She would take the bus to Tia Juana, the border town between the U.S. and Mexico. There she bought the tortillas and the chiles. Beef was hard to come by so she made cheese and black olive enchiladas. I remember her peeling the chiles and complaining that her hands were on fire. If I had a dinner party, the menu would be enchiladas, salad, guacamole and tortilla chips, made from the real corn tortillas. My friends would rave. It's strange that San Diego stores didn't sell authentic Mexican food as so many natives lived there. Well, we are more cosmopolitan now, the roads are better, gasoline is available to truck things around. That was 1942 and we were at war. Since coffee and sugar were rationed, every guest brought her own tablespoonful and we would have enough to make a pot and sweeten our own cups.

Living right on the beach gave me territorial delusions. I considered it *mine!* I resented strangers using it for sunbathing or fishing. No one swam there as it was too rocky and the surf was too strong, and for me, too cold.

There were little pools among the rocks, where sea animals would get trapped, having been swept in on the waves at high tide. Pache captured these hermit crabs and other crustaceans and made us a saltwater aquarium. Every day she would trudge down to the surf and get a bucket of fresh salt water. She would spend time looking for just the right sized shell for a hermit crab that she thought might be outgrowing his present abode.

I have a vivid memory of coming home one day and spying Pache, always spotless in white uniform, and Ducky, lying on a big rock down on the beach, each flying kites, which she had made, that were way up in the sky, dark pinheads against the blue. Those two were at that moment exactly the same age. I didn't even know how to fly a kite, much less make one.

Pache took Ducky on the bus to San Diego to see a magician. He wore his sailor's uniform. On the bus they sat in front of two sailors, who immediately started a conversation with my son. One of the sailors asked him what he wanted to be when he grew up. He said, "A sailor."

Pache said, "And what is your father?"

Ducky replied, "A Marine."

"And what is your grandfather?"

"He's a Marine."

"And so what are you going to be when you grow up?"

"I'm going to be a sailor!"
Those two sailors thought that was great but Pache was miffed.

Another day, Pache got seats on the front row at a magician's show so Ducky could see everything. At one point during the show, the magician asked for a volunteer from the audience. People were slow to respond and Pache looked around to see if anyone was going up on the stage. When she turned back, Ducky was gone. There he was, climbing the steps to the stage. Everyone roared with laughter as the magician talked to this four-year-old in all seriousness. Finally he let him go and Ducky got a big hand. Pache was so proud of him.

At Christmas time she took Duck to see Santa Claus. When they got home, I asked Ducky if he had talked to the jolly old elf. He said he had. I asked him what he had said to Santa. "I asked him for a Noah's Ark."

"And what did Santa say to you?"

"He said, 'Next.'"

Unfortunately, the day came when my beloved Pache left to care for her grandson who had been abandoned by his mother soon after his birth. I was so spoiled, I started right away in my search to find a replacement. I hired a series of enlisted men's wives who were hanging around until their spouses went to war in the Pacific. These poor women would do anything to find a place to sleep. San Diego was exploding in population, bursting at the seams, and even hotel rooms were hard to come by.

This beach cottage was constructed of beaver board and the walls were so thin, the occupants had to be on intimate terms with one another in order to survive harmoniously. I hired a timid little Puerto Rican named Rosa. I always explained to the maid of the moment that her husband could not stay with us. On his time off, they would have to go to a hotel; the bedroom was small with only a single bed and I definitely did not want to share my bath with a strange man. *And* the walls were so thin, no one could have any privacy. The girls I hired always agreed to my terms.

I soon found out Rosa was pregnant; she had morning sickness and felt awful. I let her stay as I felt sorry for her but she was little help with Ducky or Posy. One day she received a package from Puerto Rico. It contained some home delicacies, native foods. She had written her mother that she had morning sickness and she yearned for the food she was used to.

Even the smell of celery nauseated her so the next morning, when I was awakened by a horrible smell, I was amazed to find her frying something dark red that looked as bad as it smelled; it was Puerto Rican blood sausage which she seemed to crave. In spite of my opening all the windows and doors, the odor hung in the air and never dissipated. Rosa savored that dish daily until it was all consumed. Finally she left my employ.

Sex was the culprit. One day Roy, Rosa's husband, appeared unexpectedly. He had a 24-hour pass. I reminded them that they would have to go to a hotel. They agreed and while they were packing her things for the overnight trip, I walked to the back house on the lot to talk to my neighbor. Halfway up the driveway I heard a terrible crash. I dashed back to the house and found Rosa and Roy standing in the hall, looking terrified. They had broken the bed. I guess they couldn't wait to get to the hotel. They left and I called a repairman. When Rosa returned the next day, she said that Roy wanted her to stay at the hotel. That suited me just fine. I paid her and happily let her go.

Another maid I remember was Bertha, a large country girl from Iowa with masses of black curly hair. Her husband had already been shipped out, (a great boon to me!) and she didn't want to go home immediately. I never ate meals with my hired help but I tried to keep our relationship impersonal and not get too intimate.

Bertha set two places at the table, one for me and one for her. I explained again that I wanted to eat alone and she said, "OK, I like to eat alone too."

She removed her place setting and put it in the kitchen on the counter, from whence she chattered incessantly throughout the meal. I gave up. I mumbled, "Uh huh" and "Nope" and tried to concentrate on my book. She just didn't seem to get it.

She told me one day that she was going to the hospital for an operation. That was why she had not returned to Iowa. The Naval Hospital was going to perform a hysterectomy on her later that week so she couldn't work for a while. Could she come back and recoup at my house? What could I say? "Of course, you may."

One of her friends came to take her to the hospital and she blithely went off, explaining I would see her in about a week.

Five days later I came back to the house after shopping with the kids. There were four or five cars in the driveway. When I opened the front door, there was Bertha ensconced on my chaise-lounge, wearing a blue satin negligee with ostrich feathers around the neck. At least six strange people were lolling in chairs, all drinking coco-colas and demolishing my "hard-to-come-by" cookies. It was quite a homecoming and Bertha was the star attraction.

She stayed with me for about a week and then, thankfully, someone collected her and she returned to Iowa.

A lot of the time I had nobody to help me. After an experience like the one with Bertha, I was willing to settle for baby sitters, who were not hard to come by.

One day, my landlady asked me to show her house to a prospective temporary tenant. She was back east visiting, and I had a key to her property. Soon a nice-looking middle-aged gentleman arrived at my door and I walked down the driveway with him to show him the house. He was chatty and told me he was from St. Louis. His father was dying in the hospital here and he had come to take the body back home when the old man had breathed his last. He hated hotels and decided to rent Mrs. Mallonee's house. I can't remember why he returned to my house with me but he did. He sat down and continued talking, telling me all about his father and how he was going to get a special train to take the coffin back to St. Louis. He owned the largest department store in Missouri so it wasn't hard to figure out that he was very wealthy.

The afternoon wore on and I wondered how to get rid of him. Finally Ducky came in and announced that he was hungry. "When are we going to eat?"

At that, this visitor asked if I would have dinner with him. I refused and said it was too hard to get a sitter. It wasn't but he didn't know that. He sat on and Ducky came back and reminded me that he was hungry and wanted his supper. In desperation I asked the gentleman if he would like to eat with us. He jumped to his feet and said, "Now that you have invited me, I'll go back to the hotel and bring dinner back for us. You go ahead and feed the children. I'll see you in a little bit."

As soon as he left, I called a girl named Nancy I knew who lived nearby and asked her to please come over as soon as she could and rescue me. She said she would arrive as soon as she finished dinner. I fed the children and was getting them to bed, when my gentleman friend reappeared with two plates of food, covered with napkins, and, tucked under his arm, a shaker of martinis.

We ate the food he had brought and he demolished the shaker of cocktails. I fixed myself an old fashioned and then, my friend Nancy arrived. The three of us sat around and talked and talked and talked. Finally Nancy caught my eye and signaled that she *had* to leave. We stood up and I thanked my man caller for dinner and said good night. He didn't budge. Nancy left and I began to get scared. What would I do if he made a pass at me?

He told me his nickname was Barty and he began pulling all the draperies shut, remarking that my house was a fish bowl. That was too much. I started telling him how wonderful Lamar was, how he was the only man I had ever looked at twice, how our marriage was made in heaven, etc.

Barty listened and then he put back his head and roared with laughter. Between guffaws he said, "When I came back tonight I had every intention of seducing you. You're damned attractive and I thought maybe we could get something going between us, but Good Lord, you have certainly let me know that's not in your plans at all. How about starting all over and having dinner with me one day next week? A friendly dinner!"

The next day I went to church and my minister, Father Glazebrook, asked me if I had met the man who had rented Mrs. Mallonee's house. I said I had and he shook his head and said, "Stay clear of him. He's a dreadful wolf and not to be trusted. His father is just like him. He's 88 and almost in a coma, but his hand keeps creeping up under the nurses' skirts when they come to his bedside."

So, when Barty called me on Monday and asked me to go to dinner, I went! I had a lovely time and he did not make a pass at me ever. He remarked that Ducky's pants were always falling down and that the child spent his life hiking them up.

"Why don't you buy him some new ones?" he asked.

"Because there are none to be had in the stores." I replied.

A week later Barty's father died and his son took him back to St. Louis. Shortly afterwards I received a present. It was six pairs of shorts for Ducky from the largest department store in Missouri.

I had another close call with a corpsman who was some relation to Mrs. Mallonee; I had met him at her house when he was visiting her. One night a week, I went to my church and served coffee and doughnuts to servicemen. Bill, this Navy enlisted man, often dropped in to chat. Of course, I was friendly. I'm always friendly! He kept heckling me to go someplace to eat after the Parish House closed at 10:00 o'clock. I always refused, giving as my excuse that I had to get home to the children. I should have been honest and told him that I didn't want to go out with an enlisted man; I would be criticized if I were seen with him. If he had been an officer, I would have gone in a minute. Often some officer who had served with Lamar would come by to give me news of him. However, I usually fed them; they rarely took me to dinner.

This night Bill became irritated with me and he accused me of being a snob. He was right. He said all he wanted to do was go to the Casa de Manana, which was close by, and get a sandwich. He double-dared me to go. I decided it would be all right as he was Mrs. Mallonee's nephew and, after all, this was wartime; I had met him in the home of an officer's wife.

"All right," I said, "but I can't stay very long. My sitter has to go to school tomorrow and I told her I'd be back early."

"That's fine," he said, "I'll get you home in a jiffy."

I called the sitter and told her I would be a little late. We got into his car and started for the restaurant. As we approached the Casa, he went flying past even as I yelled that he had overshot the turn off. "Where do you think you are going? The Casa de Manana is back there!"

"I know," he said, "we're not going there."

"There's nothing open this time of night except the Casa."

"I know a place that is open," He said. "Just trust me."

We drove fast and the lights of La Jolla disappeared behind us. He started telling me he was a psychiatrist and was very good at analyzing people. I, for instance, hadn't had sex for a long time and that was not good for me. He carefully informed me that he was sterile and couldn't get anyone pregnant. He could never have children. "It's true and sad," he said, "but, on the other hand, he was available for sex without ever getting his partner pregnant."

By this time, I was really panicked and my imagination went berserk. I would never have sex with him willingly and he would rape me and throw my body over the cliff. No one had seen me go off with him and no one would ever suspect him as the murderer for we had never been seen together. My death would be a mystery forever! Or, maybe we would have an accident. We were still speeding northward and he could easily wreck the car. I visualized the headlines in the San Diego paper, "Couple killed in car crash. Woman identified as wife of Marine Officer; the man a Naval corpsman. The accident occurred in a lonely area where the wreck was spotted at about 11:30 p.m. last night."

Finally, he slowed down as we neared Laguna Beach and pulled in to a night club that had flashing lights, indicating it was open. We went in and Bill ordered a full meal, urging me to join him. I wanted just coffee. As we waited for the food, he continued his psychoanalysis of me. It was very unhealthy for me to remain pure for a husband who might never come home. He was on his second beer, too, which convinced me I would never get home alive. I went through my life story about how much in love I was with Lamar and how I never, never wanted sex with anyone else. Surprise! Surprise! He listened, he ate, he drank, he drove me home, we said, "good-night" and I had diarrhea for two days.

Bette Davis was a famous movie star in the 40's, her career was spotted with Oscars. She lived in Hollywood, of course, but Laguna Beach was a popular hangout for the movie crowd. Mrs. Mallonee had a homosexual friend named Seymour, who often came with his enlisted friends, like Bill, to visit her. He was related to the Spanish royal family and was a bleeder as many of them were. He had a very attractive friend who was named Bill Sherry, another Navy corpsman. Looking back on those years it seems to me that for an officer's wife, Mrs. Mallonee knew a lot of enlisted men.

Seymour, who seemed to know a lot of influential people, took Bill to a party in Laguna where Bette Davis was one of the guests. When they arrived, Bette was holding court, regaling her surrounding admirers with a story. When she finished, she asked her hostess, "Who is that gorgeous young man?" She was indicating Bill.

The hostess said she didn't know him. Bette said imperiously, "Bring him here!" Bill was duly presented to the movie star and shortly thereafter they left the party together.

This was the beginning of a relationship that ended in marriage. Their courtship was a little wild. He had no money to squire her around to restaurants and parties, so she opened a bank account for him, which blew his mind until he saw how little she had put in it. It was all of $200.00.

She bought him clothes so he would look sharp when they dated and shortly thereafter they were married. She became pregnant and they had a little girl, the only child she produced from various marriages. Bill had an affair with the baby's nurse and Bette divorced him in a flash. Ah me! Fame is so fleeting! I think I saw this child once on television. She was grown, didn't look like either of her parents and was bashing her Mom.

Two of those war years finally passed. I had a call from Lamar. He was in Hawaii and would arrive in San Francisco in about a week. He was coming home for R and R. Mother and Boppie were in San Francisco and he wanted me to be there when his ship arrived. I contacted Pache and she said she would come and watch the children so Lamar and I could have a two-day honeymoon. I bought a new dress, told Mother I was coming and all went according to plans. Pache arrived, I took the train to San Francisco and arrived there one day sooner than Lamar did.

That night, Boppie took Mother and me to a well-known Chinese restaurant. I had my usual old-fashioned before dinner and then Boppie recommended beer with dinner. I don't really like beer but I was willing to try it. I didn't know the old saying, "Whiskey on beer, never fear. Beer on whiskey, rather risky."

That night I was sick as a dog and the next morning, I was queasy and I felt awful. Lamar arrived on schedule and he was so excited at the prospect of being with me and celebrating in the town known for its wonderful food. He had been on K-rations a long time. He was disappointed to find his wife peaked and not interested in food of any sort. Nevertheless, we went to The Blue Fox, one of the city's best and most expensive dining places where Lamar had a wonderful meal and I just toyed with my food. Then we saw "Oklahoma" in the theater, which was super and even I forgot my queasiness.

The next day we took the train back to La Jolla. Lamar was so joyful at the prospect of seeing Ducky again and making the acquaintance of his 18 month-old daughter. When we arrived at the house, there were our children impatiently waiting for us as Pache had prepared them for the big moment. Posy took one look at this father who smelled of pipe tobacco, had a booming voice and scratchy mustache. She said one word, "No!" and fled to the kitchen.

Ducky asked, "Did you kill any Japs?"

Lamar said, "Not that I saw."

Then Ducky asked, "Did you get wounded?"

Lamar said he had not been wounded. Whereupon his son asked him, "Then what did you come home for?"

How's that for a homecoming after striking blows for liberty for two years? Posy's attitude was explainable. There had been no men in my life. But Ducky! I guess not many men that we knew had come home unless they were wounded. If Lamar was hurt, he didn't show it. Ducky was soon all over him, but Posy stayed aloof.

Lamar had one month's leave and then he was ordered to a different outfit, the Fifth Division, which was being trained at Camp Pendleton, a Marine Base close to San Diego. He had barely reported for duty when he came down with malaria. He was hospitalized and his family used their valuable gas rations, burning up the road to visit him in the hospital at Camp Pendleton. He recovered in time to go to Hawaii with his outfit. General Edson made Lamar his artillery Officer for Fleet Marine Force, Pacific. They were soon back in the South Pacific in the War zone. He was promoted to Colonel and received a new job. He became operations and training officer for the Third Amphibious Corps and went to Guam. The troops were training for an invasion of Japan. This never took place as the bombing of Hiroshima and Nagasaki with the atomic bomb brought the war to an unexpected end.

Instead, his outfit went to China. Chang Kai Chek was in command of the Chinese Nationalists, who were fighting the Japanese in North China. Lamar's outfit was given the job of holding the airports and seaports to protect the passage of troops. They were stationed in Tientsin, where they lived in real luxury.

Lamar never ceased to be impressed with how well the Japanese accepted the American Occupation. They were so disciplined, there were no hostile overtures and the people bowed respectfully when the occupying troops arrived. The Americans threw out the German nationals and occupied their apartments and took over their Chinese servants. On a scale of 1-10, Lamar gave their accommodations a 10! Certainly, for wartime.

Once he wrote home and told me he was desolate because their Mess had lost their cook, who could make the best Wall of China in the city. That, in case you would like to know, was a peanut brittle basket filled with whipped cream! No one that I knew had seen whipping cream since the war started. Sugar was rationed and desserts were not commonplace. My heart did not bleed for my husband or his fellow officers.

Lamar was in Tientsin when the Japanese signed the peace truce. All the Japanese officers surrendered their swords and one was given to Lamar as a keepsake. He kept this hanging on the wall of his study for years. The officer who had relinquished it had tied a rag on the handle, giving his name and address. To lose your sword is to "lose your honor." I'm sure he hoped against all hope to get it back one day. And he did!

Years later, in the early sixties, Lamar, softened by age and released from loathing of the enemy, wanted to return it to its rightful owner. He sent the little rag with the Japanese inscription to the Military Attache in Washington for translation. The Embassy wrote back and suggested Lamar return the sword to the Mayor of the town, where the Japanese officer lived. He would have a special ceremony and present it to the owner with pomp and circumstance. This Lamar did and subsequently received a gift of tea and seaweed in beautiful lacquer boxes plus a scroll of thanks, about ten feet long. The gentleman also sent some newspaper clippings of the ceremony. The Japanese officer was a solemn and tough-looking man. How many people do you know who would do something as nice as Lamar did?

Finally, Lamar was allowed to come home. He had accumulated 40 months overseas and the authorities thought that was enough. He agreed. So we had another homecoming.

Parenthood

This time he arrived by ship in San Diego. Ducky and I met him and spotted him on the deck. He made motions indicating a smaller child, wondering where Posy was. I explained with gestures that she was asleep. When he had disembarked and we had returned home, Posy deigned to approach her father and sit on his lap. We were making progress.

Lamar had orders to Washington to Marine headquarters. No one ever wants to go to the Capital for duty; it is one of the most expensive places to live and housing is always a problem. We did not complain. You go where Uncle Sam sends you and you don't make waves.

When Lamar told me we were leaving for DC in two days, I said it would take me two days to clean out my desk, which, incidentally, belonged to Mrs. Mallonee. If it had belonged to me, I would have shipped it full of stuff! I hadn't straightened it in two years. In two days we left California.

Washington was a madhouse. We would not get government housing, there were no rental properties available and no motel would allow a guest to stay more than two or three days. The answer? I went to Camp LeJeune where Boppie was Commanding General and visited my parents while Lamar went to Washington and looked for a house to buy.

Boppie and Laolo had big beautiful Quarters and two stewards to cook and clean. I didn't think our visit would be too hard on Mother. They had invited us often but I sometimes wonder how thrilled they were to have us; Ducky was eight and Posy was four and a half. We had a wonderful time and eventually, Lamar called and said he had bought a house. He sounded very excited and described the property in glowing terms. He was particularly taken with the seven rooms in the basement as he intended to invest in power tools.

We had never owned a house before and my parents hadn't either. As soon as the sale was concluded, we could occupy the premises. I would meet him in Barcroft, VA.

While waiting for Lamar's word to come that we were to join him, one night at Camp LeJeune, Mother and I went to the movies. Boppie opted to stay home and babysit his grandchildren who were in bed. I drove my car which had a visitor's tag attached to the windshield. When we arrived at the base theater, Mother insisted I park in Boppie's special parking space. It was next to the entrance and she didn't like to walk any distance, which would have been a necessity if I had gone looking for a space for the common people. We parked and entered the auditorium. The lights were still on and we found our way to the seats reserved for the Commanding General and his guests. Suddenly, a voice came over the loud speaker, "Will the owner of a Blue Buick with license plate number 461-978 please report to the box office?"

Mother and I paid no attention as we were talking. The loud speaker repeated the message, this time adding the info that the car in question had a California license. The light bulb came on! That was my car! I started to get up but she put her hand on my arm and said, "Oh, just ignore it; it's not important."

I stayed seated, the lights stayed on and again, the voice, irritated this time, boomed out, "Unless the owner of the blue Buick comes forward and identifies himself, there will be no movie shown here tonight!"

Catcalls and whistles followed this announcement so I timidly rose from my seat and went to the box office, amid the stares of several hundred people. The Marine Police were gathered and I had to explain that I had the wife of the C.O. with me and she asked me to park there. I think they called Boppie to be sure I wasn't lying and then I was allowed to return to my seat. The lights were out and the film was being shown and my tail felt very pinned down. You know I am so frightened of the LAW.

I remember little about that visit except Ducky caught an eel and the cook fixed it for dinner. It looked like a snake and I disgraced myself by refusing to taste it. Ducky was so proud of his catch. I'm sure Mother didn't touch it either as she wouldn't even look at a picture of a snake.

One afternoon, Boppie and I took the children for a walk. The trees were festooned with Spanish moss that grows in that part of the country. Boppie grabbed some and stuffed it up under his uniform cap, turned it around backwards, and chased the kids, acting silly. The Spanish moss looked like grey hair and a beard and Duck and Posy were squealing. A sedate colonel and his wife appeared and nearly died at the sight of the Commanding General in uniform acting like that. Boppie had so much fun in him, he didn't care a bit.

Soon I had word that our house was available for occupancy so I went to Washington with great expectations.

9

Post-War Years

When we arrived in Washington, we stayed in a motel, waiting to finalize the house sale. I called my dear friend, Kay Sherman, whose husband also had received orders to the Marine Corps headquarters. They had bought a house in Falls Church and I made arrangements to meet at her house the following morning so we could go together to inspect what was to be my new abode.

Lamar went to work at headquarters and I took John and Posy to Kay's. Linda, her eldest, Ducky's age, now had a twin brother and sister who were almost Posy's age. The Sherman house was lovely, a white colonial with green shutters, set back from the road on a lot with tall trees. The property was large enough that they could keep a pony for the children and there was a pond in the back yard complete with some ducks, which rushed us and began to peck at our feet.

I admired everything and could hardly wait to see what we had bought. We left the children, under the care of her day worker, playing in the garden, and drove to the address Lamar had given me. As we approached the section in Northern Virginia called Barcroft, we noticed that the houses were less attractive and not too well kept up. Soon we found Eighth Street and started looking for 4708. We spotted it readily as Lamar had said there was a stone wall across the front of the lot. The wall looked handmade and was enhanced with four large stone flowerpots. Seated in two of them were rather scruffy urchins, looking very much at home. We asked them if the Kinchloes, the owners, were at home. They informed us that they didn't know, they were just neighbors. Later, when I planted those pots with flowers, the neighbor kids continued to sit in them and I never had a bloom.

No one answered the door, so Kay and I returned to the car. Neither one of us had said a word. I thought it was a dreadful looking place and I couldn't forget that we had *bought it*.

Finally, Kay broke the silence. "It's only 8:30 in the morning or I'd suggest going someplace for a couple of dry martinis."

I nodded dismally and said, "One good thing about service life is that nothing is forever. We can sell this place when we are transferred, thank God, Maybe our duty in Washington won't last very long."

Kay allowed as how it could maybe be fixed up a bit but as for its location and general looks, there was little we could do; I was stuck with it. We returned to her gorgeous property where I drooled and would have killed for it.

I want to say that Lamar had never before been faced with the purchase of a house and real estate prices were horrendous after the war, especially in Washington. He jumped at the first thing he could afford because rentals were so scarce. There had been no building in four years and the Government had grown immensely. So, I forgive him!

Well, we finally moved in and made a thorough reconnaissance of the property. Mr. Kinchloe was a carpenter and had built many additions to a small two-story concrete box while he and his family continued to live in it. He started with the basement and dug out those seven cinder block rooms that had so impressed Lamar. That completed, he added a den, a dinette and a pantry to the main floor. Then I think he got tired. Upstairs he had converted one room into a bathroom, thank goodness. There were outhouses in that area so he probably had one when he moved there. That left three small bedrooms, the largest of which we took for our room as we had a double bed. It was so small, we could never close the door and on one occasion, I ran into it in the dark and gave myself a beautiful black eye. When I told my friends I had run into a door, they thought I was being funny.

My first priority was to take an interior decorating course from the Marine Corps Schools. It was by correspondence and I could do it at home. Because Lamar was an officer, he was qualified to give me the exams and see I didn't cheat!

On its completion, I had all the confidence in the world. Armed with so much knowledge, I wanted to tear out all the partitions and make the rooms bigger. That was not in the budget, so all decorating would have to be within the limits of the rooms as they were. We had to buy furniture so we kept everything "color-coordinated" and I used a "bridge," a hunting print I had bought Lamar because he was so horsey. The draperies were unbleached muslin, which I had dyed a scarlet to match the print and the sofa (the most uncomfortable daybed you ever sat or slept on.) And the chairs were upholstered in a red print and a blue solid to match the blue broadloom rug, which showed every footprint and was my anathema for all the years I owned it.

I rented a sewing machine to make the draperies, and when it was delivered, asked the salesman to fill 15 bobbins with scarlet thread. He looked alarmed and asked me if I knew how to use this machine. I said I knew enough to thread it and sew straight ahead and put a new bobbin in when I ran out of thread. He didn't really like leaving this expensive article with me. It could hem, roll, pleat, gather and make buttonholes and all I wanted was to sew, "straight ahead?" Weeks and fifteen bobbins later, I had five pairs of red draperies and Lamar had used his workshop to make valance boards. We were settling in.

That Christmas I bought Lamar a red leather lounge chair which matched everything perfectly. I bought a dining table for five dollars for the dinette and painted it with Pennsylvania Dutch designs. Lamar told me the table was not worth five dollars. It took him months to put it into serviceable condition. I painted plates of food; lobster, crab, grapes, cherries. Then I painted glasses of wine with roses in them and silverware, everything with painted shadows. Carried away with this new hobby, I bought two corner cupboards and painted them in the same manner. I tried to stain the floor maple to match the chairs I had bought at the Salvation Army but in my ignorance, used the stain so thick, the floor was painted, not stained.

Next I attacked the yard. There was room for a vegetable garden and I was itching to grow my own. Imagine! Fresh corn and teeny weeny string beans! And my own strawberries! There was a plot that had been a garden so I asked my neighbors, a plumber named Charley Dove who had the deepest sideburns and the slickest hair I had ever seen, and a policeman, another neighbor, who drank bourbon straight from the bottle, what I should do to have a really good garden. They joined me in the yard and showed me how to "turn over the dirt." You take a shovel and go down twelve inches, turn it over and break up the clods. Neither neighbor offered to help but they leaned on the fence and gave me endless advice. They urged me to get some good sheep shit. I am so prissy I was horrified at their using the word in my presence, I failed to hear where you could buy it and what it was called commercially. I found out later that sheep manure was very available, so I dutifully bought some. I wouldn't want to lose face with my new neighbors. Their garden hints didn't keep me from making the usual beginner mistakes. I planted too little corn and we had one meal only from that effort; we got four ears. The birds ate all the strawberry plants so we got nil from them. The lettuce was bitter and the beans got some rust or scale on the bushes so they didn't bear. I hadn't heard about spraying. I needed my Boppie who was one of the world's best gardeners; he knew everything about gardening, but he was still commanding Camp Le Jeune and not available.

Our son John, still called Duck, was becoming a pyromaniac. He burnt a hole in Lamar's lounge chair, he burned up the shower curtain, he made a small fire under the front porch, which happened to be wood, where I found him and spanked him. His crowning achievement was brought about by my neighbor burning his leaves in a right sizable yard. Duck wanted to help and had been hanging around, watching and admiring. When the light began to fade, the neighbor went into his house for dinner. Not Duck; he decided to finish the job for him. Soon the yard was ablaze and the fire department was called. They extinguished the burning leaves and admonished the assembled crowd to be more careful. The neighbor was very kind and didn't seem unhappy with Duck, but Lamar and I worried that matches had become a real problem. Like most things in life, this stage ended with as little fanfare as it had started. Duck became sated with striking matches and there were no more crises of this particular variety.

We had been entertained so many times by the Commandant of the Marine Corps and Mrs. Vandergrift at receptions and dinners, I was getting embarrassed because I had been trained to return social engagements. One night we were with one of the general's Aides, Jeff Fields, so I asked him what I could do to repay my social debts. He informed me that the Vandergrifts never went to private parties as they had so many official functions they had to attend. They cherished their few free nights at home alone. "If you want to make brownie points," he said, "ask them to dinner and they will be pleased that you invited them; most people don't. You are perfectly safe. They won't come."

The next morning I called Mrs. Vandergrift and asked if she and the General could have dinner with us one night. I was more than a little disconcerted when she asked, "What night, dear?"

I said, "I'd like you to choose the day. You are much busier than we are. Any night next week."

"How would Thursday be for you, dear?"

"Oh, fine," I said, wondering how all of this had come about.

I must tell you Mrs. Vandergrift was an interior decorator. She received big bucks for her services and she had wealthy clients. Just the thought of her driving up in front of our house and spotting the bathtub and trash in the next door yard and those atrocious empty stone flower pots, was enough to give me shingles or ulcers. I had given her the latest hour for dinner that I dared, eight o'clock. Would it be dark by then?

I spent every minute of the next week getting ready for the big event: I cleaned silver, I washed goblets and good china, I bought the most expensive food items and the best wines, I cleaned and straightened the house umpteen times, admonishing the children to not touch this and that. I was worn to a frazzle as the big night approached. I had convinced my day worker that I needed her to serve the dinner and she complied. At least, I wouldn't be hopping up every two minutes to serve, clear and refill plates and glasses.

Thursday night arrived. The children had been fed and were up in their rooms. Praise the Lord! It was almost dark and my guests hadn't arrived. They would not see the trashy yard next door. I had invited that mistaken aide and his wife to join us and help make conversation. They were coming with the Vandergrifts.

Finally, we saw a car in front of the house. I saw the Marine driver helping one of the ladies descend. As I opened the front door, Mrs. Vandergrift smiled and said they were a little late as they had been lost. They had driven around the block several times and Martin, the driver, had said, "Let me ask at this house." Weren't we lucky! It was your neighbor's. They said they were from Kentucky and enjoyed having you next door."

Good grief! Martin had to have seen the interior of their house, complete with the hog killing debris from their morning activity. Duck had come in dragging a bloody pigtail which had been given him by the neighbors.

The Vandergrifts were friends of Mother and Boppie and they were most gracious about the dinner and my puny efforts at decorating. Looking back, I'm sure the only reason they accepted my invitation was to be nice and to write my parents that they had been to our house. I never let Jeff Fields forget the panic he had caused me. He probably couldn't figure out why they came either.

Mrs. Vandergrift had remarked that we had the same flat silver pattern, Gorham's Fairfax. I told her she could borrow mine if she ever needed it for a big dinner. She thanked me, but said she had 36 of everything and her dinner parties were never larger than that. My tail felt pinned down as I had eight of most things and only six of some items like cocktail forks and grapefruit spoons.

Lamar had been chosen that fall to attend the National War College which opened its doors for the first time in 1947.

There were students from the Army, Navy, Marine Corps, Diplomatic Corps and a few foreign officers from Canada and Great Britain. Of course, we were socially active and there were parties every weekend. One of the British couples, Brigadier and Mrs. Batten, invited us to dinner. We had met them and looked forward to getting to know them better.

The night of the dinner party the weather was cold and blustery. Our usual sitter arrived about six in the evening and remarked there had been a few snowflakes. We left for Falls Church and by the time we arrived at the Battens, the ground was white with snow.

This was before TV and hourly radio weather reports. The evening news would have alerted us but we had left home before it was broadcast. When we arrived at the Battens there were no other cars in front of their house. Had we made a mistake in the time?

We rang the bell and Betty Batten greeted us but seemed surprised to see us.

"Are we early?" I asked.

"No, but everyone else has called and cancelled. The storm warning frightened them."

"We haven't heard any weather warnings. Maybe we'd better go home." I said.

"No," she said, "we have this dinner all ready. Come in and we'll eat right away and then you can start back."

So we stayed and after we had eaten, I helped Betty with the dishes and cleaning up. Then we hurried to get on the road. Lamar started the car but the snow was so heavy the wheels just spun. He tried everything he knew but nothing worked, so we retraced our steps to our hosts' house to call the AAA. The Battens let us in and Lamar repeatedly tried the AAA number.

It was always busy. Finally, he decided to get a garage on his own. None answered or were willing to come to our aid. Eventually, the AAA number responded and a voice told us there would be a twelve-hour delay before they could service us.

The poor Battens were stuck with us. We called the sitter who disgruntledly told us the buses were still running in Barcroft but she would stay all night and wait for us to return. Betty said we could sleep in their bed. Since they had only one bed; they would sleep on the floor in the living room. We argued and argued but they insisted we use their room. We had no sleeping garments, no tooth brushes and we were mortified that our hosts were lying on their living room floor. The next morning after a stressful night, at about eleven o'clock, the AAA people hauled us out and we went home. I'm sure the Battens fell into bed and didn't even change the sheets. Our dear sitter, an elderly monster, charged us full rates for the 18 hours we had been gone. This was at the beginning of Lent and I always gave up smoking for Lent. If I could have had a cigarette at any moment of that awful evening, I would have been a better camper! The Battens smoked up a storm, but my Marston heritage - stubbornness - wouldn't let me break Lent. Ordinary day-to-day I can take, but in a stressful situation, give me my nicotine, please!

That winter we returned to see our psychic guru, Mrs. McLaren, for another seance and in the course of either Lamar's or my interview, the crystal ball revealed that the neighborhood we were in was hazardous to Posy's welfare. On answering in the affirmative a query about woods being adjacent to our property, Mrs. McLaren advised us to move. She saw boys doing unsavory things and she worried for our little girl. Since some of those boys had written the f-word on our sidewalk, I was a little alarmed too.

We started looking for a house in a better neighborhood. Now we had a good excuse! We found one in an Alexandria suburb and put our Barcroft house on the market. I discovered I was pregnant, which didn't surprise me as I had decided the month before we wanted another baby. Why did I decide this? I'll tell you what I think! We both came from families that had three children; we were programmed into this script. If our parents had three offspring, so would we! Being pregnant and moving don't go together in my case; I could anticipate trouble. We sold our house very promptly so we escaped the consequences of breaking the first three rules of successful real estate bargaining. Location, location, location!

Before we left this den of iniquity, our children had their first real encounter with spirituality. One Sunday afternoon a gentleman arrived at the front door and asked if John and Mary were at home as they were not at Bible School and he was worried. I'm sure I must have looked surprised. We always attended church and Sunday School for the children at an Episcopal Church that we had joined. What Bible School was he talking about?

He explained he was the pastor of the little church up on the corner and John and Mary had been attending regularly all week their annual Vacation Bible School. Didn't I know? The graduation ceremony was that evening and the children were needed to practice their parts. John had a stellar role. How my children could be so involved and I not know about it, is a mystery. Maybe they thought I wouldn't approve, but a better guess is that I was busy packing and they, with complete freedom to roam, hadn't bothered to tell me.

That evening at seven o'clock Lamar and I, as dutiful parents, escorted our children to the church, one block away. There we were greeted by everyone with smiles of welcome. On the wall were many charts, each with a child's name at the top. All the boys had puppy dogs on theirs and the girls had kittens. I spotted the one for Duck. Attached at the bottom were paper cutouts of bones, one for each day he had been present. There were seven. Posy had a kitten on hers and attached to it were paper cutouts of bowls of milk. She had seven bowls also. My offspring had perfect attendance. I was pleased in spite of myself.

The children sang a hymn. It ended with a riotous line about shooting the devil dead and at that point, the children grabbed Bibles and held them aloft triumphantly. Not too dumb, I realized the Bibles were the guns. That was a rousing song and the children enjoyed singing it.

There were prayers and some speeches and then the pastor announced that John Curry had the floor. My son calmly got up, went to center stage and proceeded to recite the alphabet, prefacing each letter with a scripture verse that started with that letter. Lamar and I sat there, not believing what we heard. He was going to be in 3rd grade that fall and he could memorize ALL that? I was no student of the Bible and could not be sure, but I don't think he made any mistakes. At the end there was a hearty round of applause. Now I understood why the pastor wanted him there for the closing ceremonies. He was the star of the show.

We didn't lose any money but we didn't make any either when we sold our house in Barcroft. That's unbelievable in Washington, D.C. Just the agent's fee would increase the selling price. Most people would have made some profit. We were so anxious to get out and move to the house at 3512 Cameron Mills Road, we settled for the first offer that matched our buying price. The new house cost considerably more, but the neighborhood was good.

The day we moved I gave Duck and Posy a lecture on being friendly to the children in the new neighborhood. They were accustomed to Service kids who were just as anxious to make friends as they were. Civilians seemed more suspicious of newcomers. I told them that they would have to take the lead as they had more experience making friends. As we pulled into the driveway, I saw two boys about Duck's age playing ball in the yard next door. I said, "Now's your chance. Go over and introduce yourself and be friendly."

Duck dutifully dislodged himself from the back seat and slowly walked in the direction of the ball players. Soon I saw them in conversation. Later, I went and called Duck to come and get dressed to go out for supper. When he came in, I complimented him on his social graces and said, "Now, wasn't that easy? You can make new friends so easily. I'm proud of you."

"Oh, Mom," he said, "that was no sweat. Those boys' father is in the Air Force. They're not hard to get to know."

Weren't we lucky to have service people next door? No more rusty bathtubs or hog killings! Wow! The Springers, our neighbors, became close friends and when Bowie was baptized the following August, Mrs. Springer acted as godmother for the real one, Alice Williams, who lived on the West Coast.

What are my memories of Alexandria? First, we were so poor; that house was really more than we could afford. Service people usually groan when they receive orders to the Capital for it is such an expensive place to live. Real estate, in particular, was exorbitant as the population was constantly changing and each time a house went on the market, the realtor's fee ups the price. The Cameron Mills house had a defective refrigerator and we never had the funds to buy another one. Two years later, we sold the house with that lousy piece of equipment still in place, never warning the new owners as the old owners had not informed us. We had been forced by law to leave our beautiful new fridge in Barcroft. Stoves and refrigerators were always necessary inclusions in unfurnished houses for sale.

John was in fourth grade and had overnight acquired a new name. I discovered this one day when a strange to me youngster arrived at the front door and asked for Freckles. I told him there was no one by that name living there. He peered in the door and yelled, "Yes, there is and there he is!"

He was looking at Duck at the top of the stairs. My son casually descended and whispered in passing, "This is my name now." Just like that, "Duck" was a thing of the past. We learned to use the new one quite easily as he was covered with freckles.

Posy was five in November and was allowed to enter first grade. She was ready. After all, she had started nursery school at two in La Jolla and was bored with the routine now that she had been a "student" for three years.

She made friends with a little girl up the road. That child's problem was she had a younger sister for whom she was responsible day and night, it seemed. This moppet always had sniffles and a runny nose. In addition, her diapers were always heavily soiled and drenched. But the worst was her odor. It was unbelievable! Her mother and I had a running contest to see which one of us could get our children dressed and out of the house and at the other's front door first. I lived in fear and trembling that I would have to change that child's diaper. Why I didn't worry about Posy coming down with colds and flu, I can't imagine. I never saw those girls with dry noses.

I was back in the hands of Dr. Mundell, the great OB/GYN specialist. Happily, I had no trouble carrying this baby. One day in October, Lamar asked me how much this pregnancy was going to cost us. I said that I had no idea; Mundell and I had never discussed fees. On the next visit to his office, I casually asked the good doctor what he would be charging me. He gave me the usual hospital costs and then quietly named this huge fee for his services. After a few moments I just as quietly asked him if he could recommend a good abortionist. His face whitened as he was a very good Catholic. I continued, "We simply can't afford that. We don't have that kind of money."

He took me seriously and with a look of panic said, "Now don't do anything foolish. I'm sure we can arrange something satisfactory to both of us."

I replied, "I thought you gave special rates to service people."

"Oh," he said, "I had forgotten you were a Marine wife. Of course, I'll only charge you the minimum. Don't ever mention that word, abortion, again."

My baby was due in early January. On December 11, I started my labor and that threw all my Christmas plans into a cocked hat. Shirley was coming to watch the children and stay for a week after the baby came. All Christmas plans came to a halt and Shirley was alerted to come immediately.

Lamar took me to the brand new George Washington Hospital which was planning an official opening three days later. There I was surprised, disappointed and irked to find this third infant was not in such a rush to be born three weeks prematurely. Bowie lollygagged for about six hours and finally made his appearance, a fine bouncing boy of seven pounds, a welcome income tax deduction we did not expect. When it was time to release me from the hospital, I think Lamar had to borrow money to get me out of hock; Christmas presents had just about cleaned us out.

After Shirley left we changed all of our sleeping arrangements. We put Bowie in Posy's room and she moved in with Freckles. Bowie had so much paraphernalia; crib, changing and bathing table, chests for diapers and clothes, a rocker to rock him, etc. All of that was crowded into our bedroom at first. John should have had his own room. He was neat and methodical and Posy was a pack-rat. His things were always fouled up and he resented her. It affected their relationship adversely and it continued that way for many years.

As soon as Lamar dared, he requested duty *anywhere* except another tour in Washington. He was assigned to Maxwell Air Force Base in Montgomery, Alabama. Joyfully, we set out for our new life. We had a new car, a Studebaker, and we would have a lovely set of quarters. We had sold our house and refrigerator and would have government furniture, which would include a fridge that worked!

Maxwell Field is Air Force and our beautiful house was on the airfield. Our first night, I was awakened by such a roar I was sure the roof had been sheared off. The house shook, the doors rattled and we rose to survey the damage. There was none. A big airplane had just taken off for parts unknown. Lamar said we could expect a lot of this. My reaction was to moan that I couldn't live in a house on the airfield; I would never get any sleep. He promised me I would get used to it and I did. After a few weeks, I never heard the planes. I became immune to the noise. During our stay at Maxwell Field, I often forgot to warn my house guests and I would be puzzled at the bags under their eyes at breakfast the next day.

In the Cameron Mills house, I couldn't afford a weekly day worker. Here I had a full-time maid who lived in. It was wonderful to wake up in the morning and smell coffee and bacon cooking.

Our quarters were quite large. Each child had his or her room. Our bedroom was huge and we had a private bath. On the first floor, there was a large living room with fireplace and long windows. This opened onto a glassed-in porch. Across the hall was the large dining room, which opened into a pantry, then the kitchen. Off the kitchen, was a maid's room and bath.

I thought I was living in the lap of luxury. I had a new car, a full-time maid! Wow! My next door neighbor, who was Air Force and received more pay, had two maids and a Cadillac!

Our tour at Maxwell was so pleasant. Lamar taught amphibious operations at the Officers' School and spent a lot of time as the Scoutmaster, training a troop which turned out to be outstanding. My duties were mostly social, entertaining and attending functions. I played a lot of tennis in a group of wives, took up painting and studied with a local artist, worked with the Little Theater, not acting but being prop mistress again. We joined the local Episcopal church and enrolled our three in Sunday School.

On the airfield mushrooms abounded so we collected them and terrified our guests when they dined with us. "Are you sure these are edible?" they would ask. I'm sure some people left them on their plates.

I painted the kitchen bright yellow, too yellow, but after lightening it twice, I gave up and suffered every time I walked into the room. Eventually, I painted Early American figures, a la Peter Hunt, on all the cabinets and they remained there until our next duty change. I bet the quartermaster painted that kitchen the minute we cleared the Base!

We really enjoyed our two years at Maxwell. Some fleeting memories would include Bowie riding his tricycle down the block at rush hour, stopping traffic. The M.P. corralled him and asked who his father was. He said his Papa was a Boy Scout. By contacting the Scout headquarters, they finally found out who he was.

Another was Posy and her next-door friend who wanted to bicycle to Texas. Lamar told Posy she could if they could bike all the way around the airfield. They couldn't make it, so he was off the hook.

On the 179th Marine Corps birthday, November 10, 1950, we hosted a party at the club, inviting all the Navy and Air Force personnel in the school. I ordered a huge cake with the Marine emblem displayed on the top in icing. By the time 179 candles had been lit and the cake wheeled into the ballroom, there was not a vestige of the beautiful emblem visible. I was so disappointed no one saw the decoration, as it had been obliterated by the candles.

Mittie, our pretty Gullah maid, was soon spotted by the black airmen who tracked her down to our quarters. They would call for her and if John answered the phone, he would act silly and make dates with them and never tell Mittie.

A production of the Little Theater improved when the Director, a submarine commander, invited his father, a Broadway producer, to come and give the play some polish. He changed everything two nights before the opening night and threw the leading lady into such a panic that she arrived drunk as a hoot owl the opening night of the performance. The sparse audience had such a treat that the next night, the house was packed! She sobered up by then and the crowd was disappointed.

The beautiful doll house that Lamar made Posy took him one year and two months but it was a thing of beauty with a staircase, fireplace, columns, window boxes, cedar closet and lights.

After two years at Maxwell Field, Lamar received orders to Hawaii. He would be chief-of-staff to General Franklin Hart. Our transport would leave from San Francisco on January 10th. We would drive across the continent, which took ten days. This was in the early part of December so the packers were notified and we began packing and preparing for a hectic month. We decided to have Christmas early as we would be on the road on the actual day. So we bought a tree and decorated it, wrapped all the presents, opened them and the next morning, the packers arrived and everything was out of the house by 5:00 p.m. Bowie's friends wondered why Santa came to our house but not theirs.

Christmas Day we were traveling through some midwestern state and we started to look for someplace to eat

Christmas dinner. Was that a joke! We couldn't find even a gas station open. Finally, at 10:00 o'clock at night, we found a railroad station restaurant open and ate the few things left from the menu. Bowie slept through the meal, stretched out on two straight chairs.

Now, on to Hawaii.

10

The Rocky Years

I call this period The Rocky Years because up to this point in Lamar's and my life together we had just accepted whatever Uncle Sam told us to do, feeling that we had little control over our own destiny. Increase in rank arrived from time to time and we viewed it as the natural order of events. Now Lamar was unknowingly moving into a world of what I call "intrigue and diplomacy." We were so naive we knew nothing about this world as it existed but we were on the verge of finding out.

My father occasionally had vendettas with other high-ranking Marine officers, but I attributed this to the fact that they had known one another for so many years and so intimately, they knew one another's weaknesses and faults. They were never in awe if their contemporaries eventually acquired august rank. Unfortunately, some officers put on airs when they finally became colonels or generals. Lamar would soon be on the list of officers to be considered for promotion to be a general officer. His fitness reports had been routinely excellent throughout his career (much more impressive than my father's and he became a major-general) and we felt Lamar's selection would be automatic. This new job as chief-of-staff to General Hart was a surprise as we didn't even know him and we wondered why he had picked Lamar for the job. General Gruenther of the Army had asked for Lamar to be on his NATO staff in Europe, but the Commandant of the Marine Corps, General Lemuel Shepherd, said he had other plans for him and did not let him go. Were these they? Hart's choice of Lamar indicated he had heard good things about my husband. We decided Lamar's reputation as an officer had probably preceded him.

We met the General Hart and his wife, Katherine, when we boarded the transport in San Francisco for Hawaii and Pearl Harbor. We were traveling with them and several others on his staff. We found out later that these other two couples were routinely part of his personal baggage. Wherever the General was ordered for duty, he automatically had them transferred with him. This was the first time we had ever encountered anything like this. We soon deduced that these couples were the "inner circle" of his "court" and it behooved us to be nice to them; they wielded a lot of power with the General through Katherine, his wife.

When we went aboard ship to our stateroom, we noticed many written regulations tacked up on the door, informing us, among other things, that "anyone caught carrying alcoholic beverages on a U.S. ship would be court-martialed." Liquor was absolutely forbidden on board. We had in our baggage one bottle of bourbon which we had brought for our evening old-fashioned cocktail, habitually consumed before dinner every night. We decided we'd better toss it overboard as soon as it was dark enough that we wouldn't be observed. That evening as we went to dinner we gave our delicious bourbon "the deep six," mournfully, I must admit.

The next day, the Harts invited us to their cabin before dinner for a drink. My face must have reflected my surprise as I said I thought it was against the ship's rules to have liquor aboard. She laughed and said that injunction was never taken seriously. By regulation the notice was always posted but no one paid it any attention. When I told her we had thrown our liquor overboard, she thought that was the funniest thing she had ever heard. I felt like a country hick, not the world traveler I had always considered myself. I had traveled on other transports, but I had been below the legal age for drinking alcoholic beverages.

We cocktailed every night in the cabins of the knowledgeable "inner circle," mortified that we couldn't return the courtesy. We promised to make up for our lack when we docked in Hawaii.

Don't ask me what my three children did during that voyage. I have not one single memory of them doing anything good or bad. Our job was to "get to know" the Harts. We had been told they could be "difficult" so we were walking gingerly against great odds, as the other staff personnel were already so intimate with them. All I know is none of my children got sick or hurt or in trouble and they ate three square meals a day and anything else that was offered to the passengers, which was plenty. I think they all enjoyed the trip as there were movies every night and a snack bar was open 24 hours a day. John and Posy were avid readers and John was a superb baby sitter for Bowie, whom he seemed to love.

When we arrived on Oahu, there was a welcoming band, a hula dance troop, lots of flower leis, brought by military people, and word that our quarters were ready for occupancy. Someone had made up our beds, filled the fridge with breakfast for the next day. What a wonderful custom. There were kitchen utensils, linens and enough silverware and crockery to keep us going until our own household effects arrived. Of course, the whole first week we had dinner every night with one or other of the welcoming families. Later, we had the opportunity and joy of extending the same courtesy to other families when they arrived. The quarters at 41 Halawa Drive, Makalapa, were nicely furnished in rattan and the rugs were grass or straw. We were just down the hill from the Harts, who had the luxurious set of quarters reserved for the Commanding General.

After we had settled in and had been wined and dined, our new life took shape. Lamar was busy from morning to night, learning his new job and new boss. John, a sophomore in High School, entered Punahou School, which he forever after considered the best of the four high schools he attended. As usual his report card was covered with A's.

Posy, aged 10, attended the base elementary school. She was never the brain that John was, but her grades were always perfectly satisfactory. My only memory of that center of learning was a certain May Day celebration. Posy came home one day and told me she had to have a very elaborate costume and described it in detail. I dragged out the faithful sewing machine and worked like a beaver. When the costume was finished and I showed it to her, she said she didn't need it as she didn't have a partner for the May Pole dance. I was so disappointed, I told her to tell her teacher to find her a partner or she would rue the day. The next day Posy came home and said she had a partner. Mollified, I calmed down and attended the big event, anxious to see my talented daughter in my creation flying around the May pole. When I arrived at the school yard, there were a lot of poles and many groups dancing around them. Finally, I spotted Posy's class and walked over closer to observe better. Posy's partner joined her and he was 8 inches shorter than she and as black as the Ace of Spades. Technically, she did have a partner but I hadn't realized until then that the Navy was desegregated. I was shocked. My Southern blood boiled. Happily, it didn't seem to bother Posy one bit.

Bowie was five years old and attended a nursery school. There he learned to do the hula, fell in love with a beautiful little girl who could have made two of him, and graduated at the end of the year in cap and gown with a diploma. As part of the ceremony, he did a right nice hula dance.

Since Lamar was Chief-Of-Staff, we did a lot of entertaining and were very busy socially. The Harts expected us to attend all of their affairs; luncheons, dinners, receptions and luaus (Hawaiian picnics.) Politicians and journalists who came out to the Islands on junkets had to be entertained, as well as visiting military brass from other countries, VIP's from the States. I was a lady-in-waiting to Katherine, who might call me on the phone and ask me to come up to her quarters and zip up her evening dress. We were considered "family." I figured we were learning our job at a pretty good rate. Somehow the sheer fun of our service life was leaving us though, and we knew we better be treading carefully as the Selection Board would soon be breathing down our necks. This was getting to be serious business.

Always there was an undercurrent of suspicion that I could feel emanating from the "Inner Circle." They were pleasant enough to our faces (they had better be, Lamar outranked them) but we didn't trust them.

Of course, there were many other couples we knew in Makalapa, the residential division in Pearl harbor where we lived; some were old friends from other duty stations that we enjoyed immensely. We all learned to do the hula, we went to the beaches on picnics, worked with the Little Theater, played tennis, partied in the good Chinese restaurants, a few of us went painting under the aegis of a Chinese marine artist, doing seascapes on the beach, our easels lashed to big stones to keep them from blowing away. I could do all these things because I had a Japanese maid named Jeannette who lived in and baby-sat Bowie at night and after nursery school and cooked dinner and breakfast. From eight in the morning until 4:00 o'clock, she was a clerk at the post exchange in Pearl Harbor.

Every day, Jeannette brought us a present, something from the exchange. Usually it was chipped or part of a broken set, or put on the sale table for some unknown reason. Our house soon became filled with this junk but I was impressed with her generosity. No maid of mine had ever given me anything before. I didn't want to hurt her feelings by discouraging her gifts, so we displayed them prominently. She also bought herself a new blouse or skirt every day. This she would wear the following morning to work. Then it was washed and joined its sisters in an enormous heap in the corner of her bedroom, where it waited to be ironed. When we left Hawaii and Jeanette was packing up her things, that pile was stuffed into suitcases, as it was, still unpressed.

Jeannette was goodhearted and pleasant and she gained forty pounds she didn't need while she worked for us. I have seen her on occasion concoct eight large rice balls to take to work for her lunch. I never had a maid who didn't gain weight when she was in our employ.

The Korean War was in its final throes and Lamar was champing at the bit to go out and be a part of it. His forte was not being part of the palace guard and he asked his General repeatedly to let him go to Korea. After one year, Franklin said he would let him go. This chief-of-staff had not turned out to be a "yes" man. He wanted to get out where the action was and as soon as his replacement arrived, my husband flew off to the war zone.

I decided to stay in Hawaii while he was overseas. We moved into a Wherry housing apartment off the base. It was small, had three bedrooms and one bath. It would be home for the duration of my husband's duty in Korea. I must say, the Harts continued to be lovely to us and always included me in their social events. I never felt completely left out of the social circle but I had no duties and, subsequently, had more time to paint and do what I liked. My official duties were at an end.

Before Lamar left we went as a family to a Naval installation at the north end of Oahu for a day's outing. The beach was excellent and we had decided to have a picnic there. In the park area where the picnic tables and restrooms were located, there were some old concrete gun emplacements, and the children enjoyed playing around them. After we had eaten our lunch, I told the kids not to swim too soon as they might get cramps. They nodded their heads and scattered like marbles to do "their own thing."

The surf was wild that day and not many people were in the water. I spied Freckles, as we called him, walking in the surf and mentally noted that he would probably soon be in the water and I would keep an eye on him. There weren't more than five heads out there in the waves and I could check them periodically. After a few minutes I did a head check. I counted only five swimmers so I scanned them carefully and did not recognize my son's. I told Lamar I was going down closer to the water and see if I could spot Freckles. He was not concerned at first but soon became as alarmed as I when I verified that our son was not in the water. We started searching the camp, calling his name and asking everyone if they had seen a young boy with a lot of freckles in dark blue trunks. No one had seen him. By now I had decided he had drowned and I was mentally attending his memorial service at the Episcopal cathedral in downtown Honolulu. I felt I could not live through this tragedy; it was more than I could bear. I looked up and there he was, standing next to me, grinning. He had decided not to swim and had gone down into one of those gun emplacements to look around. Eventually, he heard someone calling his name and came out to find out what we wanted of him. I didn't recover for a week; imagination can be a terrible thing.

I remember two very nice vacations we had in the Islands. Once we flew in a little plane to the Island of Hawaii. The volcano had just erupted and it was a sight to behold, especially at night, as the orange river of melting lava wended its way down the mountain to the sea. There was a government camp on the Island and we had a cottage there for a week. Highlights of the trip were trekking across the lava fields, walking on the black sands caused by lava flowing down to the ocean. We took a trip to a rain forest where the vegetation was lush. There we swam in a mountain pool with orchids floating in it below a spectacular waterfall. Last but not least, was the sumptuous food in the dining room, three times a day. And there was the ubiquitous snack bar open every hour on the hour. The kids loved it.

The other vacation was at Bellows Field, an Air Station on the other side of the Island. There were cottages on the beach and we spent a Thanksgiving Week there. Our neighbors cooked their turkey Hawaiian style by wrapping it in Ti leaves and burying it under and over hot rocks. It didn't look very appealing, but it was certainly thoroughly cooked. I think we cooked ours traditional style. For a week we just loafed and swam in gorgeous weather and sunbathed on a perfect beach.

In those days of the early fifties, there were only two ways to travel by car to the other side of Oahu: one, go around the Island; the second was to drive up over the Pali, a high mountain where the early natives had tossed over their enemies in conflicts in the past. The view is spectacular from the summit.

I shall now recount two episodes that occurred during our stay at 1029 Reeves Street, Moana Loa, our Wherry Housing address. The first was the result of my answering an advertisement in some art magazine, offering a course in art by correspondence. I had to draw a copy of some image, send it to them and they would inform me if I had any talent. If I did, I would be eligible to enroll in their school. I thought I was talented but I wanted to hear them say it! I hadn't the slightest intention of taking any course. Boston is pretty far from Honolulu so I felt perfectly safe sending them my sketch.

A couple of months later, I was surprised when I answered the front doorbell and found a complete stranger standing there. He introduced himself as a representative from the Famous

Artists' School in Boston, MA. He asked to speak to Mary Curry. I said I was Mary Curry. I must have looked very surprised, but I couldn't think of anything to do except invite him in. He entered with alacrity.

I must tell you that Posy had a pet parakeet which had the run of the apartment; it was not caged as its wings were clipped and it could fly only short distances. Also, John had a castle of white mice which he kept out on the screened-in porch. He had been given express orders to keep those mice "in the castle." Since one of them had attacked the parakeet, they were not allowed the run of the porch. He disobeyed me and made an exit on the back of the mouse cage so his mice would not be so crowded and could roam the porch for their constitutionals. And his mother could not see how they were getting out of their house. The stage is set for the salesman's visit.

He went to his car and brought back some beautiful art books that covered the four-year course that I had been talented enough to qualify to enroll in. We sat side-by-side on the sofa as he explained how the course was set up. I told him I really didn't have time to take this, but he insisted on showing me one gorgeous book after book.

The front door burst open and Bowie and about four little friends traipsed in, demanding cookies. They found the cookie jar and armed with refreshments, surrounded us to "see the pretty pictures." Crumbs fell on the slick pages and the salesman and I both worried that the books would be grease-stained. In the middle of all this, Posy's parakeet flew down and landed on my lap. My visitor looked alarmed and jumped up. Then I saw him staring at the sliding doors to the porch. I turned and saw three white mice climbing up the screen. By this time, the parakeet had perched itself on his shoulder and tried to nibble his ear. His face was white as a sheet. He grabbed his books and said, "Mary Curry, I agree, you are too busy to take this course. Maybe in later years."

I never saw anyone leave as quickly as he did. I learned that day that you are never safe from the world of enterprise. He had certainly not come from Boston but very possibly California.

Anyway. I'm sure there was no representative in the Islands. At that time, Hawaii was not even a state yet.

I did continue to pursue my art education in Honolulu; I joined a still life drawing class offered by one of the instructors at the University of Hawaii. After two sessions, Professor Morella told me I was so advanced he wanted me to draw the human figure. Flattery will get you anywhere with me! He told me to come to his sculpture class and draw the model.

The next week, there I was and my professor told me to sit down front, five feet away from the model, who was a sailor making a few extra bucks and he looked scared to death. He was naked as a jaybird except for a discolored and very limp jockey-strap. His pose, decided upon by Morella, forced him to keep his hands clasped behind his head and perspiration was pouring down his face and chest He looked so ill at ease I felt very sorry for him. I was as embarrassed as he. As I sketched, he watched every stroke of my pencil. I made a point of not staring too closely at his crotch as he was my first nude model and I was embarrassed. After an hour, Morella came over to give me criticism. He seemed pleased with my drawing but told me the whole crotch area was too vague. The model and I out-blushed each other. I was told to hold my pencil out as a measuring tool. "Look! Measure! Be precise!"

I don't remember any other model, so I was probably nearing the end of our tour in the Islands. I did study painting earlier under John Young, a well-known marine painter, whose work I admired but couldn't afford to buy. The next best thing to purchasing a painting was to paint with him and learn how to get those special effects his works had. Painting on the beach in oils, using an easel that is weighted down with rocks so the wind won't capsize it, is quite a feat. I never got a "John Young" out of it, but I had a ball; art was becoming very important in my life.

The other event that was memorable was a crabbing expedition. The children and I would go out on a pier at Pearl Harbor with a bucket, a net, lots of string and old smelly fish-heads, scrounged from the butcher and reused over and over, the gamier the better. In between crabbing expeditions I would keep them in the freezer.

On this morning, I had taken the three children and we all had our strings hanging over the end of the pier, waiting for that enticing nibble that told you there was a crab on the end of it, munching happily on a delicate "tete du poisson." I don't remember whose line it was but the commotion on the end of it was terrific. Someone grabbed the net and it was lowered gently to encase the crab. When it was pulled up, there was an enormous Alaskan crab which filled the net! Wow! That was so unusual we ended our crabbing expedition and took our catch home to cook it. Our kitchen was tiny but I got the dishpan, filled it with water and put it on the stove to boil. The children disappeared, as usual, to do "their thing" but I couldn't wait to cook this beast so we could have crab salad for supper. Finally, the water boiled and I emptied the bucket's contents into the dishpan. Well, the crab found it too hot so he crawled out, flopped on the floor, his antennae wiggling threateningly. I knew those claws could take off a finger or a toe, so I hopped up on the kitchen counter and yelled out the window for help. Some man heard me and came running. The crab had backed himself into a corner ready for action and I stood on the drainboard, not knowing what to do next. The good Samaritan who had heard me yelling found a big brown grocery bag, urged the crab into it, closed the open end and plunged the whole thing into the boiling water. Unable to escape, our dinner expired, and allowed itself to be cooked for the recommended time. When it was cool, we picked out the meat and had enough crab to make a salad for eight people. That was a unique crabbing experience as we never did catch another Alaskan.

At Christmastime, a special boat would bring fir trees from the mainland. One had to meet it when it docked or the pickings were slim. I was among the first arrivals and asked for the biggest tree available. I got it and when it was delivered, three feet had to be sawed off before it would fit in our living room. That was great as we had enough greenery to make a wreath and decorate the whole house.

John was qualifying to be an Eagle Scout. He wanted to surprise and please his father when he came back from Korea.

The Rocky Years

This was pretty imminent as General Hart had alerted me that Lamar would be coming home a little early. He had orders to 29 Palms Marine Base in California as Commanding Officer. Franklin confided that this was a General's billet. We were all excited and, as usual, looking forward to our next duty station although we loved Hawaii.

John was enthralled with fireworks. They were easily available as the Orientals, so numerous in the Islands, use them in all of their celebrations. John and his friends could purchase them when they went into Honolulu to school. The night before Lamar was due to fly in to Pearl Harbor, we all went to the movies in Makalapa, to an outdoor theater not too far from where we were living. John and Bowie walked and Posy and I went in the car. John had some firecrackers (unbeknownst to his mother) and he told Bowie they would explode them after the movie, probably on the walk home as it was against the law to have them on the Base. I think these were called cracker bombs. You throw them and they explode on contact with whatever they hit. Bowie wanted to "just hold one" and finally John gave him one just to shut him up. All thru the movie, Bowie asked John repeatedly, "Now? Can I throw it now?" John told him to wait. "Not until the movie is over. I'll tell you when."

Finally, the film ended and the lights came on. The usual Marine Police were on duty to keep order and direct traffic. Suddenly there was a loud boom that sounded like a bomb going off. M.P.s arrived and closed in on John and Bowie who were down in front of the screen. They were immediately surrounded. I joined them reluctantly and acknowledged the culprits as my offspring. "Ma'am, we will have to take them down to the Police Station. You will have to come too."

Frantic, I said, "Their father is coming home tomorrow from Korea and this young man is to receive his Eagle Scout award. You can't arrest them."

I don't know who came to my aid but Lamar's rank and position served us well, and after a stern reprimand, my sons were released to me. On the way home, John kept shaking his head and saying, "What a dumb kid. He has to wait until the lights are on. In the dark, no one would have known who had thrown that cracker bomb."

My reply was that I didn't even know he had those fire crackers. Where did he buy them? Didn't he know it was against the base regulations to have them? It was definitely time his father came home!

The next day, Lamar returned and the Eagle Scout award took place as scheduled. I don't think we told him about the cracker bomb right away. We knew it would ruin his homecoming to hear his sons had been arrested.

Our orders to 29 Palms never materialized. They were changed and Lamar was ordered to Parris Island, South Carolina, as chief-of-staff to a General Silverthorn. We didn't care but I know Lamar did; this was not a General's billet. Everyone said this was just interim duty as Lamar would be made General in the fall.

We had to take the children out of school in the middle of the year. We would fly home on the Navy Mars plane and land in San Francisco in January, which complicated the clothes problem. None of the children had any winter clothes that fit them since we had been in Hawaii for two years. We would leave in Hawaiian cottons and I had sweaters and jackets for the children in a suitcase which I would take with me on the plane. It would be chilly in San Francisco and we had to wait there for our car to arrive on a transport. Lamar was in uniform and I had on seasonal dark clothes and a trench coat. We bid our friends farewell and took off on a long, overnight flight on a Mars plane, a Government aircraft, not too luxurious. The following morning as we prepared to land, my suitcase could not be found. It turned out that it had been left by accident on the runway in Pearl Harbor. My children would arrive in summer clothes to go by taxi to the Marine Memorial Club in San Francisco. They did, wrapped in blankets from the plane. We must have looked silly, getting out of that cab with flower leis up to our ears, Posy in a muumuu and Bowie in a pair of overall shorts.

We booked two rooms, left Posy and Bowie there in John's charge, and went out and bought them all winter clothes so we could go downstairs for dinner. I remember that stay as being a challenge to Lamar and me, keeping three children occupied in a hotel for at least a week. They took judo, used the exercise room and the pool, attended double feature movies, and they ate and ate and ate!

Finally, our car was delivered to us at the Memorial Club. We packed all of our gear and went down to the Hotel entrance to put it in the car for our cross-continent trip. Lamar opened the trunk and it was chock-a-block full of shells and driftwood, lovingly gathered on the beaches on Oahu over a period of two years. Lamar was so frustrated he began throwing it all out on the sidewalk while the rest of us wailed. Our gorgeous shells had to be discarded.

At last we got all our baggage in the trunk, all five of us in the car and we started on our trek across the continent again. A repeat of our trip two years previously. No time to sightsee, of course, just straight ahead and faster, the same way we had crossed the country to catch that transport. Parris Island, here we come! By this time, after a week at the hotel in San Francisco, our children had learned to look at the prices on the menu and then look at the entrees. The more expensive it was, that's what they ordered. One good thing was that John had a bottomless stomach. What the others couldn't eat on their plates, he finished off with gusto; not much was wasted. Posy says she gained 10 pounds on that trip and I believe it.

At last, we arrived at Beaufort, South Carolina and found we had a wonderful set of quarters. They were huge and very attractive. General and Mrs. Silverthorn were lovely people and we soon were enjoying our new duty. Lamar's position as chief-of-staff meant we had to entertain a great deal but the Officer's Club was a boon. The chef cooked items for me, sent me bartenders and waiters for receptions. I had a wonderful black cook who loved to entertain. She was thrilled when I told her we would be ten for dinner or that we would have fifty for cocktails.

We were "at home" one day a month and all newcomers called on us at that time. I remember one couple came every month. They were the first to arrive and the last to leave and they hovered over the buffet table the entire two hours. I know they were eating their dinner at my house so she wouldn't have to cook when she got home.

John went to a public school in Beaufort, where his teacher murdered the King's English. He yearned to be back in his beloved Punahou School in Honolulu. One day he was so fed up he started correcting his teacher's grammar. He did this several times and she finally blasted out at him and said, "John Curry, if you know so much, come up here and teach the class yourself!"

"I'd be glad to," said John, getting up with alacrity. Whereupon, he took over the class and taught the remainder of the period. This must have endeared him to that poor woman.

Bowie rode the base school bus. An airman always rode on the back to keep order and to protect the children getting on and off and crossing the street. One day at the lunch hour, Lamar and I noticed that the airman was approaching our porch with Bowie in tow. Lamar went to the door and the poor man was embarrassed to complain that he tried to get Bowie to sit down but he refused. "Sir," he said, "he refuses to obey me as he says his father is Chief-Of-Staff and I'm just a private." Lamar told the Marine he would discipline his son, which he proceeded to do with the help of a switch. How soon service children learn about rank! I was reminded of my own childhood and of how snotty I was. Bowie was barred from the bus for a week and I had to drive him to school and back.

Beaufort, South Carolina, is a charming town. It is old, full of lovely antebellum mansions, miraculously not destroyed by the Northern Army as they drove on to Charleston, which was an important seaport. The townspeople were lovely to the military personnel. We were wined and dined in elegance. I remember crab and shrimp feasts that were superb.

No one could have been nicer than General and Mrs. Silverthorn. They were both great Christians and encouraged the many chaplains of different denominations to hold joint Bible studies at their quarters. We often attended these and found all the different opinions refreshing and educational. The boot camp for raw Marine recruits is at Parris Island and the need for chaplains is obvious. Boots are very roughly treated and not all of them stay in the Corps. It's too tough.

The chief chaplain was a hypnotist and thus was useful to the dentists. So many recruits have bad teeth and need so much corrective work, they dread dental sessions; the chaplain would hypnotize them into feeling no pain.

One night he brought one of his good subjects to our quarters and we invited some friends to join us. The good minister put on quite a show. He put his subject to sleep and told him he would be unable to pick up one of my coffee tables. Then he awakened him and thanked him for his cooperation. After a few minutes, the chaplain offhandedly asked the young man to bring the little table over and sit it in front of him. The Marine jumped up and reached out to lift the table from in front of the fireplace. He couldn't pick it up. We looked and this 175 pound man was straining and perspiring. He couldn't budge it. Finally, the chaplain released him from his hypnotic state and requested again that he bring him the table. This time he carried it in one hand. He also was put to sleep and taken back to his childhood. At one point he was so young, he couldn't read a simple three letter word.

The chaplain said he would hypnotize us if we wished. I tried to let go but I was a lousy subject. He didn't succeed with me but he had better luck with some of our guests. Lamar wanted him to hypnotize me into liking butter! The chaplain told him that was a bad move; if I was psychotic, I might find something else to replace the butter and that was risky since it might be worse.

The Selection board met and to our astonishment and dismay, Lamar was not selected to General. We couldn't believe it. When the list was released, some of the newly selected were unbelievably poor officers. Other excellent officers had been passed over. What was going on? Eventually, word trickled down to us that this was all politics. Members of the board wanted their cronies selected and some of these candidates had more friends than Lamar did. It was as simple as that. No one could believe it. "Well," everyone said, "this will be rectified next year. Another board will set straight this fiasco and Lamar and these others will be picked up."

Our new C.O. was announced. He was a General Pollack whom we knew slightly from our Quantico days. He always carried his chief-of-staff with him as part of his personal baggage (Shades of Franklin Hart!) Lamar would have a new billet, which turned out to be the Amphibious Base at Little Creek, VA.

Soon we were packed up again and traveled up the East Coast in the hurricane, Carol. We spent the night in Wrightsville Beach, awed by the huge waves engendered by the high winds. The next day, we arrived at our destination and started a new life. Lamar would be chief-of-staff to a General Jack Horner. This was a Naval base, commanded by an Admiral. Here we would wait out the year until the next Selection board met and the terrible mistakes made this year were rectified.

What was memorable about that year? Our quarters were unusual; an old wartime hospital had been converted into five sets of housing. The General had the lion's share and Lamar and three other officers shared the remainder. As quarters they were pretty nice. There was a living room, dining room, kitchen, two baths and three bedrooms and a large screened-in porch They were nicely furnished and we had no complaints. The entire complex had communal corridors in the basement, lined with unused rooms, which we could claim if we wished. Posy had one for her dollhouse which Lamar had made for her in Maxwell Field. It was so big, it needed a room of its own. I chose one for an art studio and there I painted happily. Others we used for storage. Those corridors were a help to the children mostly. They skated back and forth between the apartments That was much faster than walking around the outside. And great in bad weather!

John was a sophomore in Princess Anne High School. It had to be better than the Beaufort one. He went out for basketball and attended every game, but I don't think he ever got to play. I have memories of picking him up late at night after the games. He always rode a city bus and was usually sitting on the curb, tired and discouraged, waiting to get home to bed. Posy attended sixth grade at an elementary school in Virginia Beach and was in love with horses. The highlight of her week was taking equitation lessons at a nearby stable with her new best friend, Jane Horner, the daughter of our General and boss. The rest of the week, the two girls wore bridles in their mouths and "rode one another." How? By galloping around, taking turns being the rider and holding the reins, which were on the head of the other!

Bowie went to a private school somewhere off the base. He hated to wear caps. Every day, he got in the station wagon that came for him, wearing a cap. Many days he returned bareheaded. Since the school had a policy that all children should have their heads covered out-of-doors, I spent my life buying caps, two or three at a time, so Bowie would not come home or go to school hatless. Eventually, the unforgivable occurred. He arrived home with a girl's scarf on his head. He was mad and his eyes were filled with tears. He got out, tore off that scarf and went storming into the house. All the other kids had laughed and teased him all the way home. Things like this seemed to happen to Bowie.

We were active in the Little Theater as usual. I was prop lady for one of the productions, a farce called, "My Three Angels." This was a period piece so some of the props were hard to come by. One item we needed was a wicker suitcase, popular a century ago. There was an officer's wife who had been in Hawaii with us who loved antiques and had a house full of them. I called her immediately and inquired if she had such an item. She told me that she didn't. I remembered we needed an old-fashioned black umbrella so I asked her if she had one of those, by any chance. There was a long silence and then she said, icily, "I had one in Hawaii but your little boy burned it up when he set fire to my garage."

I could have died. I remembered Bowie at the age of five and one of his friends had found some matches on the street and decided to burn something. The open garage facing them had some junk in it and they decided an old silk umbrella would do very nicely. So I had another pyromaniac on my hands. That poor woman never really liked me after that incident and I never asked her for any more props. She was childless and didn't understand the perils of parenthood.

Amphibious troops are called alligators. Little Creek was an amphibious base. The Commanding General's wife had to do something civic so she instigated a day center for the enlisted men's children and called it The Wee Gators. The Navy Relief Ball was to make money that year for the Center. Because I was an "artist," I was commissioned to sketch a Deep South Plantation and garden, the motif for the dance. I got carried away and sketched wisteria all over the place. What could be more Southern than wisteria? It turned out the Officers' Wives Club had to make the paper flowers for the decorations. Did you ever look closely at wisteria? It is made up of thousands, maybe millions of tiny lavender petals. We made paper wisteria blossoms until we went blind, all the wives scowled at me for months. We could have made gardenias much faster, or even better, magnolias, but Polly had sketched wisteria.

Eventually, the next year rolled around and another selection board met to rectify the mistakes made the year before. This time, the Commandant himself got into the act and instructed the members to select a certain candidate who was down the list. No one, period, was to be picked up who had been passed over the year before. The Commandant would be retiring this year and he wanted his colonel made general while he was still in a position to help him. Next year would be too late. He would be gone and he had no assurance another board would select his man. I swear I never knew that selection could be so political. Never again would I automatically consider high ranking officers the best in their group. My husband and several other excellent officers never got a shot.

Before long Lamar had orders to ROTC duty, a usual end-of-the-line billet. Having been passed over twice, he would be forced to retire with thirty years' service. We were going to Northwestern University in Evanston, Illinois. It would be our last tour of duty before retirement.

Lamar went west ahead of the rest of the family. Besides learning his new job and meeting all the faculty, he spent every spare minute house-hunting all summer, a discouraging pastime as everything the agents showed him was so expensive. Then he was lucky for he was offered a faculty house, located next to the university, practically on campus.

That summer, as I waited for news that we had a house to live in, I stayed with Mother and Boppie in Lexington and all three children went to different camps; Laolo, my mother, was not well enough to have children foisted on her routine. John at sixteen became a counselor at Camp Good News on Cape Cod, owned and operated by a Chaplain Wyeth Willard, Lamar's wartime chaplain in the Pacific. That was a memorable summer as John found the Lord, or better, the Lord found him. He became a dedicated Christian, the first member in our family to succumb to our Almighty Father completely. I take that back! Lamar was always a good Christian.

As John tells it, Camp Good News was an evangelical tool dedicated to saving souls of children, many from the slums. Normal children from middle class families were sprinkled liberally among them and paid high enough fees so the "dead end kids" got a free ride. All campers were evangelized equally. John was assigned a tent full of boys to supervise and teach, among other subjects, the Bible. At one point, he was teaching the ethics of a Christian life and one little boy asked him if he was a Christian. John assured him he was. Whereupon the moppet asked him why he didn't live like one. John was floored; he thought he did. This started him thinking about how he must be falling so short of the mark that this boy thought he was a pagan. He resolved to live every moment of the day for a month as a true Christian. He soon discovered he couldn't do it for a full day. It was the beginning of Wisdom for him and this son of mine started on his road to dedicating his life to Christ. By the time he joined us at the end of the summer, he had decided to be a missionary.

Posy attended a camp run by two elderly Southern ladies. It was a disaster for her as they gave demerits for leaving the cabin barefooted and for buttering a biscuit without first breaking it. The Girl Scout camps she had attended before didn't care if she ever wore shoes and as for the buttering the biscuit bit, even at home our manners were not as strict as that. This was sort of a "finishing school camp" and Posy was miserable. She developed a horrible case of boils and the authorities wouldn't even let her swim. Betty and I went to see her on visitors' day at the end of the first two weeks, and she had hysterics when she saw us. She seemed so frightened of doing the wrong thing. How I hated leaving her there, but I knew Mother was not well enough to have any child around as a steady diet. The worst part of my farewell was the knowledge that I wouldn't see her for another two weeks. The road up the mountain was so rut-filled and rocky, Betty was terrified that her station wagon would get bogged down in the mud. She vowed not to come back until we had to retrieve her at the end of camp.

Bowie, too young to go to camp for any extended period, also spent six weeks at a boys' camp called Camp Nimrod. He was just out of second grade and he must have been homesick. He was a good trooper though, like the other two, but he was awfully glad to see us when visitors' day rolled around and we went to see him. I remember he was in a swimming meet and won a blue ribbon for swimming under water the entire length of the pool. I think he was close to drowning. Everyone watching was amazed that he could hold his breath that long; he wanted so much to please us.

My summer was a piece of cake; Betty and I played every day, often including Laolo, picnicking with friends, shopping, cooking, berry picking, mushroom hunting, going to an occasional movie. Buffy always went his own way, fishing, hunting beaver, talking to cronies downtown, writing to politicians to complain about everything. He managed to be around the house a lot too. He ground his own wheat and cornmeal, made biscuits hard as nails, put up peaches and wine berries, cooked up some of his favorite messes and put up with his sister-in-law who drove him up the wall with her smoking and cracked ideas about spending money. Worst of all, I was a true women's libber. He thought I was a bad influence on Betty and I guess I was. She was always so intimidated by him and I tried to put starch in her soul by urging her to stand up to him in arguments. I succeeded for only very short periods; her feistiness soon evaporated in his presence.

I was still a confirmed churchgoer, so I sang in the summer choir at R. E. Lee Memorial Episcopal Church, where the minister, Tom Barrett, was a jewel of a preacher. No one in the Letcher family attended church for the National Church had desegregated and Buffy had resigned as a warden in disapproval. Out, Sunday School! Out, Young People's Group! Out, Sunday Service! And most of all, out all monies in pledges!

With the end of summer, our family group was reunited and we left Virginia for our first foray into the great unknown midwest. All our lives we had lived on either one Coast or the other, barring duty in foreign lands As usual, we looked forward to our new duty station. Evanston, Illinois, here we come!

11

Interlude In Indiana

When we arrived in Chicago, we drove along Lake Michigan Drive, looking out at the Lake, at the whitecaps, whipped up by the ubiquitous wind that gives the city its name, the Windy City. The traffic was so horrendous that I informed the three Curry cubs in the backseat that they better get a good look at the landscape as they might not see it again until we left Evanston for good in two years. Coming from a town of 9000 people in Virginia, those eight lanes of cars traveling at sixty miles an hour really cowed me. Lamar, thank goodness, was accustomed to the ways of the big city, having lived in its environs for a few months, and he drove like a "pro." When we reached the outskirts of Evanston, there was no letup in the pace or number of vehicles; the traffic was no better. The sound of the screech of brakes, demolishing the tires, will always be the theme music of our stay in Evanston. I was going to have to learn how to drive all over again.

Lamar drove us by our new domicile so we could see what it looked like. It was most unimpressive. Lamar had said it wasn't much to look at but the location was perfect, being right on Long Field, where so many of the university's sporting events took place and all the pep rallies were held. Northwestern University skirts Lake Michigan and the college gymnasium was directly across the street from our house. Lamar could easily walk to his office, and an excellent elementary school was located three blocks away from our house so Bowie could walk there. If location was the most important thing about a house, then 618 Lincoln Street would be perfectly satisfactory!

But the house was ugly! Three stories high, grey stucco with a front porch open to the weather and a flight of concrete steps leading up to it. There was a parking lot on the Lake Shore side of the house and three or four better-looking residences on the other. We're not snobs but we had lived in more attractive houses. There were no shutters or window boxes to soften that stark grey look. There was a small garage at the end of an overgrown driveway at the rear of the house, but no car of that era would ever fit in it. That was not a first for us; the garage of our atrocity in Barcroft was of the same vintage.

We had been invited to spend the first night with an Admiral and Mrs. Anderson, who had befriended Lamar during the summer. The Admiral and his wife lived in a huge house not far from our location and we somberly drove there.

They were lovely people and we appreciated their hospitality. Lamar told me their only child had entered the Navy as an ensign during the Second World War and was mortally wounded in action. His father's ship happened to be nearby and the boy was taken there and died in his father's arms. Such a sad story. I had been so blessed. I had husband, father, brother and brother-in-law in the Pacific for four years and they had all come home, not one even wounded although Boppie had come home with malaria. The master bedroom in that lovely house had TWO antique four-poster beds, one for each of our hosts. And they were huge beds. The spaciousness of that bedroom impressed me mightily.

The next day we moved into our house. Our household effects had arrived and we unpacked everything. Since this was an unfurnished house, the first we had ever occupied except for the Barcroft and Cameron Mills in Alexandria ones, we made an estimate of what we would need in the way of furniture. The list was formidable. We had no dining room table, chairs or buffet; no sofa, tables, rugs or mirrors. We had enough beds but we needed dressers and chests of drawers. We planned to attend auctions but a good friend of Lamar's, Dean Bill Bradford and his wife, Cissy, said the way to buy furniture in Evanston was to attend house sales, garage sales, and frequent the Salvation Army. They had furnished a 22-room house that way.

I was bewildered but Cissy and two of her friends, Dorothy Desposito and Joan Evans, attended these sales weekly and they would be glad to take me along.

So began a lasting friendship and a moneysaving hobby. Every Thursday these two would study the paper and since they knew the area, they would check the good neighborhoods for interesting items and off we would go, looking for bargains. They knew their merchandise too and did not let me pay too much for something that caught my eye.

My first purchase was a sofa. Cissy talked me into it as it was a "Colby," whatever that was. The price was $90 but she said that was too much. She offered them $30, which they refused. Cissy gave them my telephone number and told them to call me if they changed their minds which they did that evening. It was mine for $30! Someone with a truck picked it up and delivered it to us. I had it recovered to suit my decor and I kept it until we left Indiana fifteen years later, when I gave it to Posy. As Cissy said, "It was good goods."

From the Salvation Army store I bought a 52-inch round solid mahogany pedestal table with six leaves in a case on rollers to store them and the store threw in six or eight caned dining room chairs. The price? $80! Another buy was a scratched and scarred bureau for $12. Cissy said the hardware on it was worth more than that. I painted it white and antiqued it and it was quite handsome. Little by little we furnished that ugly house.

Posy and Bowie had their own rooms, Lamar and I had ours and John had the third floor to himself: two bedrooms, one which he used as his study, and a private bath. He called the third floor his eyrie. Another bedroom on the second floor was our T.V. room where we lolled on that atrocious blue daybed I had bought way back in Washington after the war. All house guests had to sleep on it, unfortunately. Four of us shared a bath, complete with a tub with claw feet and a rinky-dink shower with a canvas curtain. In defiance, I painted those claw feet nails bright blood red. Outside the bathroom window was a ladder attached to the ledge so we could escape if the place caught on fire. It was probably installed by the university to comply with local fire regulations.

Another purchase we made was an old upright piano which we bought from the ROTC Department, of which Lamar was the boss. It cost $20 and that was about its worth. The sounding board was cracked so it wouldn't hold its tuning but we didn't know that when we bought it.

For All Our Days

We discovered that Evanston was a very materialistic place. It is on the Gold Coast and money was King! Our friends considered our house pretty awful. Posy, a sophomore in high school, brought a friend home to spend the night and she never came back. Bowie was in a Cub Scout patrol and his third grade friends were ashamed to come to our house for meetings. John never brought friends home. He was considered weird because he rode a bike to school; every other senior had a car. Evanston High School was a super school but the students were snobs. Posy was looked down on because her sweaters were not cashmere; this was our first sortie into a civilian world and it was a shocker; we were learning that service people had different values. Washington DC, where we had been stationed, was unique in that so many government people lived there. Not having much money was common in that area.

Lamar and I survived OK because he was head of a department at Northwestern and that gave him social clout. The university embraced us in spite of our lack of money as the Navy contingent always lived as poorly as we. They understood. We were entertained, reciprocated and were part of the scene. We had no complaints.

Our poor kids were struggling to make their way. John and Posy did pretty well; John's scholastics were so impressive, even Evanston High took notice. At our first Parents' Night, every one of his teachers sought us out to rave over his performance; each instructor insisted that our son must major in the subject that particular teacher was instructing. Lamar and I were amazed that John could do so well in such an excellent school as he had made so many changes. This was his fifth high school in four years.

Our Posy was being noticed also. Her artistic talents had been spotted, she was a member of the Ravinia choral group that sang with the Symphony, and she had made the water ballet. And she was beautiful! And her grades weren't bad either. She was doing OK except her sweaters came from Sears.

Poor Bowie, he was having his troubles. He was the new kid on the block and he had attracted a bully. Every morning and evening this creep would wait for him and harass him as he walked to and from school. Our son didn't tell us or we would have taken care of the situation. Instead, he suffered in silence and tried to fend off the bully by himself.

One afternoon, a woman called me on the phone and asked me if I had a little boy about eight years old. I said I did and asked her why she wanted to know. She asked me if he was wearing a red sweater and Navy blue pants. When I said he was, she told me he was hiding in her garage and wouldn't come out. She gave me her address, right across Long Field, and I dashed over and retrieved him. My poor son had been suffering for weeks and hadn't told us a thing. When we notified the school, the bully was identified, he was chastised and the trouble stopped.

Bowie was in a school of overachievers and he was having a struggle. Eventually, the school told me they thought he needed psychiatric help. We took him to Great Lakes Naval Hospital and the doctors told us he checked out perfectly normal; his parents must be sick!

Next, the doctors discovered Bowie had a slight curvature of the spine and recommended we take him to a specialist in Chicago; he might have to wear a brace.

A doctor was selected and we made an appointment with him. On the appointed day, it was raining cats and dogs so he wore his new yellow slicker. We took the subway into the city where we had to change cars, so we went down the stairs to the platform and waited for the car that would take us into the inner city. Finally it arrived. I opened the door, jumped in, turned to Bowie to take his hand and he was out of reach. The door snapped shut and I sped away, leaving my moppet all alone. I was frantic! There was no attendant on the car, but all the passengers gave me the same advice. I was told to get off at the next station, run up the staircase, come down the other side, catch the next car going in the opposite direction, get off at the first stop and hopefully, I would see that yellow slicker! He would be across the tracks but I could tell him to wait there and that I would come and get him. I did all that and when I stepped out of the car, there he and a policeman were waiting for me. The policeman had anticipated my actions and had taken Bowie up the stairs and over to the opposite side. My son was perfectly calm, but I was a wreck. When we arrived at the doctor's office, that gentleman said Bowie was too young to fit with a brace. End of diagnosis! Returning home, I never, never let go of Bowie's hand until we got in our car. We never went to Chicago again!

Being the "perfect" mother I was, I always attended PTA meetings and usually ended up being a home room mother for all three of my children's classes. Bowie's school was a small one, with only 250 students. I attended the first PTA meeting right after school opened in September. The main subject that evening was the yearly school musical which would be produced in the spring. There were about thirty people in the auditorium and I couldn't help wondering where the actors would come from. I thought, doesn't a musical take a lot of talented people?"

The assembled multitude was told to submit original scripts and songs! I thought they should have their heads examined. What did they expect?

Well, I could hardly wait to go back the next month and find out what was happening. Those parents submitted five original scripts and 80 *original songs!* This was not your ordinary PTA group; these people were Evanstonians, most of them outstanding in their respective fields. I was told later that the school never had to go outside their organization for a guest speaker; these children were the offspring of giants.

Finally, a script was chosen and there were tryouts for the parts. Yes, I tried out for the chorus. I'm a ham! The next morning someone called and asked me to play the *lead!* All I could say was, "But she's an 18-year-old and I'm forty-five!"

"That doesn't matter," she said.

"Well, it does to me. I refuse, but I'll be glad to be in the chorus."

Actually, the lead was played by a 55-year-old and she did very well. She had a strong voice and was so petite she could fit into a dress, donated by one of the group, worn by Elizabeth

Taylor in "Giant." She wore a wig which concealed her nearly white hair. She got away with playing the part very well!

I am always impressed by people who do things well and that play was as good as The Music Man which had not yet surfaced on Broadway. I had one line in the play and we never rehearsed it. On opening night, I stepped forward at the appointed time and said with a great deal of conviction, "Abbie, you forgot your lox bunch!" Whereupon I handed her a small wicker basket containing her box lunch. Mother later told me she had a one-liner in a play once where she took three steps forward and said, "A very wise decision." *She* didn't flub hers, either!

That winter John caught some kind of flu or virus. We called a local doctor and he prescribed some fancy antibiotic. Instead of curing him, it made him desperately ill as he was evidently allergic to the drug. All of the membranes in his mouth and down his throat sloughed off. His temperature soared and we were frightened to death. Lamar called an enlisted man who worked in his office and the two of them got him to the emergency room of the Great Lakes Naval Hospital where the doctor immediately admitted him. The next day I went to see him. He was in a ward with a lot of enlisted men. The medicos had stripped him naked and packed him from head to toe in ice, to bring down his temperature. It was the first time I had seen my first-born naked since he was seven years old, male modesty being what it is.

Poor John. He was sick for about six weeks. When he was out of danger, we worried about his school work and grades. When I called his teachers, they told me not to worry about his assignments and projects. He had entered the Westinghouse Scholarship contest and he was worried about making some sort of box, I think, to take pictures *in the dark!* They told me, "Just get him well."

Eventually, he was well enough to return to school. Nothing seemed to have suffered; his scholastic standing did not change. He received word he had won a Westinghouse Scholarship and would go to Washington that spring to compete with the other winners for placement: All the winners would receive money prizes. We asked him if he had done the experiment and he admitted he hadn't. However, he was sure it would work.

I never knew what John would say or do. One night on the way to church, he asked me if he could drive. I said I would be thrilled to let him drive when he got his license. Whereupon he pulled a license out of his wallet and said, "Will this do?" On his own, with his own money he had been taking lessons without telling us. That was typical of John; he was so independent and he liked to spring things on us.

He began to get a lot of publicity from the Westinghouse contest. Colleges sent him brochures and he was offered scholarships frequently.

About this time he had to register for the draft. Since he wanted to be a medical missionary, he declared himself a conscientious objector. He was called to plead his case with the authorities. He was positively gleeful; he could hardly wait for the appointed hour. When he appeared, he convinced them and was declared non-fodder for war. I think he was safe anyway as long as he was in college making good grades; good students were not being drafted.

Lamar and John stayed up all one night making that darn black box for the trip to Washington. He was supposed to demonstrate how it worked. It never occurred to us that it wouldn't work. John's brain was so much smarter than ours, how could we doubt him?

He went to Washington and conquered. He won fourth place and a sizable scholarship. I still don't know if he ever demonstrated that black box or if it did or did not work!

Since he was a Christian and was considering being a missionary to China, he was intrigued with Brandeis University in Massachusetts which was 78% Jewish. He was challenged by the opportunity of being a "minority" student. They snapped him up and he requested "foreign" roommates. He got his wish. The school billeted him with a group of Asians and Africans in a castle of their own.

With John off at college, we rented the third floor to various Northwestern students. One was named Wally Cox and looked exactly like the movie star by that name, except our student was twice as tall. He was shy, never opened up to us and we hardly ever saw him. Another was a Mexican named Francisco who was just as elusive. Once a week I would change their sheets and towels and do little else. Cissy, who had students on her third floor, told me she just collected the dirty sheets at the top of the steps and left the clean ones for her lodgers to hassle. I soon discovered I would make a terrible boardinghouse madam; I hated working for other people. It was demeaning. Those two students' lodging fees paid our rent so I put up with feeling demeaned.

The second winter Posy wanted to learn to drive but had no free time at school. We decided to let her go to a driving school in Evanston. I took Posy down to the school which was located right in the middle of Evanston. When I went to pick her up, she looked awful. I asked her what was troubling her and she told me the instructor had seated her in a car, explained where the brakes, clutch, starter were located. Then he asked,

"Do you have any questions?"

"No," she said.

"OK, let's go." He said.

Thereupon, she had hysterics. The thought of driving out that door into all that traffic when she had never driven in her life before threw her into a panic.

He began again and took her through the instruction much more slowly and she learned to drive very well.

That summer Bowie went to Boy Scout Camp. It was up in Michigan so we decided to go up and visit him after he had been there one week. I think John had returned to Cape Cod for the second time to be a counselor at his beloved Camp Good News. Papa, Posy and I arrived at the camp and were directed to

Bowie's tent. It had rained all that week and we found him sitting on a wet bed in wet clothes with a drippy nose. He couldn't find the key to his trunk so he had been wearing those same wet clothes for a week, sleeping in a wet bed every night! Why he wasn't dead, I'll never know. I don't believe an adult had checked that tent or its occupants once! Lamar was furious. He broke the lock on the trunk, got Bowie into dry clothes, stripped the bed and we took everything down into a small town where there was a Laundromat. There we washed and dried sheets, blankets, pillow and his *filthy* clothes.

Lamar and John had such good experiences with the Scouts, he couldn't believe a scout camp could be that bad. We had rented a cabin for the night so we took Bowie there with us, giving his mattress a little time to dry out. We didn't like leaving him another week, but we thought it might be worse for him if we brought him home. It would be one more failure in his life so we reluctantly left him. He survived the second week all right.

Bowie was singing in our Episcopal Church Boys' choir. He was paid money and it was serious business. The choirmaster took boys if they could read the words of the anthems and hymns and carry a tune. This Bowie could do. Thus started a long career for him singing in church and school choirs.

That Christmas Eve when we went up to Communion at the Midnight Service, Bowie, sitting in the front choir stall, looked at me and didn't know me even when I touched him and smiled. He was out like a light, asleep with his eyes open.

This was Evanston, so the parishioners of the church were mostly wealthy Gold Coast residents. When we had our annual bazaar, some of the items were so valuable we had to have police officers to guard the place and direct attendance; only fifty people were allowed in the parish house at a time. We had fur coats, silver and gold items and, one year, a car in good condition.

This year I was assigned to the jewelry table. Someone more knowledgeable than I had appraised the stuff and everything was marked. Three of us stood ready to take in the money. The first batch of customers was released by the police inside the parish hall. We soon had a crowd around our table. Right in front of my eyes, two women at opposite ends of the merchandise table had grabbed a gold bracelet. They argued, they refused to let go of the bracelet and we had to call the police to break it up. The women turned out to be two dealers who had spotted a "real find." Both were escorted to the door and the bracelet had its price raised.

When Lamar and I celebrated our 25th Wedding Anniversary in Evanston, we invited the Navy contingent and their wives and some close friends to dinner. We bought a case of champagne and the 18 or 20 of us polished it off. We drank it before, during and after dinner and no one got tipsy. What a wonderful way to celebrate. We all felt so witty and clever, so sharp! Bowie came downstairs and formally went around and greeted each guest. Later, someone told me he was wearing large white gloves on his feet. With all that champagne under my belt, I never noticed!

The Baron Von Lupin, German attache to Chicago, and his wife, our next-door neighbors, became our close friends. Their neighbors, on the other side of their residence, were a Baptist preacher and his family. They disapproved of all the liquor that the von Lupins served at their parties. Once, when the Baroness' maid was ill, she put a slew of empties in a wheel barrow and carted them down to the alley behind our houses. She was mortified to see her neighbor spying on her behind a curtain.

Once the von Lupins took us as guests to the theater in Chicago to hear the Heidelberg Chorus. We sat in a box and in the adjoining one was a woman that I was sure I knew; her face was so familiar. We chatted and I told her I was sure we had met somewhere but I couldn't remember the occasion. She asked if we had lived in Germany and I said, "No." I asked her if she had lived in France, Hawaii, or La Jolla? "No," she said. Mostly she had lived in Chicago. Finally we gave up.

That night, after the concert and we were back home, I turned on the telly for the late news. There was my theater neighbor, broadcasting her evening report. My TV was a black and white one so her red, red hair did not show up. I watched this woman's program regularly and had always thought her hair was brown. I felt like a ninny, not recognizing her when we were face to face. I imagine this happens a lot to celebrities. They get accosted by strangers because they look familiar. Wasn't she nice to play along with me!

At Christmastide, the von Lupins invited us for lunch and in our honor they lit all the little candles on their tree. They would never have used electric lights; candles were traditional in Germany. As soon as we admired them, they extinguished them right away. They lit them for very short times only.

That Christmas we sent to Maine and had fresh lobsters flown in for our Christmas dinner. It was expensive but fun! I have a snapshot of the whole family, wearing lobster bibs, pigging out.

I was still taking art lessons. This winter I was working with a portrait painter. He would not allow us to use any earth colors on our palette. That left purple, green, blue, orange, alizarin red and maybe, lemon yellow. From these wild colors, we had to mix skin and hair tones. It was a challenge, but I discovered you can arrive at brown and black if you mix enough colors.

Besides being head of the ROTC, Lamar was attending classes and working on a Master's Degree in mathematics. He would be forced to retire at the end of this tour of duty and he had to earn a living doing something. He had always enjoyed teaching and mathematics was the subject most in demand at that time. Not Lamar's favorite, but he did very well and was offered a job at Culver Military Academy in Culver, IN.

We made a trip there and were sufficiently pleased with the school and faculty to decide we would go there in retirement. One problem! Posy would be a senior in high school and Evanston had chosen her for a special course in Art at the Chicago Institute of Art. We had some counseling and were told, "Children are always better off with their parents than staying with friends." Some of our friends had invited her to live with them that senior year. Posy would be allowed to attend the military school, one of five girls with five hundred boys!

Just before we went to Culver to be interviewed and "looked over," Lamar and I had a shock. We had received a letter from the Dean of Students at Brandeis University, telling us our son, John, would not be welcome back at school the following year. Why? He was a very fine student, getting exceptional grades but he was proselytizing all the Jewish students, trying to convert them. "Brandeis considered itself a nonsectarian, interdenominational institution and John was a discordant element" the Dean wrote.

We were so shocked we went to see our minister and asked him for advice. He told us our son would have no trouble getting into any Christian college in the United States; anyone would love to get him. That was small comfort to us. Our wonderful son was under some sort of cloud and we were miserable. Finally, Lamar wrote Dean Hazelstein and asked him to give us a detailed account of these incidents that had resulted in his dismissal as a student. Very quickly, a Dean with a different name wrote Lamar that there was no Dean Hazelstein at Brandeis. He was confounded at these charges and he had called our son into the office and asked him who he thought would have done anything as dastardly as this. John said that he had. He had stolen some paper with the Dean's letterhead, he had written the letter himself. If anyone would examine the original closely, the date would be self-explanatory. It was dated April First! What a guy is my son John!

Culver beckoned. We told Posy there was a Black Horse Troop there and she could ride horses as much as she liked. In another year, Bowie would be eligible to be an 8th-grader cadet. We looked forward to our future. Being attached to a military school, Lamar was expected to wear his uniform and the school would have a military ambiance.

The Culver experience was interesting. We lived in faculty housing, a duplex two-story apartment that was situated in Faculty Circle. There were four or five single homes, and we shared our duplex with the Zetty family, the school's choral director, his wife and three little girls. There was also a six-apartment building in this Circle, occupied by faculty members. It was a little like living on a Base. Across the road was the school, a complex of beautiful red brick buildings, set in an attractively landscaped area. It was more impressive than many colleges I had seen: a lovely chapel, a large auditorium; a huge gymnasium; different classrooms and dormitories; a medical infirmary, extensive stables, a parade ground, a riding hall. All of this was on Lake Maximkukee, where the Naval cadets studied navigation in the summer months. The school even owned a three-masted schooner. Evidently, a lot of money had been poured into this institution of learning.

The town of Culver was minuscule. The shopping section was two or three blocks on one street. There was an elementary school which Bowie attended the first year we lived there. There was a weekly newspaper and I bought everything we ate at an A&P. We were living in the "sticks" and the worlds of the school and the town were miles apart.

The Culver cadets came primarily from wealthy midwest families. True, some boys were on scholarships but many had been born with the proverbial silver spoon tucked in their mouths. It cost as much to attend Culver as to go to an Ivy League college. Scholastically, it was excellent. If a student was poor in a subject or not too terribly motivated, he would get a lot of individual attention and tutoring. The boys' parents got their money's worth.

Posy was having an unforgettable experience. She was attending classes, usually the only female in the classroom, she was pretty and attractive, and the boys loved it. All doors were opened for her, her books were carried, her coat held for her, and wonder of wonders, she had a crush on a cadet, a Big Man on Campus, who seemed equally in love with her. Along with all this, she was chosen to sing the female lead in the musical, "Oklahoma," the school's dramatic production of the year. Those five faculty daughters came in handy in a situation like theater.

Posy was doing well in her scholastics, too. Her art instructor, a sculptor, thought she was terrific, and her English teacher was so impressed with her creative writing, he insisted she major in English in college. But that role in "Oklahoma" put her on the map. Her drama coach, Bill Martin, must have been a genius. She acted well, she sang like a bird, and she looked beautiful. The production was so outstanding, the Board of Trustees was flown in for a special showing. Her performance was outstanding!

Incidentally, all those horses bored her to death; she had discovered *boys*. We decided to enter Bowie in Culver Military Academy the next year. He would live at home with us but he would be a cadet. He would get a much better education.

Posy graduated and was accepted at all three colleges to which she had applied. One, Washington University in St. Louis, MO originally tore up her application when they received it. A girl from Culver Military Academy? Culver finally contacted them and they apologized. By now she had changed her mind and wanted to go to Cal. Tech. because her boy friend was going there.

That summer she worked as a waitress at the Culver Inn, making enough money to go out and visit him in California. His family had invited her and she was very excited about going. That trip was a disappointment. Posy came home so disheartened, she really had little interest in going anywhere. We persuaded her to try Indiana U. for a year; if she didn't like it, she could transfer. She was not sorority-minded but the campus was so huge, she had to join one just to belong to something. She wanted a degree in art and got one, but she wasn't prepared to get a decent job when she graduated. Lamar and I should have helped her more but we didn't know it at the time. On the rebound from her boy friend, she became involved with a most unsatisfactory man who dominated most of her time. She went to summer school her last year so she could graduate in January and get married. Fortunately, she saw the light and changed her mind before we made wedding plans.

John, at Brandeis, sent us one of his roommates, a Nigerian named Azuka, who was on his way to a summer job in the Midwest. We agreed to the visit and awaited nervously the young African's arrival. John had encouraged us to invite the faculty to see Azuka's slides and hear his lecture about his homeland. John alerted us he had a native costume and he could wear that if he liked. We invited some of the more liberal instructors and their wives to come to a soiree and meet Azuka. There were no black students at Culver.

I mentally visualized a tall, majestic black, wearing a colorful turban and a bright African print. He was the son of the Finance Minister so I was unprepared when I opened the front door to a very small, very black young man in a short-sleeved white shirt and blue jeans, carrying a large suitcase, which I recognized as the one we had given John for Christmas. This was Azuka!

Since he expected to give his lecture in the clothes he was wearing, after dinner, I suggested he wear his "costume." He agreed with alacrity, went upstairs and soon reappeared wearing what looked like flowered pajamas. Not much improvement.

Guests started to arrive and conversation was difficult as Azuka had quite an accent. Finally, we settled down and the slide show began. There was no sound track and our houseguest made no remarks so the guests would venture a question now and then. Such as,

"What is that a picture of?"

"Oxen drawing a cart."

"Where is it, Azuka?"

"I don't know. It is not in my country."

These exchanges were quite frequent. Someone had given Azuka these slides and he knew nothing about them. Finally, the show was over and everyone could get up and drink coffee and eat cookies. People were nice to him, and the chaplain even invited him to come and talk to some of the cadets the following evening. He did, wearing his flowered pajamas, which John called, his "clown suit." One little aside. When John came home for Christmas, he was carrying an old beat-up cardboard suitcase that had to be tied shut with some cord. We asked him, "How come?" and he said he and Azuka had traded suitcases because Azuka's books were so heavy, the cardboard one would have broken open. I wasn't as Christian as my son. We were always so poor, paying for three kids in school, it had been a real hardship to buy that luggage for John. Such are the experiences of parenthood.

The following fall, Bowie became a Culver cadet. He was a member of the choir, played the cornet in the band, taught himself to play the guitar, acted in the musical "Guys and Dolls," where he displayed good acting ability. Culver saw that he was accepted at a respectable college, Trinity in San Antonio, Texas. We couldn't ask for more.

We stayed at Culver for four years. In that time, Lamar taught math, counseled a company of cadets, coached the company football squad, taught math in the summer schools.

Lamar had a student named Baker who seemed pretty dense about math. Patiently, Lamar explained some concept to his class but poor Baker never seemed to grasp it. One day he told the young man, "Baker, if I ask you this one more time and you can't answer me, I am going to shoot you."

A week later, the class was having a review. Lamar knew Baker would not be prepared so he brought to school a toy pistol, loaded with blanks, which he had hidden under his desk. When he arrived at the concept that Baker had trouble with, he looked right at him and asked, "Well, Baker, do you know the answer?"

The cadet blushed and shook his head. Whereupon Lamar reached into his desk, pulled out the pistol, aimed it at Baker and fired. The boy looked petrified as he thought his instructor was really shooting him. Then everyone laughed. A month later, poor Baker committed suicide. Lamar felt terrible. This poor kid had real problems, about which Culver knew nothing.

That spring, the maintenance crew put raised concrete bumps in the road that ran through our housing area. This was to discourage the cadets with cars from speeding in that part of the campus. We occupants didn't like them so we just drove around them on the grass. The school retaliated by putting huge rocks at either end of these bumps so we couldn't drive around them. Easter was in the offing so we fought back. Posy, Carter Bays, the son of one of our neighbors, Lamar and I obtained some latex paint in many colors from the Theater Department and, come Easter Eve, about midnight, we painted those huge rocks. Lamar had made a Bugs Bunny out of plywood, painted it and stuck some carrots in his paw. Then he made a sign to nail above his head which said, "What's up, Doc?"

Easter dawned and the world awoke. There were all those rocks looking like Easter eggs. No one ever found out we had done the mischief. Someone in the apartments said she saw a light in the Currys' house about 2:00 a.m. Maybe we had done it. Everyone roared with laughter at the idea of General Curry doing anything that undignified. It took quite a while for that paint to wear off. When we moved the next year, there were still traces of it.

The next year we moved into a different faculty apartment, the second-story of a big Victorian house on the Lake. We called it our tree house. The windows were so enormous and the house was so light, everywhere we looked, there was a vista of tree branches with glimpses of the lake. It was beautiful and quite secluded. The rooms were spacious and after that little cracker box in Faculty Circle, we were luxuriating in the openness of our living quarters.

The chaplain at Culver, heard that the Bishop of Southern Indiana, John Craine, was looking for an administrator. He investigated and soon my husband was invited to come to Indianapolis to be interviewed. We were invited to have dinner at the Country Club so they could observe us and decide whether we were suitable. We evidently passed the test and Lamar told General Spivey we would be leaving right after graduation that June. He was extremely nice and told us Bowie could finish and attend his senior year at "faculty rates" the next fall. That was a godsend as we dreaded putting our son in a public school in a big city after the excellent teachers he had at Culver.

We went house-hunting in Indianapolis. We were looking for a three or four bedroom house on a bus route (I was planning to go to art school and get a BFA.) I knew the winters were treacherous in Indiana and I was a sissy about driving in ice and snow. I might settle for three bedrooms but nothing less than that! We were soon discouraged as the houses we were shown were so dull and they all looked like railroad cars. One day I told Lamar to go out with his good Episcopalian agent and I would try someone else. An agency sent me out with a woman who soon discovered I wanted a not-the-run-of-the-mill property. She took me to see an attractive modern bungalow with all kinds of perks. It had been a "Home Show" house, built to show off a lot of new ideas in building; it had a cathedral ceiling in the living room, heat ducts in the ceilings, two fireplaces, an electric window in the kitchen, a paneled den, a glassed-in porch with a patio in an attractive stockaded fenced garden, nicely landscaped, and *two* bedrooms. We went through agonies over that paucity of sleeping quarters. We reasoned finally that with John in medical school, Posy at IU and Bowie at Culver, we didn't need so many bedrooms. (We did, of course, but we really liked that house!) It was owned by the widow of a General Electric Vice President. We didn't try to bargain for it. I took Lamar to see it and we bought it that afternoon. We were afraid someone else would buy it. It was too small and there was no bus line anywhere near our house, but we bought it anyway!

Moving day finally arrived. Our household effects were loaded on a van and we followed it from Culver to Indianapolis. Arriving at 201 West 73rd Street, we found the dear widow had made no moving arrangements and was lying on the bed with a wet towel on her forehead. What to do? The movers put our stuff out on the lawn, packed the widow's things, moved her to the apartment, came back and moved our gear into the house. Honest! It was that simple, all done in about eight hours!

So commenced our new life. I had one friend, Bea Van Dusen. Her husband, an Army Colonel on active duty, had been stationed at Culver too but he had been transferred to Taiwan. Their only son, Roy, had graduated from Culver and had decided to do his military stint before going to college. He was stationed somewhere nearby so Bea decided to stay in the States. We clung to each other as we didn't know anybody else in the city.

Lamar was working into his new job. It was new for the Diocese too so he was feeling his way and sort of creating the job as it developed. We were meeting his new cohorts on the Bishop's staff, getting to know them and even entertaining a little.

That summer I had taken a course in watercolor at John Herron Art Institute. I applied to enter in the fall as a full-time student. I was fifty years old and scared to death. I had to submit a portfolio of artwork and get character recommendations, like any freshman. I did all that was expected of me and I was accepted. That September I started on my quest for recognition; I was going to be an artist, a real artist.

Lamar came home one day and complained that he had pains in his arm. He didn't think it was serious but that night, he didn't sleep very well. The next morning, he had an appointment with a man about some Diocesan matter. While the two of them were talking, Lamar mentioned his discomfort and the man, who happened to be a medical doctor, told him he should go to a hospital and have his heart checked. When Lamar left work, he went out to Fort Benjamin Harrison Hospital and asked if someone could check him out. Someone did and immediately hospitalized him. He told the nurse not to bother me as I was in class, but to wait until late afternoon to call me at home!

Shortly after I arrived home, the nurse called and told me my husband was in the base hospital with a heart attack and he wanted me to bring him a few things from home, such as his shaving gear and his reading glasses. When I heard he had been there since the middle of the morning, I was shocked. Suppose he had died?

Lamar had never been sick before so I was scared to death. I found him in a room with another patient. I knew he was in good hands as the doctor said he would recover, but he wanted to keep him there so they could watch him for a while. I went to see him every day he was hospitalized, right after my last class for the day. Finally, after about two weeks, the medico let him come home but warned him that he had to take things easy for a while, working just half a day. This bugged Lamar because he had been working such a short time for the Bishop, he felt the Diocese wasn't getting its money's worth; he felt he was getting medical leave much too soon. After about a week, he started working full-time again. I worried about him and started him on a salt-free and fat-free diet, which he disliked but accepted philosophically.

A few weeks later, he came home early. I think it was the day of the Army-Navy Game and he wanted to watch it on TV. It was the weekend of Thanksgiving and the weather was cold and damp. I was painting in the basement and didn't hear him come in. He went outside to get the mail and the door closed behind him and locked. When he came back he couldn't get in. He rang the bell but I didn't hear him down in the basement. Finally, he came around to the window of the area where I was painting and I saw him. By the time I let him in he was chilled to the bone and was having chest pains again. I drove him to Fort Ben Hospital and this time he was in much worse shape; he was given the VIP's room, right next to the nurses' station and the medico called in a civilian heart specialist, a Dr. White.

That whole period was a nightmare. Lamar was so ill, the hospital told me to get our children home as he could die. He had a very high temperature, was out of his head and had pneumonia. He was in an oxygen tent and had a lot of fluid around his heart. He passed the crisis and our three children returned to their respective schools. Thanks to antibiotics and a fine doctor, eventually he recovered but then he had a blood disease around the heart which kept him in the hospital until the spring. He was there for five months.

One day I came back from my daily visit to your father and there was a winter wonderland all over the side yard. A water faucet had frozen and water had been spraying out and freezing for a few hours. The bushes were covered with ice and the grass was a skating rink. I found a plumber and got it repaired.

Next, the furnace malfunctioned and an oily mist came up from the basement and went through the whole house. The night that happened, Bea Van Dusen had come over to have supper with me and she noticed that my neck was dirty. She thought I was so worried about your father that I had not had time to bathe regularly. She even saw black all around my nose. She was wearing a white wool dress and when she went home and was getting ready for bed, she discovered she was as dirty as I was. She called and alerted me to call a furnace repairman. The result of that was he discovered the furnace was malfunctioning and I had to move into the Hotel Marriott for two weeks while it was repaired and the dirty mess was cleaned up. My house was a "disaster area." Our homeowners' insurance paid for my entire house to be washed, everything to be dry-cleaned, even things in trunks. Also my stay in the hotel. As it turned out, the whole house should have been painted as that oily scum never really washed off. Months later, everything still looked dirty and dingy.

How we made it through that winter, I'll never know. I went to school every day, went to visit Lamar at the hospital every day, did my homework and studied and somehow, kept my sense of humor. Lamar recovered and returned to work. He learned how to take care of himself and life resumed.

The next year John Herron became part of the University of Indiana. We students were given the choice of sticking with an arts program or becoming bona fide college students. The latter meant we would study everything needed for a B.F.A. That sounded so neat, I went for it. I would get a degree from a real University. I'm so glad I did. I enjoyed every subject I studied.

Unfortunately I soon suffered from freshman trauma; I lost my religion, which I now think, I had never had. I became an agnostic. I stopped singing in the choir at Saint Alban's, refused to go to church, became a hippie and a war-dissenter. I read Betty Friedan's book, "The Feminine Mystique," and considered it my bible. I might have tried marijuana if I hadn't been afraid to mess with drugs. I would have gone to Washington to object to the Vietnam War if Lamar had let me. I really didn't want to shame him! After all, he was a retired Brigadier General and I had been a Marine all my life.

Betty, my sister, had plenty of money, while we always seemed to be poor as church mice. Since she was a painter also we had a lot in common. Once a year we would go off together on a trip to some exotic place and paint. Buzz would pay her way and she would pay my part of the trip. I was chagrined at first but soon took her charity in stride and enjoyed myself immensely.

Once we flew to Mexico to San Miguel d'Allende for a two-week course in art. The instruction was mediocre but we had a ball. We would paint all morning, return to the hotel for lunch and then go sight-seeing or shopping all afternoon. Evenings, we would converse with the other artists and critique each other's work. Mexico was so beautiful and San Miguel was very old and interesting, being a walled town and a national monument. It was a town of shops and many artisans displayed their wares, hoping to sell to the "gringos" from the United States and Canada. I discovered a wonderful Mexican artist named Orozco. He was having a show at the museum and I yearned to paint with his talent and individuality. If I could have afforded it, I would have bought one of his paintings.

Another year we flew to the island of Tobago, off the coast of Trinidad in South America. This was where the movie "Robinson Crusoe" had been made four or five years before our visit. Originally a possession of Britain, it had been given its independence but had not yet been discovered by the world's tourists. There was nary a golf course or discotheque or Hilton. The beaches were beautiful and varied, the natives spoke English with a British accent, the only amusements were bird-watching, snorkeling, driving around the island to admire the flora and fauna and socializing with the other guests at the little inn where we were staying.

To get to Tobago from Trinidad, it was necessary to take a small plane over to the island. Arriving in Trinidad, we had a whole day to shop there which was great as it is a "free port" and merchandise from all over the world is "duty-free." Betty was in seventh heaven, buying Liberty prints from England as she was quite the dressmaker. The hotel called a taxi for us and the driver took us to the best English shops in the city. We finally released him as we wanted to lunch in town and the streets were full of taxis of every description. We would have no trouble finding a replacement. About three o'clock we were tired and decided to go back to our hotel. We hailed a cab and told the driver to take us to a certain hotel. He nodded and smiled. As we drove out of the business district, he pointed to a gas station and told us his friend, Frederigo, was the proud owner of it. We nodded and said something like, "That's nice."

The next thing we heard was our cabbie telling us that Frederigo was going to meet us at the Hilton Hotel in one hour for cocktails. We had noticed that he had been talking on a C.B. radio as we were driving along. Betty and I couldn't believe our ears. We said, "Oh no, we can't meet anyone for cocktails. We are very busy and have too much to do."

This driver got very upset and insisted that we had a date with his friend and he would be mad if we were not there when he arrived. I finally told him I was in Trinidad on official business for the United States and my country would be more upset than his friend if I did not show up for a reception. He looked sheepish, growled a little and drove us to our hotel.

When we entered the lobby, we told the girl at the desk of our strange encounter with the taxi driver. She told us we should have telephoned the hotel for a cab as many women come to Trinidad for "a little fun and sex" and that cabbie thought we were looking for dates!! The hotels know their clients better and protect them from such types. Evidently, just getting into that cab in downtown Trinidad gave the alert that two "fresh" ones were available.

The next morning we flew to Tobago and went to the Robinson Crusoe Inn. This was run by a Dutch couple, brother and sister. The inn was the unofficial British Club and every evening, the English residents would gather for coffee, drinks and some singing around the piano. As guests, we were welcomed and made unofficial members.

One of the other guests at the inn was one of Queen Elizabeth's ladies-in-waiting. She was traveling with another woman and her six-year-old son, who was a dead ringer for Christopher Robin of A. A. Milne fame, even to the white linen hat which he wore in the sun. She owned an *island*, and was in the process of having a generator plant installed there as she had no electricity. She impressed me with her casualness; she had a kinky, flyaway perm and never set it; she went barefooted in the dining room; she wore old beatup shorts and invariably had her elbows on the table. How I yearned to resurrect my Mother there so I could say, "*She* is real aristocracy and just look at the way she behaves!" Mother's conversation when I was growing up often started with, "What would the Queen of England say?" I have now learned that the higher you are on the social scale, the less you pay attention to what other people think. Only the peasants worry about being properly dressed and following conventions. Does that imply Mother was a peasant? She would turn over in her grave.

Our daily routine consisted of breakfast in a dining room with no screens, where the waiters put out dishes of sugar for the little yellow birds who came to the tables and unashamedly ate it right under our eyes. The coffee was so delicious, I asked the waiter if it was grown on the island. He shook his head and said, "No. It is Nescafe, instant." I couldn't believe it then, but I know now that these big food companies can foods differently for foreign countries. I could almost swear that coffee was South American and freeze-dried right there in Trinidad.

After breakfast we prepared for the beach. The night before, the decision had been made by the assembled guests as to which beach we would grace with our presence, rocky coast? Quiet water and little ripplets? Big breakers for surfing? A fishing beach? About eight of us would get into the inn's oversized station wagon with our gear: painting equipment, fishing rods, bathing suits, sun hats, beach towels and lotion; and off we'd go. A big black driver would get us there and back and in the interim, prepare a delicious lunch, complete with icy-cold rum punches that made us all sleepy. (They were made with 150 proof rum!) Back to the inn and long siestas, during which Betty and I read to each other silly books by Alexander Woolcott or Bennett Cerf. We would laugh until we were crying and hurt all over. Betty would try to shush me between gales and say she wondered what the other guests thought we were doing as she was certain they could hear us.

At five, we would get dressed and go down for "tea." This was the hour to go bird-watching or drive around in a rented car or go to the village and shop.

There was a lady on the Island who fed birds, period. Tourists were welcomed so Betty and I went calling. Remember, no screens on the doors or windows on Tobago. We drove up to her house where we found her sitting on a terrace, watching a native boy crack open coconuts and papayas and spread their meat out on the ledges for the birds. Our hostess gave us a tour of the house. There was bird food in large bowls on the tables, (mahogany!) And the inevitable bird droppings everywhere, on the dining chairs where they had perched, splattered over the upholstery seats, white evidence on mirror and picture frames. In one room there were lots and lots of bats, hanging upside-down, snoozing until dark, when foraging for food would begin. Betty was a bird-lover but we agreed that woman was going a bit far.

We thanked the lady and went home to dress for dinner. The cocktail hour would begin at eight-thirty and dinner was at nine. After the meal, we would all congregate in the spacious living room and singing would commence. Kirk, our host, a repressed would-be-performer, made those keys dance and soon we would be dancing too.

One night when we had been there about one week, I noticed a gentleman who seemed quite taken with Betty. He monopolized her the whole evening and I could see she was enjoying the attention. When we went up to bed, she seemed worried that her new friend was so in love with her, she wondered if maybe we shouldn't leave. He spoke of being so enamored he wanted to marry her. She slept little that night and seemed nervous about seeing him again. The next morning, we took a cab and went to town to make arrangements to go snorkeling. Coming out of the ticket office, we ran smack dab right into Betty's "lover-boy." He looked at us without recognition, swept past us into the shop and we stood there, not knowing whether to laugh or cry. Betty said, "He was drinking pretty steadily but he didn't *seem* drunk." We both thought our experience would make a neat short story. That evening he was "courting" someone else. I'm glad we didn't go home precipitously.

We did snorkel and it was one of the big highs of my life. We went out on the reef in a small motorboat with two other couples. A huge pitch black native was our guide and trainer. We wore jeans, tennis shoes and long-sleeved shirts. And snorkels!

Then we went overboard and put our faces under the water. There was fairyland. I never saw such gorgeous fish in my life or coral in so many colors. It was magnificent. I kept talking to myself in my snorkel. "Oh, look at that one! Do you see that black velvet fellow with sapphires all over him?" Of course, no one could hear me but I was in heaven. Before we left, the guide took me off, guiding me through the coral beds, my feet floating out behind me, his huge hand steering us through the water, his feet bare, toughened by years of no shoes. When it was time to leave, I begged the rest to leave me there; nothing in the future could ever top that experience.

When we had to leave Tobago to go home, we decided to spend the last night at the airport as our plane took off at six a.m. We booked a room at the airport motel and arrived in time for dinner. We noticed a lot of men milling around the courtyard and I asked the clerk if there was a convention of some kind. She shook her head. We decided to eat early as we thought all these men would be occupying the waitresses soon enough. We had a table by the window where we could see the planes and we noticed the men were still there. Unbelievably, one young man took a chair and insolently sat facing us and never took his eyes off of us. We were embarrassed and were on the verge of asking for another table when I noticed he wasn't there anymore. Thank heaven! Then I looked up and there he was in the dining room, headed for our table. We ignored him and he passed and re-passed our table several times. Eventually, he left. When we asked for our key at the desk, I commented on this man's behavior. The clerk shrugged and said, "Many American ladies like escorts in the evening. They are lonely widows, yes?"

My four years at Herron were a wonderful experience. I loved being part of those young people's lives. So many of them were really talented and had so much imagination. They were products of the 60's and their language was foul, their sex lives unconventional, their clothes unbelievable, but they had a wonderful spirit and took their art education very seriously.

Our third year, we had to decide whether we would be painters or printmakers. I chose painting and fifteen of us were given a house behind the museum, where we painted everyday all day long. I shared a room with two young men, Danny Coble and Larry Spaid. I know our instructor was horrified to get me in his group as he didn't like me very much and he had a penchant for "boys." He was unmarried, treated the male students very well and ignored the females he was assigned to teach. He never liked my work and was very complimentary about all the boys' paintings although some of their work was sloppy, poorly executed and always late!

We had to enter shows regularly so we had to paint incessantly. Once Danny had nothing to send to a show in South Bend, so he threw together an atrocious canvas, just using up the paints on his palette. We had to price our work for insurance purposes and Danny put a huge price tag on his "mess." Later, he heard from the museum that his painting had been ripped when it fell off the truck and he received a check for the full amount of its price. We all laughed over that and raised the prices on our work when the next show came along.

Danny loved antiques and Indianapolis had wonderful "house sales." One day, during noon break, we drove to a big mansion nearby. He was looking for a wicker baby carriage as his wife was expecting. We arrived and went in and I saw some people from church. They approached and I introduced Danny. Then I became aware of how he was dressed. He had Indian blood and his hair was long and straight. That day, he was wearing a black Indian hat with a large brim. His coat was a World War I wool American army jacket, riddled with moth holes with half of the buttons missing, that he had bought at the Goodwill, and he wore old puttees over his blue jeans. I'm sure they never forgot him. I was so used to how the students dressed, his garb didn't bother me.

Larry bought an old moth eaten fur coat at the Goodwill Store. He ripped out the sleeves and wore them over his boots; the remainder he wore as a jacket but it always flapped open as the buttons were missing. The lining was a shredded mass of stringy silk. Add to this various splotches of different colored paint as he was a sloppy painter. When he won the Hoosier

Interlude In Indiana

Salon Art Show's first prize, that is the costume he wore when he was interviewed on television. His entry! Ten two-by-fours, painted in primary colors, carried to the second story balcony of the museum and dropped randomly on the exhibition floor beneath. They looked just like pickup sticks for a colossus. Well, it was original and different!

I invited a group of my fellow students to dinner. My only request was that they avoid foul language as Lamar can't abide it. They promised and arrived dressed in clean clothes and shampooed and bathed in our honor. I was so proud of them I could have burst. When they left I asked Lamar how he liked my friends. He said, "They're OK but their language is awful."

I realized I had become so accustomed to their vocabulary I didn't even consider it "bad." They had really tried to not use four-letter-words but a few slipped out automatically.

The house we worked in was a firetrap. Turpentine, oil paints, cans of house paint, alcohol do not sit well with fifteen chain smokers who are not above flicking live butts on the floor. We had orders not to smoke but the instructors were as culpable as we were, coming in and giving us criticism, smoking their ubiquitous cigarettes. One day we heard we were going to be inspected by the Fire Dept. Our floor was a mess of butts, oily rags, candy wrappers and foam cups. I borrowed a broom from a janitor and went to work sweeping everything into a closet. Our radio was blaring and both boys were yelling over the noise. Suddenly, everything was quiet. I stuck my head out of the closet and there was a police officer and two men in civvies The inspectors had arrived. I was wearing an old beat up painting smock and I looked too old to be a student. They thought I was a cleaning woman and told me to go on with my work. The whole place smelled like a smoking car. Did we pass? I guess we must have as we never were reprimanded. Of one thing I am sure: none of the other rooms were in any better shape.

Along about this time, Posy decided she didn't want to marry her young man after all. What a glorious reprieve! We were so excited we took her out to the best restaurant in town to celebrate. She was on the point of graduating with a B.F.A.

No job in art had materialized so she took a position with some securities company as a secretary. Eventually, she and a friend, Nan McLaughlin, took an apartment together so Lamar and I were in "an empty nest." We were both so busy we hardly had time to realize it.

John graduated from medical school with much honor; he had two degrees, one in Medicine and the other, a Doctorate in Biology. He married Betsy LeBleu, who was a school teacher in Houston. She kept him clothed and fed for a year while he did his residency. Then Uncle Sam, who had picked up his school bills, had his claws into him and sent him to Vietnam as a Lt. Junior Grade, where he struck blows for Liberty. He was attached to a unit of Marine artillery. He did a good job, walking off with a Bronze Star for his peaceful efforts in training young Vietnamese girls to be nurses for their civilian countrymen. Lamar and I were so proud of him.

After his tour in 'Nam, he came back to Bethesda Naval Hospital, where he started the tissue bank which collected spare body tissues and bones to be used in reconstructive surgery. He also was working on bone marrow transplants for youngsters with leukemia. When he had paid his dues to the Navy, he resigned and took a job with Fellowship House where he and Betsy were hosts and had the opportunity to work in Christian Ministry, which was very close to his heart.

Bowie was attending Trinity University in San Antonio, TX. Soon he was up to his ears in theater because he could sing and play the guitar. On graduation, he joined the Dallas Players and led an erratic life, traveling in a van with three other players, with a repertoire of four or five dramas, playing in churches and schools. It must have been a hard life as those four people spent every waking moment together even if they were not 100% compatible. I hope that Bowie writes the story of his life someday. I sure cannot and will not, but I've read novels that paled in comparison.

Posy married Denny Neidigh and called us from their wedding trip. They had eloped and now I would never get my share of all those wedding presents that everyone in the world owed us. Over the years, Lamar and I had responded to hundreds of wedding invitations. Posy's wedding would have been our chance to recoup some for our own! Of course, that hurt us. We were stunned; mostly, that she would get married and not tell us. Young people just never realize how much these things hurt until they themselves are parents.

After their honeymoon, they rented a nice little house not far from us and it was fun having them so near. Their first baby, Michael, was born the following June and I had to miss my graduation from Indiana University as that was the same day Posy was released from the hospital and I was bringing them home. I didn't care; I.U. meant nothing in my life. I had attended Herron Art Institute; that was my Alma Mater.

The next winter I had a job teaching artistic anatomy at the Indianapolis Art Center. Anatomy had been my least favorite subject in school and I had worked just hard enough to get a passing grade. This was just retribution for my inattention. Now I had to teach it! And, in so doing, I learned it thoroughly. We had to draw the human body from memory, front, back, and side, showing all muscles that could be seen with the naked eye. This required a nude model for the class and I had to interview prospective models, meeting them in off hours and asking them to strip and pose in complicated postures. This was somewhat embarrassing, but I put on a very professional air and hoped the poor model didn't realize how inexperienced I was. I had failed to do this with my first model and when he appeared on the model stand, we noticed he had a dreadful rash all around his groin. It was repulsive to look upon and my poor students, all lovely ladies from the upper echelons of society, were horrified. I was too. I wondered if he had some venereal disease. After the session, I told the young man we had a female lined up for the next week but I would "call him." I never did.

I was going great guns, entering all the big shows and winning some prizes. One particular prize gave me much pleasure; I took first place in the State Fair, beating out my instructor, who did not even place. Forgive my bragging but that man had almost destroyed my self esteem. My marks in Printing had kept me off the Dean's List for four years. Except for the grades he bestowed on me, all the other instructors' grades would have guaranteed my graduating with honors.

Into this busy and rewarding life, Lamar threw me a curve ball. He was tired and wanted to retire. If anyone deserved a rest, it was he. He had worked for forty-one years, survived two heart attacks, learned a second profession and earned his living at it for nine years. If he wanted to retire, I was all for it. Then came the shocker; he wanted us to sell our house, buy a motor home and travel all over the country like vagabonds. We could use, as an excuse for our madness, that we were looking for a place to retire, hopefully on the beach, somewhere like Florida. This last was the cheese in the mousetrap. How I wanted to live on the beach! Indiana had been good to us, but we weren't Hoosiers. Our three children were grown and leading their own lives; they were no longer dependent on us. It was time for us to think about ourselves and the remaining years of our lives. Neither of us knew anything about trailering or recreational vehicles but we could learn. After all, we were both service brats and had been on the move most of our lives. If we didn't like it, we could always quit, couldn't we? Thus, we reasoned, we could try something new. Who knows, maybe we would never have to pay real estate taxes or cut grass again!

12

Nomadic Madness:
Too Small to Live In & Too Big to Drive

When Lamar told me he was tired of working and wanted to retire, I was not surprised and I urged him to do it. He had had a military career of thirty years behind him plus four years of instructing at Culver Military Academy plus nine years of working at an entirely new career as the administrator of the Episcopal Diocese of Indianapolis. He was the survivor of two heart attacks and a lengthy convalescence from an infection of his heart. I couldn't but agree that it was about time he slowed down and relaxed for the rest of his life.

We were sitting on the sofa in the living room of our Indianapolis home. He arose, went into his study and came back with a magazine. I glanced at it and saw that it was a copy of Popular Mechanics. He showed me an article about a truck van which had been converted into a mini motor home. It was the lead article and there was a picture of the vehicle on the cover. Then he timidly asked, "How would you like to travel around the country in that?"

My reaction was one of amazement and, I must admit, consternation. We have always felt, both of us, rather above those "plebeians," who live in trailers, neatly parked in rows like elongated match boxes, some ornamented with doll picket fences, potted plants and a liberal sprinkling of cats and dogs. The usual tenants might be seen sitting around in their undershirts, sprawled on their ubiquitous plastic lawn chairs found for sale in every supermarket. Their proximity to their nearest neighbors seemed one of the worst aspects of this type of living. "It must be awful to live so close to strangers," I would think, as we passed these parks, "There but for the grace of God, go I," and I always arrived home feeling a little conscience-stricken as I drove up the driveway of our attractive contemporary home in suburbia. Thank God we didn't have to live like that!

Lamar was talking about our staying in these trailer parks as we traveled around the country. When I realized he was serious about wanting to live in a tiny cramped house on wheels, I marveled more and more. Here was a man who so loved and admired his Alma Mater, the U.S. Naval Academy, but chose the Marine Corps for his career over the Navy as he couldn't stand the idea of "being cooped up on board a ship," a man who frowned mightily at the idea of living in a duplex house and sharing a wall with another family or who refused to consider renting an apartment for six months to "leisurely look for a house to purchase." In other words, he was a man who liked his *space*.

One day we sat down and made a financial estimate of how much we would have to live on if he retired. The picture wasn't too grim. Probably we would have to sell this house, find a smaller place not in Indianapolis (too cold), stop losing our heads completely over Christmas and, in general, "pull in our horns" financially. But we weren't going to starve. The next day Lamar told the Bishop that he was retiring but he would stay until someone was found to replace him. We put the house on the market and began our search for the right vehicle, which would be easy to drive and maneuver, yet roomy enough to be comfortable. Ha!

The Church advertised for a bursar and soon had a likely prospect. Some buyers seemed interested in our property so we decided the time had come to go and look at that intriguing little motor home that had tugged at my husband's heartstrings. We bought a couple of trailer magazines and were amazed at the number of people who did this sort of thing as a way of life and how numerous the manufacturers were that catered to this particular type of madness. We discovered the Ford Explorer motor home was manufactured in Indiana, so we journeyed north to South Bend to examine one at a dealer's shop.

When first we saw the little vehicle, it seemed just perfect. I figured I could drive something that size. The dealer unlocked the van and we stepped inside. The roof was so low we couldn't stand upright. In a crouched position, we oohed and ahed over a three-burner propane gas stove, no oven; one double bunk bed in the rear (Lamar snores so we like separate beds); a four cubic foot refrigerator, the freezer space was so small I doubted I could get more than one tray of cubes in it. There was a monomatic toilet in a shower stall behind a door, no curtain separating it from he rest of the bath, and the storage space was so cramped, I couldn't visualize our modest wardrobes ever fitting into it. As Goldilocks said, "It's too small!" I don't like to bash this little rig; for a weekend trip for a couple, fine!

But we were going to *live* in this car for weeks, months, maybe years! In spite of my Piglet temperament about driving large vehicles, I was going to have to think bigger. We went home somber and reflective.

From the ridiculous to the sublime. We heard about a 21-footer that was for sale secondhand. We went to see that. This was more like it; we could stand upright, there was a four-burner Magic Chef stove, an eye level oven, an eight-foot refrigerator; twin beds, a separate shower stall in the bathroom, gobs of storage space and even a couch to lounge around on and watch TV. The owner insisted that I drive it and I did, around one neighborhood block in South Bend. Somehow, driving that huge vehicle, I was amazed that the back of it followed me around corners. I did not find it difficult to maneuver. I was suddenly a happy camper!

Lamar really liked this model but it was secondhand and we were suspicious of anything not new. Back to the drawing board. Actually, we probably could have been happy with that particular rig. We didn't know all new motor homes have kinks and this particular one's kinks had been discovered and removed.

Back in Indianapolis, the word was out and we began getting calls from recreational vehicle agents. One gentleman drove one up to our house and we were most impressed. It had everything the neat Travco in South Bend had to offer, but it was brand-new and still in our price range. It was a Banner and we decided to buy it. When I think what babes in the woods we were, I blush with chagrin. We knew so little about recreational vehicles, we should have looked more, studied more and dickered a lot more. That thing cost a mint!

Well, we sold the house very quickly so we had to vacate within the month. Trying to decide what to keep after so many years of marriage was difficult. Happily we had three children, two of them married, so Posy and John came and relieved us of a lot. Then we had to put everything we owned and wanted to keep in storage for a later day when we would be tired of the motor home and would need to furnish some place somewhere, hopefully not too large.

We were ready to take off on our great adventure. After transferring our household and personal effects to the Banner which was sitting in our driveway (a lot of things were discarded because there just was no place to stash them) we made a short trip to the southern part of the state, to Evansville, for a church conference. Right after leaving our driveway, we drove about two blocks and discovered the door to the rig was wide open and swinging merrily in the breeze We pulled over to the curb and rectified that and continued on our way. Lamar and I soon learned to make a checkoff list of necessary duties before starting the engine.

Arriving in Evansville, we proceeded to the TV station, where we were welcomed by the director. He insisted we hook up to his water and electricity so we moved closer to the building. I heard water sloshing and found the shower stall full of Joy suds and dirty dish water. Lamar hadn't removed the rubber cap that allows drain water to escape without polluting the fresh water holding tank. However, he had had the foresight to buy a collapsible canvas bucket and except for getting thoroughly sprayed in the process, drained the water from the shower stall.

Lamar took a shower before retiring and decided the best way to accomplish that was to soap the body before stepping into the stall, then turning the water on to rinse. The stall was too small to do much maneuvering. Of course, the whole bathroom had to be wiped down with towels afterwards.

Lamar left early for a church breakfast and I ate a solitary meal. This time the coffee perked and I fried my usual egg and bacon in the electric fryer. I noticed the can of frozen orange juice was defrosted but the ice cubes were still intact in the freezing compartment.

I walked uptown and bought a tape (Bert Bachrach) to try out our new stereo tape player. After reading all instructions carefully, I decided to wait until the technical genius got home. I am a mechanical ignoramus.

I wanted to go to the Art Museum but after looking at the map, I figured it was about 12 blocks away. That was 24 blocks in all and the sky looked like rain.

Back to the rig. I had to plan something to facilitate meal preparation. I had a space 18 inches square by the double sink and that was it. Lamar would have to make me a board to go over the sink. And maybe something to cover the stove burners would be a help. Just finding space to use a mixing bowl was a problem. I was determined that all these things could be rectified in time.

This conference was the last official act Lamar accomplished for the Diocese and he was given a hero's sendoff from the church officials. The next day we bid them a fond farewell and returned to Indianapolis to sign contracts, straighten and clean the empty house and prepare for departure.

Our last night in Naptown, we spent in Posy's and Denny's driveway. How I hated to leave my daughter. I realized how lucky (I didn't know the word "blessed" then) I had been to be so close to one of my children. They had all left home and now we were leaving them.

The next morning, Denny helped Lamar hitch up the little yellow Volkswagen, which we had bought as our "dinghy" to go ashore in, and we gaily took off. Three blocks later, we turned the corner onto Meridian Street (the main drag in Indianapolis) and found our Bug was off its hitch and the wheels were locked. Good grief! We separated the two vehicles, removed the hitch and returned to the place where we had bought it and demanded a replacement. The hitch was unstable and set too high. It took all day to get it fixed right. Back to Posy's driveway for the next night.

The next day we finally got out of town without any more mishaps. Our destination: Washington, D.C. to visit John and Betsy, our son and daughter-in-law. We made about 50 miles that first day and found an acceptable trailer park in Greenfield, Ind. *Until* the first train came by, about 50 feet from our rig! All night trains passed and woke me up. I counted *six*! That night I learned something very important: trailer parks are generally located in lousy areas; people dislike their proximity so they are usually right on the highway or in a lowly part of town. Trailer magazines don't tell you goodies like that!

One thing we forgot to watch for was foreign objects when coming in after dark and parking between the usual trailer park "white posts" which define your "space." We were too close to one and knocked it askew. A fellow camper helped us by removing it completely until we had swung clear and then he replaced it for us. The Banner got its first dent and scrape marks.

The next night, we stayed in a court in Cambridge, Ohio. We had made only 200 miles. I had a real tub bath in the Court Facilities and felt clean for the first time since leaving our house at 201 73rd Street. The incessant roar of trucks on the highway kept us from sleeping very well.

We decided to clean out the monomatic tank as the court had the facilities. Of course, we did it all wrong; we didn't open a particular valve and all the chemical water backed up in the shower stall. Lamar finally got it flushed out and refilled it and I mopped up the debris. Lamar was so dirty, he took a shower in the bath house while I fixed lunch.

After eating and re-hitching the yellow Bug, we finally got away. The scenery that day was spectacular; the hills were so beautiful, the flowering trees and the red and white barns looked like Brown County paintings; every rise was a challenge to the artist in me. I decided there were good things about this way of life.

Arriving in the D.C. area we found a mobile home park and parked the Banner for the night. Some of the rigs in there were straight out of Cannery Row. One mobile home looked homemade and was patched in several places. It was decorated with pieces of driftwood, rocks, dreadful statuary, a few wan flowers and a pair of red tennis shoes drying in the sun. It looked as though it had been parked there for twenty years. The next morning, we took the VW and went in to Washington.

John and Betsy were living at Fellowship House where they were employed as Spiritual Papa and Mama. It was a large mansion which had been turned into a gathering place for religious leaders from all over the world. Betsy was general manager and John was official host!

We stayed three days in the area, making a trip to Easton and St. Michael's. We went in John's car; it was wonderful not to maneuver our big bus through the little old towns.

We ate wonderful seafood, smelled the salt air and listened to the seagulls squawking. I would have been perfectly willing to stay right there and live. But we had just started on our search for a spot so we had to go on and see what was to be seen on the "other side of the mountain."

Saturday, we four went to Annapolis in the Banner to watch a Navy-Duke football game. We parked in the huge parking lot and fixed lunch. It began to rain a little and cars began to arrive in profusion. The occupants put on raincoats and tried to have picnics from their station wagons. They all looked so miserable and I began to feel like Noah and his Ark; all snug and everyone else drowning.

Betsy and I were not interested in the game so we took the VW and went into town to see my first cousins, Mary Ellen and Tootie, who lived in their parents' historic home.

Every time I go to Annapolis I feel like a ghost. We lived there for six years when I was growing up and I always thought of it as home. Now it has grown enormously and the streets seem narrower, the houses smaller, the front yards closer to the streets. Everything has shrunk! I never see anyone I know so I feel invisible. It's a very strange feeling.

When the door to 110 Duke of Gloucester opened and my cousin greeted us, I felt alive again. Forty years sloughed off and I was a teenager.

For All Our Days

Everything was unchanged. It's a lovely old eighteenth century house with wide-planked floors and old glass window panes. The outside bricks were brought over from England as ballast for the sailing vessels that had carried tobacco and cotton to the Old Country. On the walls were Grandfather Worthington's paintings, done when he was a young man before the Civil War.

Memories of Mother, Aunt Mamie, her sister, Aunt Ellie, their aunt, and ourselves as children flooded in. The dining room with its lovely old furniture and cabinets full of old Canton china seemed peopled with ghosts: Mother teasing Aunt Mamie about her weak coffee, Cousin George consuming two quarts of milk for lunch; the invariable fare of sardines and soda crackers as a meal, the way Mother and Aunt Mamie were so in tune that every word spoken between them sent them into gales of laughter, incomprehensible to everyone else. My sister, Betty and I have the same rapport and it is a joy.

After a long talk, exchanging family news, we wended our way back to the stadium and awaited the end of the game. It was still raining and little groups huddled around their tailgates and seemed loath to separate. The whiskey was still flowing. The game over, Lamar and John were entranced; Navy had won with a last-minute spurt.

As the stadium cleared out, we took to the road again and made a new discovery; driving in the dark in the rain is no fun in a motor home. The side mirrors and the rear window got fogged up; visibility was almost nil! When we finally got back to the trailer park, we put Banner to bed, transferred to John's car and went to a great restaurant for seafood.

The next morning we drove to Lexington, Virginia, to see my sister and her family. She had been sick but seemed much better.

Lexington is a very interesting place. I have been visiting there since the late 40's and it doesn't seem to change much. It's small enough that the people are concerned about one another but with two colleges here, it is not provincial. The natives call the town The Heart of the Confederacy. The never ending stream of young people and University professors keep it modern thinking. Also, because it is Southern, the ambiance is gracious and friendly.

After five days we left for Mountain City, Georgia, to see Lamar's older sister, Shirley. There was no trailer park but we found a mobile home park. Parked on an incline, we took all the food out of the fridge and put it in Shirley's, used no hookups as nothing works unless the rig is on flat ground.

Shirley has a 150 year old log mountain cabin. Over the years she has added, subtracted and changed things and the place is very attractive and comfortable. We spent our honeymoon here and the place is right out of a novel by John Ehle about mountainous stock. There is no industry and the folk speak but are leery of strangers. Shirley, who has lived here for forty years, is still not "one of them." In spite of her 80 odd years she lives here alone and takes care of herself. Perhaps her days are numbered as she seems frailer each time we come but she's a remarkable woman; intellectual, warm, liberal thinking, and in spite of no TV and a poor radio, reads periodicals and books with the aid of a magnifying glass and keeps abreast of what is going on in the world. Lamar takes her to church and she is as well-groomed and attractive as a Grande Dame. In fact, she is a Grande Dame, one of the few I have ever known.

We stayed with Shirley, but the last night we slept in the rig as I had washed all the bed clothes and towels we had used at Shirley's.

My trip to the Laundromat was interesting. I'm not very familiar with Laundromats so I needed a lot of help from the mountaineer women who were engaged in the same activity. I was so interested in their *wash*; homemade cotton patchwork quilts and rag rugs, one of which I was told was 20 years old. I can't sew on a button straight so I was impressed.

One old woman in her seventies hauled in about ten old beat up blankets and was washing them in five machines. She told me she was two days out of the hospital and turned down my offer to help her load those heavy wet things into the dryer.

Another younger mountaineer woman looked me straight in the eye and said, "When I'm pregnant I wear my hair in a ponytail. I jest cain't get used to hit flowing 'round my face.'" I assured her that her long black hair would look nice either way but I'm still wondering why she wears it in a ponytail only when she's pregnant.

It rained for three days and as Shirley would say, "It keeps opening up and then shutting off." Finally, a brisk wind blew the moisture off the mountains, the sun came out and everything looked washed clean.

From Mountain City we went to Atlanta where we have various relatives. My brother Jack lives there in a Holiday Inn and Shirley's only son, Cat and his wife, Virginia, live in one of the suburbs. We stayed in a trailer park and Lamar and Jack went to a Navy football game. We had dinner at a restaurant called L'Abbaye, an old converted church. The waiters wore monk's habits, the communion rail was a bar rail, tables were placed throughout the Nave. I hope the church had been deconsecrated.

13

The Glory Years

After two and one-half years of wandering around the USA and exploring parts of Canada and Mexico, Lamar and I decided we needed some "port" where we could stash our seashells and miscellaneous gear that we had collected during our travels. After much discussion, we decided to find a place in Lexington, Virginia. We would continue to winter in Mexico and spend the summers in the States. My dear sister Betty and her family were in Lexington, and since Lamar and I could not afford that spot on the ocean that I so coveted, then I would at least have my wonderful sister to pal around with for three or four months a year. Lamar would be happy anywhere as long as he could play with his ham radio uninterrupted.

We contacted Betty and she found us a little house on two and a half acres, ten minutes from town. There we could park the rig behind the house where no one could see it. (We didn't consider it an eyesore but some people don't like them cluttering up their neighborhoods.) Our landlord would buy the house as an investment and rent it to us. He even offered to take care of those two and a half acres of grass, which had worried me a lot as grass-cutting was not Lamar's favorite past-time nor mine either. This was in 1972.

We drove the Travco to Lexington and stayed in Glen Maury Park in the little town of Buena Vista which is located six miles from Lexington. We had to wait a few weeks until the house was ready for occupancy. In the Park we had a flat trailer space, restrooms and showers and plenty of privacy, at least, during the week when the Park was deserted. Weekends we had to share the facilities with strangers. And, after a few weeks, we became quite possessive about the Park and resented it if other campers did not keep the facilities neat and clean.

Every day, Lamar worked on his ham activities and I went off in the Volkswagen Bug to play with Betty. We had a great summer, picnicking at Goshen Pass on the Maury River, lunching with Alice Shell and Betty's best friend, Gillie

Campbell, shopping in Staunton and Roanoke and socializing at night with our new and old friends. Lamar, Buzz and Buddy Shell had all fought in the Pacific together and now were all three retired Marine Corps Generals. Buddy was the only *real* General to serve as such. Lamar and Buzz had honorary rank bestowed on them at their retirement from the Corps.

That fall with our household gear from Indiana out of storage and arranged to our satisfaction in the Meadow View house, we obtained house sitters, a W&L visiting Law professor and his wife, Bob and Louise Campbell, from Ann Arbor, Michigan. Then we bid farewell to Lexington, packed up the Jolly Green Giant, made our usual calls on relatives in Georgia and friends in the Alamo Campground in San Antonio and returned to La Floresta in Ajijic, Mexico.

When we returned to San Antonio, either going to Mexico or returning from there, bittersweet memories of Bowie when he was attending Trinity University always flooded our thoughts. We wondered where he was and if he was all right, since we had lost contact with him for two years.

The next spring in Mexico, I received an Easter card from him. It had no return address and the note with it sounded almost as though it had been dictated. It didn't sound like him at all. The zip code on the envelope indicated he was in or near Winter Park, Florida. For the first time in two years we had a hint as to his whereabouts. We decided to leave Mexico early and go to Florida and look for him. We figured he would be involved in religious activities and some church person would recognize his photograph.

When we arrived in Winter Park, we started investigating the Fundamental churches as we were sure he was not attending a mainline one. No one at any of the churches we investigated recognized Bowie's picture and their comments were very discouraging. We were told that the whole Florida Coast was populated with little religious sects, many camping on the public beaches.

The Glory Years

We were so discouraged we gave up but since we were in the vicinity, we decided to continue south and explore the Florida Keys. There we found a charming Trailer Park with delightful people and there we stayed until it was time to come back to Lexington.

After our first year on the road, we had decided to buy a better motor home. Our choice was the Travco, which was more streamlined and, we thought, better made than most of the boxy ones. Every time we had passed one on the highway we had said to ourselves, "He's OK and we're not OK."

We finally ordered it in Atlanta, GA as we could stay at Warner Robin's Air Force Base Family Trailer Park which was close to Macon, where we had so many relatives. There we stayed for two months, waiting for our green watermelon with a cream bellyband to be assembled.

Betty and Buzz came to visit us for a few days and we socialized with Louise and Fred Williams, Lamar's sister and brother-in-law, their children, Ann Shirley and Beth, and their husbands, Ed Pendleton and Buck Blanks.

Finally, we were informed that our new domicile was completed and was on its way from Michigan. The day it arrived, we moved into a guest room on the base, stripped the Banner of our belongings and were ready when our Jolly Green Giant came barreling up to our space. Business completed, we started moving our possessions into the new rig. There just wasn't room so, we had to discard things we really cherished.

Having bade everyone in Georgia farewell, we took off for San Antonio, pleased as punch with our new "look." Poor Banner! We hardly gave her a perfunctory goodbye; because we had had so many problems with her.

Driving in Mexico always poses challenges. We had to get over the border, which involved bribing the inspectors with cigars, pesos and humble attitudes. Once past the Inspection Point, we had to contend with bad, narrow roads, infrequent gas stations in one area, no gas for 200 miles, unsafe parking places, livestock on the highways, and poor Mexican drivers.

For All Our Days

After a few years, we had the trip pretty well organized and always followed the same route and stayed in the places that were familiar to us. When we crossed high mountains or drove through tiny towns with narrow cobblestone streets, we unhitched the Volkswagen Beatle and drove singly, Lamar the rig and Polly flying along ahead of him in the Yellow Bug.

It always took us three days to get from the border to La Floresta Trailer Park in Ajijic. The countryside we drove through was arid and sparsely populated. There was no vegetation except cacti, Joshua trees, or Spanish swords. Occasionally, we would pass a hut made of corrugated tin or adobe, clothes flapping on a clothesline, tin cans holding various plants, maybe a burro grazing on such little vegetation.

What on earth did those people do for food or water way out there? Approaching Guadalajara, which is a big city, the shocking filth would become more obvious. We would see in the fields clumps of white, which turned out to be hundreds of plastic bags, discarded by the inhabitants, indissoluble, never collected. In the U.S. we are so accustomed to cleanup crews policing the highways, the sight of so much garbage and trash left unattended was disturbing.

Skirting the city of Guadalajara, we approached Ajijic, which is 15 miles south. We climbed a small mountain and, as we drove over the top, there before our eyes was fairyland; a beautiful lake down below, rimmed with mountains, lush trees, some flowering, and houses, red-tiled roofed with gardens, church steeples, the little town of Chapala.

The village of Ajijic is a few miles past Chapala and our winter home was up on the side of a mountain, with a view of the town, Lake Chapala and mountains beyond spread out before us. The trailer spaces were landscaped with flat gravel pads, tile patios, flowers everywhere and native gardeners sweeping up leaves and bougainvillea blossoms. Every pad had a view. It makes me sad to know that the park is extinct, that area now covered with small vacation houses, built for the middle class citizens of Guadalajara.

The Glory Years

Many of the same people came every year to La Floresta and, on our arrival, we were always greeted by old friends. They came from the northern part of the USA, Canada, the Midwest, the Northern States, even Southern ones like Texas. We were all snowbirds, escaping the North American winter weather.

Once we had parked our motor home, we unfurled our awning, unpacked from the storage pod up on top of the rig our outdoor table and chairs, knowing we would see nary a drop of rain during our stay. Ajijic has a rainy season from May to September when the hills turn green but we never saw them that way; they were always as brown as the cattle that had a way of wandering onto the roads uninvited, causing many accidents. By April, most of us would have returned north to spring plant or to pay our income taxes.

So began a season of carefree living. We enrolled in Spanish and art classes, easily available in the school at the bottom of the hill, taught by the native Spanish or Indian instructors, sightseeing and shopping in Guadalajara and Tlaque-Paque (we called it "lock your pockets," a town of shops) eighteen miles away, going to the open markets in Chapala and Ajijic, attending American films, which were shown once a week at the local theater, where we took cotton for our ears as the sound was always turned up for "foreign" films, and plays put on by the local Little Theater (in English as the American colony numbered at least 3000.) We attended all the religious pageants, so colorful and frequent, with their Spanish and Indian costumes, went bathing in the hot springs down the road in Jocotopec, dining in the local restaurants, buying the hot French bread right out of the brick ovens, listening to the Mariachi bands and singers. Then, add to all this, the parties given by friends in the trailer park and in Ajijic.

Of course, everyone shopped like mad, buying the handmade pottery and glass, embroidered clothing, woven serapes and wall hangings, jewelry, linens, on and on. Mexico is a shopper's paradise. We felt very fortunate to live the way we did.

Eventually, Lamar's health interfered with our routine; his hearing was getting bad and his eyes gave him trouble so he didn't feel safe driving the Jolly Green Giant. I was not going to drive that six-ton truck 3000 miles. The time came when we realized we couldn't go anymore. We sold our beloved Jolly Green Giant and became permanent residents of Lexington.

There Lamar attended Robert E. Lee Church regularly and soon was serving on the Vestry. I had no interest in church functions. I had not gone to any church services in 14 years except to three Midnight Christmas Masses, one on Sanibel Island, one in San Antonio, one in Puerta Vallarta, Mexico. All three were memorable for different reasons. On Sanibel, I thought the congregation very cold and unchristian as they ignored Bowie's gestures of friendliness in "passing the Peace." In San Antonio, the whole congregation sang Handel's Hallelujah chorus with gusto, which amazed me, and in Mexico the organist at the cathedral played "Jingle Bells" and "Santa Claus is Coming to Town." At a High Mass!

I must tell you how Bowie resurfaced into our lives. One summer day in Lexington I was talking to John Curry about my worry concerning Bowie. I told John one of us could die and no one knew how to contact him. He said he knew a dentist and his wife in Washington, D.C. who were supporting Maria's ministry. Maria was the woman who had persuaded Bowie to travel with her to Bermuda to win that country for God. We hoped that this dentist would know how to reach Bowie. John said he could get their telephone number. I asked him to get it for me which he did.

I called and talked to the dentist's wife. At first she refused to give me Maria's address as she had promised not to share it with anyone. When I told her I was Bowie's mother and had not spoken to him in two years, she relented and gave it to me. She told me they were living in an orange grove in a trailer which they were outfitting with a loud speaker for an upcoming mission trip to Bermuda.

When I hung up I was so excited at the prospect of talking to my son, I could hardly wait to telephone him. Then I began to think that was not such a good idea. He did not seem to want to contact us, so I would honor his wishes. If we had an emergency, I knew now how to reach him. In some very strange way, I had released him to God.

The next weekend John and Betsy said they were coming down to see us. They arrived at about 11 o'clock at night and I noticed they had another man with them. Wondering who he was, I went to the door to let them in. They had brought Bowie! I nearly fainted. I don't know why I didn't have a heart attack. I know I was in shock. We sat up and talked for hours and they explained what had happened.

A day or two after I had not called, Bowie decided to leave Maria and her ministry as he felt he was not serving the Lord but serving Maria. He walked down to the highway and asked a passing truck driver to give him a ride. He had decided to go to Washington to see John. Of course, he had no idea where his parents were living so he never thought of "coming home." He asked the driver of the truck where he was going and he replied, "Washington." That was where John and Betsy lived. So Bowie had a ride all the way to DC. There, John was just a phone call away and Bowie made contact with his brother. One interesting aspect of this incident was my complete non-recognition of God's hand in these events; I thought it was just a coincidence. It never occurred to me at the time that God was rewarding me for not interfering in my son's life and his decisions.

All was not a bed of roses; Maria followed Bowie to Lexington and tried to persuade him to return to Florida with her. Bowie was staying with us. He stood firm about leaving her ministry and she finally left.

During his stay with us, he met a lot of young Christians and brought them to the house where Lamar and I had the opportunity to get to know them and become fond of them.

John and Betsy, both devout Christians, decided to take Bowie under their wing, so to speak, and found him a job in Washington doing Christian work in a halfway house. But all of that is his story and I'll let him tell it.

Back in Lexington, we continued to see some of those young church people that Bowie had enjoyed when he came home. One of them, Eric Sisler, berated me one day for not doing enough things for Lamar. When I asked him what he was talking about, he said my husband wanted to attend a certain church conference but he wouldn't go because I wouldn't go with him. Eric thought I was very selfish because it meant so much to Lamar.

This offended me as my husband had never mentioned wanting to attend any church conference. When I asked him about it he said he knew I wouldn't go, so he just put the idea out of his head.

After thinking that over, I asked him how much he wanted to go and he said, "Very much."

So I told him if this meant so much to him, I'd go but if I felt uncomfortable when I got there, I would leave and let him come home with some friends who were attending. He agreed to this arrangement and we told Eric we were attending.

The conference was held in Hungry Mother State Park, down in southern Virginia. I had never attended a conference of any kind before. This one was very informal, in rather rustic surroundings, a camp really. We took jeans, shirts and sweaters, no dress-up clothes.

When we arrived, I was hustled off to a cabin where I had a stranger for my roommate. Lamar was taken elsewhere and we were quietly requested not to seek out one another's company. Ye Gods! What had I allowed myself to get into?

My roommate turned out to be very loquacious, friendly and knowledgeable about religious conferences. This one started on Thursday night and ended late Sunday afternoon, so I prepared to be a good listener.

That evening we attended a church service during which we "made the stations of the Cross" and were told not to speak to one another until breakfast the next morning. I spied Lamar and timidly waved to him and he waved back.

My roommate talked until 1:00 o'clock in the morning. She told me about a miraculous healing she had had and, I must say, it was impressive if it was true!

The next morning, after breakfast, we had our first lecture on Christianity. Since this was a subject about which I was abysmally ignorant, I found it interesting. Maybe I was going to learn something after all.

This was followed by my being put in a circle of prayer. To my horror, people individually prayed *aloud!* When they came to me, I just sat there frozen until they finally moved on. Episcopalians as a rule are very quiet and close-mouthed about their religion. This must be a "fringe group" I thought. I wasn't anything but I had once been an Episcopalian, and I knew how they acted!

That afternoon there was another talk and after dinner we took communion. I liked that, especially the latter. It was so informal and friendly; more like the way the early Christians must have had it. They had a special loaf of bread and we all broke off pieces and gave them to our neighbor. The cup of wine was passed from one to another also.

There was a lot of music with guitars during the weekend and the songs were simple "praise" songs that I had never heard, but liked.

The thing that impressed me most was the caring that all these people had for one another. Everyone seemed genuinely interested in others' problems, which surfaced during discussion within small groups. Personal relationships were being formed spontaneously. In spite of my agnostic beliefs, I was beginning to be impressed.

On Saturday, during one of the lectures, I made a decision; the world that was controlled by a personal God was far preferable to a universe created by accident and uncontrolled by anyone or anything. There was no proof of either. If I put my faith in a God that did not exist, I would lose nothing; my life would be much happier and when I died, that would be the end. If I renounced Him and He did exist, I would lose everything. I asked God to forgive me for denying Him. Then, something remarkable occurred; God spoke to me. He said, "Well, it's about time, Polly."

I was so surprised I just sat there in a daze and tried to digest what had happened. I could hardly wait to go away and be alone. I sat there numbed. I had heard of people having encounters with God but I had thought they were in dreams or visions.

The rest of the weekend was rather hazy. I didn't tell anyone what had happened and I couldn't decide if I would even tell Lamar when we were on the way home.

The weekend came to an end but not before I had stood up at the closing and announced that I had thought God was dead but I had discovered He was very much alive.

We hadn't been in the car more than half an hour when I blurted out, "Gunk, God spoke to me." Then I related my experience. I don't remember what he said but he seemed to accept my story.

That was October 8, 1982, and my life has been a different one ever since. The Bible says I am a new creature and I know I am. My priorities changed overnight and I was filled with a desire to know more about my Lord and the Bible; I went to Church and nearly scared those Episcopalians to death. I joined everything in Church and loved everybody. Loving Jesus makes you love people!

That was 20 years ago. I was 70 years old and today I am 95. Not once have I doubted that Jesus is the Son of God and that He spoke to me. That's why I call these years "The Glory Years."

Of course, I thought everyone should go to Cursillo (the name of the retreat I had attended) and get turned on to Christianity, so when I came home to Lexington I heckled people mercilessly and made a nuisance of myself. I should have been locked in a closet. The church didn't know what to do with me, the great agnostic and once non-churchgoer. The bulk decided to ignore me as a fundamental ignoramus, but a group accepted me and my conversion and I was happy.

At last, I learned about the Bible and started reading it daily. I joined Bible studies, became involved in prayer groups, went to conferences, served on Cursillo teams and, eventually, the Secretariat. What a wonderful life I lived. Of course, Lamar was right there doing all these things with me.

The Glory Years

I had very little influence on my church. I can't say I convinced one single communicant of R. E. Lee Church to become more evangelical, but I loved the association of the other "reborns" and we were quite a group. We no longer have a source to initiate new recruits as we no longer sponsor weekends so our ranks grow slim.

Here I am, trying to incorporate twenty years into a few paragraphs and that is very difficult. So much water has gone under the bridge, there have been so many changes: Lamar has died, I have moved to a retirement community, our church has lived through many changes of leadership, some supportive of our group, others not.

I still live thankful that my Lord or the Holy Spirit loved me enough to speak to me that day at the Cursillo weekend. I guess I was like Thomas; I had to be shown that it was real! I was the last member of my immediate family to become a Christian and I know they all rejoiced when I announced my renewal. Their prayers had a lot to do with it.

Is my story finished? My life is not too productive these days. 95 years! That is pretty awesome, as Laura would say. The year I was 89, no one seemed to be impressed but now I am helped across the street whether I like it or not. Cataract removal has made me see how old I am. After surgery, when I looked in the mirror I thought my mother had been resurrected. Sometimes God knows what is best for us; blindness is kindness. Why do we tinker with it?

One thing makes me very happy. Everyone in my family is Christian, all my grandchildren and great-grandchildren. We all live by The Book. I think the spiritually faithful in Lamar's and my family would be pleased if they knew that. And we did have a giant or two.

I did not write about Lamar's illness and death; it was too painful for me. We had a wonderful relationship for 66 years and it was that way until the end. He never lost his beautiful ways and his mind was clear up to his death. A big part of me died with him. He doesn't seem that far away.

At ninety-five, death doesn't seem too bad. I think the world I have inhabited was much nicer than the one we have today. Our advances in technology have changed our world remarkably. Like Dickens, I say, "Those were the best of times" and the ones ahead don't promise to be very good. We were supposed to be "the greatest generation," but we had many challenges. This generation will be just as great if the times demand it. I think the future will do that.

Perhaps this country's greatness will start downwards. We have grown into an empire in 200 years. No empire lasts forever. I like to remember my ancestors were here from the beginning of our country and took part in its foundation, and I expect our progeny will be here when its end commences. What a glorious experience we have had and how blessed we have been.

Farewell

Dear children, here I end my book. Most of the things that you wanted to know and many you didn't care about are in these pages. At this time we had quite a few years ahead of us but you have been part of them so I bid you farewell. This is the year 2008 and we left Indiana thirty-eight years ago. Little did we think then that I would still be alive, that our grandchildren, some of them, would be married and starting interesting journeys of their own. This record will at least show you how the world has changed since I was born. I think I was extraordinarily blessed to be born when I was to the parents I had and to live in the time God put me here. I hope you can say the same when you are as old as I am.

By reading all the way to this point, you are to be commended; I seem to have produced quite a tome. God bless you, one and all!